DISCARDED

D1788024

NOT SHAKESPEARE

Burlesque has been a powerful and enduring weapon in the critique of 'legitimate' Shakespearean culture by a seemingly 'illegitimate' popular culture. This was true most of all in the nineteenth century. From *Hamlet Travestie* (1810) to *Rosencrantz and Guildenstern* (1891), Shakespeare burlesques were a vibrant, yet controversial, form of popular performance: vibrant because of their exuberant humour; controversial because they imperilled Shakespeare's iconic status. Richard Schoch, in the first study of nineteenth-century Shakespeare burlesques, explores the paradox that plays which are manifestly 'not Shakespeare' purport to be the most genuinely Shakespearean of all. Bringing together archival research, rare photographs and illustrations, close readings of burlesque scripts, and an awareness of theatrical, literary, and cultural contexts, Schoch changes the way we think about Shakespeare's theatrical legacy and nineteenth-century popular culture. His lively and wide-ranging book will appeal to scholars and students of Shakespeare in performance, theatre history, and Victorian studies.

RICHARD W. SCHOCH is Lecturer in Drama at Queen Mary, University of London. He is the recipient of fellowships from the Leverhulme Trust, the Folger Shakespeare Library, the American Society for Theatre Research, the Stanford Humanities Center, the Harry Ransom Humanities Research Center, and the Mrs Giles Whiting Foundation. He is the author of *Shakespeare's Victorian Stage: Performing History in the Theatre of Charles Kean* (Cambridge, 1998) and a finalist for the Barnard Hewitt Award (sponsored by the American Society for Theatre Research) for outstanding research in theatre history. He also operates out of Culture Factory, where his email address is ceo@culturefactory.net.

NOT SHAKESPEARE

Bardolatry and Burlesque in the Nineteenth Century

RICHARD W. SCHOCH
School of English and Drama
Queen Mary, University of London

PUBLISHED BY THE PRESS SYNDICATE OF THE UNIVERSITY OF CAMBRIDGE
The Pitt Building, Trumpington Street, Cambridge, United Kingdom

CAMBRIDGE UNIVERSITY PRESS
The Edinburgh Building, Cambridge CB2 2RU, UK
40 West 20th Street, New York, NY 10011-4211, USA
477 Williamstown Road, Port Melbourne, VIC 3207, Australia
Ruiz de Alarcón 13, 28014 Madrid, Spain
Dock House, The Waterfront, Cape Town 8001, South Africa

http://www.cambridge.org

© Richard W. Schoch 2002

This book is in copyright. Subject to statutory exception
and to the provisions of relevant collective licensing agreements,
no reproduction of any part may take place without
the written permission of Cambridge University Press.

First published 2002

Printed in the United Kingdom at the University Press, Cambridge

Typeface Baskerville no. 2 11/12.5 pt.   *System* LATEX 2$_\varepsilon$ [TB]

A catalogue record for this book is available from the British Library.

Library of Congress Cataloguing in Publication data
Schoch, Richard W.
Not Shakespeare: bardolatry and burlesque in the nineteenth century / Richard W. Schoch.
p. cm.
Includes bibliographical references and index.
ISBN 0 521 80015 3
1. Shakespeare, William, 1564–1616 – Parodies, imitations, etc. – History and criticism
2. Shakespeare, William, 1564–1616 – Adaptations – History and criticism   3. Shakespeare,
William, 1564–1616 – Appreciation – Great Britain.   4. Popular culture – Great Britain –
History – 19th century.   5. English drama – 19th century – History and criticism.
6. Theatre – Great Britain – History – 19th century.   7. English drama (Comedy) –
History and criticism.   8. Burlesques.   I. Title.
PR2880.A1 S32   2002
822'.809 – dc21   2001037924

ISBN 0 521 80015 3 hardback

To Joseph Lordi, star-bright

Contents

List of illustrations		*page* viii
Acknowledgments		x
Note on texts		xiii
	Introduction 'New Readings for Unconventional Tragedians'	1
1	'Vile beyond endurance': the language of burlesque	31
2	Shakespeare's surrogates	57
3	Shakespeare in Bohemia	107
4	Politics 'burlesquified'	151
Bibliography		188
Index		203

List of illustrations

1 Thomas Blanchard as Guildenstern in a provincial production of *Hamlet*, c. 1790. — *page* 2
2 'New Readings for Unconventional Tragedians', c. 1850s. — 9
3 Henry Hall as burlesque King John in Gilbert Abbott à Beckett's *King John (with the Benefit of the Act)*, St James's Theatre, London, 1837. — 32
4 'Hamlet; a *ballet d'action* in the court of Denmark, into which are introduced some strange figures and awful frights. For characters, see small bill of great William', c. 1850s. — 35
5 Extract from the promptbook for Mrs F. B. Conway's production of John Poole's *Hamlet Travestie*, Park Theater, Brooklyn, 1870. — 50
6 Edwin Booth as Hamlet, c. 1870. — 61
7 George L. Fox as burlesque Hamlet in T. C. DeLeon's *Hamlet Travestie*, Olympic Theater, New York, 1870. — 62
8 Playbill, Francis Talfourd's *Macbeth Somewhat Removed from the Text of Shakespeare*, Olympic Theatre, London, 1853. — 64
9 Chorus of fairies from F. C. Burnand's *Ariel*, Gaiety Theatre, London, 1883. — 72
10 Shakespeare begging from Tom Thumb, *Theatrical Journal*, October 1848. — 76
11 'Shakspeare and the Pigmies', *Punch*, 30 January 1864. — 77
12 'Shakspeare Packing up his Goods', *Man in the Moon*, 1847. — 79
13 Illustration from J. Stirling Coyne's *This House to be Sold: (The Property of the Late William Shakspeare) Inquire Within*, 1847. — 82
14 Playbill, *This House to be Sold*, Adelphi Theatre, London, 1847. — 84
15 Playbill, *Malone's Travestie of Macbeth*, Strand Theatre, London, 1853. — 88
16 Portrait of Frederick Robson, c. 1855. — 96

17	Robson as burlesque Shylock in Francis Talfourd's *Shylock; or, the Merchant of Venice Preserved*, Olympic Theatre, London, 1853.	97
18	Playbill, William Brough's *Perdita; or, the Royal Milkmaid*, Lyceum Theatre, London, 1856.	112
19	Hugo Vamp's 'Comic Dramatic Shakespearean Scenas', *c*. 1850s.	133
20	Portrait of Francis Talfourd, *c*. 1850s.	137
21	Playbill, *Shylock; or, the Merchant of Venice Preserved*, Olympic Theatre, London, 1853.	142
22	'A Winter's Tale for any Weather, In the form of a Pocket Opera', *c*. 1856.	144
23	Marie Wilton as burlesque Perdita, *Perdita*, Lyceum Theatre, London, 1856.	145
24	Finale, Robert and William Brough's *The Enchanted Isle*, Adelphi Theatre, London, 1848.	178

Illustrations 1–5, 8, 10–12, 14, 15, 17, 18, 21, and 22 are reproduced by kind permission of the Folger Shakespeare Library; illustrations 6 and 7 by kind permision of the Harry Ransom Humanities Research Center, the University of Texas at Austin; illustration 9 by kind permission of the Public Record Office, London; illustrations 13 and 19 by kind permission of The Harvard Theatre Collection, The Houghton Library; illustrations 16, 20, and 23 by courtesy of the National Portrait Gallery, London; and illustration 24 by kind permission of the Library of Congress.

Acknowledgments

Most of this book was written at the Folger Shakespeare Library, where I had the privilege of spending the 2000–1 academic year as a National Endowment for the Humanities Fellow. My chief thanks and gratitude go to the Folger and the NEH for the luxury of undisturbed time for thinking and writing. The staff of the Folger's Reading Room, under the leadership of Betsy Walsh, was unfailingly helpful. Georgianna Ziegler deserves particular thanks for guiding me through the Folger's collection of nineteenth-century theatrical ephemera. Valuable assistance was lent by Heather Wolfe in researching the provenance of an anonymous burlesque script. Carol Brobeck and Andy Tennant, with their characteristic good humour, untangled knotty administrative matters. Kathleen Lynch kindly asked me to speak at a colloquium organized by the Folger Institute Center for Shakespeare Studies, while the Folger docents honoured me with an invitation to deliver the 2000 Muriel Hoitsma Lecture. I am especially grateful to Richard Kuhta and Barbara Mowat for the many kindnesses they showed me throughout my fellowship year, demonstrating that venerable academic institutions can still be compassionate.

Research for this book has been funded by much appreciated grants from the American Society for Theatre Research, the Arts and Humanities Research Board (UK), the University of London's Central Research Fund, and the University of Texas at Austin. A Leverhulme Research Fellowship secured this book's timely completion. Bruce Smith graciously arranged for me to be appointed a Visiting Researcher at Georgetown University during my sabbatical year. The Harry Ransom Humanities Research Center generously awarded me a Mellon Fellowship. The two months I spent in Austin in 1999 proved crucial to the development of this project. I am indebted to Melissa Miller for curatorial guidance, Roger Lewis for an invitation to address the Faculty Seminar on British Studies, and Ben and Judy Lindfors for Texas-style hospitality. Over the past few years I have also conducted research at the Birmingham

Shakespeare Library, the British Library, the Harvard Theatre Collection, the Library of Congress, the National Portrait Gallery (London), the Public Record Office, the Shakespeare Institute in Stratford-upon-Avon, the Theatre Museum, and the University of London Library. It is a pleasure to acknowledge the expertise and generosity of the library and curatorial staff of these institutions. Within the School of English and Drama at Queen Mary, University of London, Paul Hamilton, Lisa Jardine, and Anne Janowitz provided unfailing support for this project during their respective tenures as Head of School, granting me valued research leave and release time. The continuing support and encouragement of my esteemed colleagues Maria Delgado and Paul Heritage have been invaluable.

Parts of this work originated as papers delivered to the American Society for Theatre Research, the Folger Institute Center for Shakespeare Studies, and the Shakespeare Association of America, and as lectures given at the University of California at Los Angeles, the University of London, and the University of Texas at Austin. On these and other occasions I have benefited from the questions, advice, and challenges of A. R. Braunmuller, Jim Davis, Joseph Donohue, R. A. Foakes, Werner Habicht, Russell Jackson, Shannon Jackson, Jeff Masten, Laurie Osborne, Elizabeth Richmond-Garza, John Ripley, Stuart Sherman, and Ted Ziter. Stephen Orgel and Joseph Bristow asked just the right questions at just the right time. This work's principal arguments were first published in my essay ' "Chopkins, Late Shakespeare": The Bard and his Burlesques, 1810–1866', which appeared in *ELH* 67 (2000). I am grateful to Ronald Paulson, editor of *ELH*, for permission to draw upon parts of that article. This book has benefited from the care and guidance of two editors at Cambridge University Press: Victoria L. Cooper, who commissioned it, and Sarah Stanton, who saw it through to completion. My thanks to them both for their unwavering support. Leigh Mueller has been a scrupulous and efficient copy-editor. Thanks are due also to the two anonymous readers who offered valuable guidance at an early stage in the writing process. Their suggestions have been silently adopted. The author alone, however, bears responsibility for any errors or omissions.

My residency at the Folger was made even more agreeable by the companionship of James Daybell and Kirk Melnikoff. Alan Stewart was excellent company during the many memorable evenings we spent at Banana Cafe and Mr Henry's. He has also been a good friend. Cynthia Burns, a cherished friend of long standing, welcomed me back to Washington with far more warmth than I had any right to expect. During my many visits to Washington over the past decade, Steve Holman has been a generous host. In London, Bill Patterson has been a trusted and loyal friend. My greatest debt is to this book's dedicatee, whose influence has been incalculable.

Note on texts

For the convenience of the reader, quotations from burlesque scripts are, in most instances, taken from nineteenth-century acting editions rather than from the manuscript originally submitted to the Lord Chamberlain's Office. The exceptions are those instances when a manuscript differs from its published version, as well as quotations from promptbooks and unpublished plays. The year of a burlesque's inaugural performance is provided the first time it is mentioned. All references to Shakespeare draw on *The Arden Shakespeare Complete Works*, ed. Richard Proudfoot, Ann Thompson, and David Scott Kastan (Walton-upon-Thames, Surrey: Thomas Nelson and Sons Ltd, 1998).

INTRODUCTION

'New Readings for Unconventional Tragedians'

Sometime toward the close of the eighteenth century, the comic actor Thomas Blanchard received an offer from an English strolling company to play one of the gravediggers in *Hamlet*. He was also asked to double in the role of Guildenstern. The offer was unusual. While low comedians were typically cast as the gravediggers, they would not expect to play any of the serious parts. Nonetheless, Blanchard accepted the offer; and he performed the role of Guildenstern the only way he knew how: as a clown. In the scene where Hamlet repeatedly urges Guildenstern to play a recorder, Blanchard preposterously procured a bassoon from the theatre's orchestra. The actor playing Hamlet fell about laughing, and it was 'some time before he could arrange his muscles with sufficient gravity'.[1] Recovering his composure, the tragedian carried on with the scene, anticipating that Blanchard's Guildenstern would protest his inability to play the instrument. Yet after Hamlet's third entreaty, Guildenstern unexpectedly responded, 'Well, my lord, since you are so very pressing, I'll do my best.' Whereupon he took up the bassoon and played 'Lady Coventry's Minuet'. The response, as shown in illustration 1, was uproarious. A shocked Hamlet, his hand covering his speechless mouth, shrinks from Guildenstern who tries to hand over the bassoon once he has finished playing. Judging from their laughter, the audience and the orchestra equally enjoyed the antic disruption of Shakespeare's tragedy. The only person excluded from the merriment was Hamlet, who 'had not another word to say for himself'. Needless to say, Blanchard never played Guildenstern again.

Blanchard's 'gag' ruefully confirms the prescience of Hamlet's injunction to the players that 'clowns speak no more than is set down for them' lest they 'set on some quantity of barren spectators to laugh' and thereby obscure 'some necessary question of the play' (*Hamlet* 3.2.40, 41–2, 43–4).

[1] Unidentified clipping, Theatrical Miscellany Scrapbook 11, Folger Shakespeare Library, Washington, DC.

1. Thomas Blanchard as Guildenstern in a provincial production of *Hamlet*, *c*. 1790. Note the smiling face set into the front of the proscenium arch.

Enacting the very comic transgression which Hamlet was so anxious to avoid, this production marks the late eighteenth-century theatre's incipient burlesque disposition toward Shakespeare: that comic deformations of his classic texts might claim a place upon the stage. In the decades following, the Shakespeare burlesque emerged as a distinctive theatre genre which allowed clowns to speak more than Shakespeare had 'set down for them'. This book tells their story.

Throughout the nineteenth century, nearly all the leading actor–managers in Great Britain – J. P. Kemble, W. C. Macready, Charles Kean, Samuel Phelps and Henry Irving – staged lavish revivals of Shakespeare. They did so partly to play great roles, partly to educate their audiences in history and morality through Shakespeare's plays, and partly to win respectability for themselves as gentlemanly proprietors of reputable places of amusement. These eminent tragedians were nothing if not earnest. And they were simply begging to be ridiculed. The burlesque backlash – the comic attack upon the pious pretensions of 'legitimate' Shakespearean culture – was not long in coming. From John Poole's *Hamlet Travestie* (1810) to W. S. Gilbert's *Rosencrantz and Guildenstern* (1891), Shakespeare burlesques were an especially vibrant, yet controversial, form of nineteenth-century popular theatre. Vibrant because of their exuberant humour, controversial because they seemed to imperil the sanctity of Shakespeare as a national icon.[2] Wildly popular in their own day, these plays are now little read, scarcely studied, and never performed.[3]

While this work restores an unjustly neglected series of comic plays and performances, restoration is the least of its goals. Bringing together archival research on burlesque performances, close readings of playtexts, and an awareness of theatrical, literary, and cultural contexts, I seek to disclose the centrality of burlesques in critiquing what the *Westminster Review*, in 1833, called the 'respectable humbug' of Bardolatry.[4] This

---

[2] Shakespeare burlesques are by no means limited to the nineteenth century. This enduring theatrical tradition ranges from Thomas Duffet's *The Mock-Tempest* (1674) to Anton Dudley's *Romeo & Juliatric* (2000). As staged by Cherry Red Productions at the Metro Cafe in Washington, DC, *Romeo & Juliatric* satirized 'America's attitudes towards seniors and the theatre community's lame recent rush to reinterpret all of Shakespeare's plays'. The production's catchy slogan was 'you're never too old to die young' (Cherry Red Productions, www.cherryredproductions.com).

[3] This study makes only passing reference to Shakespeare burlesques staged in America since the cultural politics surrounding those productions were not at all similar to those of British productions. On Shakespeare burlesques in nineteenth-century America, see Susan Kattwinkel, ed., *Tony Pastor Presents: Afterpieces from the Vaudeville Stage* (Westport, CT: Greenwood Press, 1998); Lawrence Levine, *Highbrow/Lowbrow: The Emergence of Cultural Hierarchy in America* (Cambridge, MA: Harvard University Press, 1988); David L. Rinear, *The Temple of Momus: Mitchell's Olympic Theatre* (Metuchen, NJ: The Scarecrow Press, Inc., 1987); and volume V of Stanley Wells' anthology *Nineteenth-Century Shakespeare Burlesques* (London: Diploma Press, 1977). On American burlesque generally, see Robert C. Allen's *Horrible Prettiness: Burlesque and American Culture* (Chapel Hill: The University of North Carolina Press, 1991).

[4] *Westminster Review* 18 (1833), p. 35.

book, in short, explores the paradoxical ways in which plays that are manifestly 'not Shakespeare' – plays like *Macbeth Somewhat Removed from the Text of Shakespeare* (1853) and *A Thin Slice of Ham let!* (1863) – purported to be the most genuinely Shakespearean of all. For all its doggerel, painful punning, and licentiousness, the burlesque styled itself as the norm to which transgressive theatrical practices should revert. As the comic playwright Sir F. C. Burnand enjoined, burlesque was the 'candid friend of the Drama' and the 'natural' extension of Shakespeare.[5] Drawing a distinction between Shakespearean texts and Shakespearean performances, the editor of *Punch* explained that burlesques were themselves a response to the occasions when Shakespeare was 'injured by the misinterpretation of self-complacent mediocre actors' or 'rendered ridiculous by extravagant realism in production' (p. 175). By its own admission, then, the burlesque actively intervened to protect Shakespeare from his true detractors. Accusations that burlesques detracted from the poet's genius were false, or so we are asked to accept. With Shakespeare thus besieged, the 'legitimate employment' of the burlesque was to 'hold the mirror up, not to Nature, but to such distortion of Nature' in order that those very distortions be rectified; that Shakespeare be returned to himself, whole and unblemished. For much of the nineteenth century, to burlesque *was* to be Shakespearean.

As the most spiritedly topical form of nineteenth-century stage comedy, the burlesque fixed its satiric gaze not only upon Shakespeare, but also upon opera, melodrama, poetic drama, classical mythology, Arthurian legend, Arabian tales, English history, the novels of Edward Bulwer-Lytton, and the plays of Oscar Wilde and Henrik Ibsen. From J. R. Planché's *Orpheus in the Haymarket* (1865) to Burnand's *Tra-la la Tosca* (1890), and from Robert Brough's *Frankenstein; or, the Model Man* (1849) to H. J. Byron's *The Corsican 'Brothers'; or, The Troublesome Twins* (1869), the burlesque exempted no area of culture from its parodic assault. Indiscriminate in taste, the burlesque never regarded Shakespeare as a uniquely deserving recipient of its mockery. Nor did individual burlesque theatres, playwrights or performers specialize in Shakespearean parody. In 1854, for example, the Strand burlesqued Kean's productions of *Faust and Marguerite* and *The Corsican Brothers* as well as his revivals of *Macbeth* and *Othello*. Robert Brough, in addition to co-authoring a burlesque of *The Tempest*, also wrote burlesques of Bellini's *Norma*, Sir Walter Scott's *Ivanhoe*, and Euripides' *Medea*. Frederick Robson, the greatest burlesque artist of

---

[5] F. C. Burnand, 'The Spirit of Burlesque', *Universal Review* 2 (September–December 1888), p. 171.

the nineteenth century, starred in two Shakespearean burlesques – Francis Talfourd's *Macbeth Somewhat Removed from the Text of Shakespeare* and *Shylock; or, the Merchant of Venice Preserved* (1853). Yet he was equally famous for his performance *en travestie* in the title role of Robert Brough's *Medea; or, the Best of Mothers, with a Brute of a Husband* (1855). And while Marie Wilton made her London debut in the title role of William Brough's *Perdita; or, the Royal Milkmaid* (1856), she appeared in only one further Shakespeare burlesque – Andrew Halliday's *Romeo and Juliet Travestie* (1859).

In light of such diversity, we might well question why Shakespeare burlesques should be singled out for investigation. After all, no one has yet written a monograph on nineteenth-century burlesques generally.[6] But of the many kinds of burlesques written in the nineteenth century, Shakespeare burlesques offer the most compelling material for critical and historical study. Because burlesques bring into popular consciousness the very contradictions of popular culture, they must aim at the summit of that culture to be most effective. If Shakespeare matters more than other cultural forms, then Shakespeare burlesques will matter more than other kinds of burlesques. Simply put, there is more at stake in burlesquing *Hamlet* than in burlesquing Colin Hazelwood's melodrama *Lady Audley's Secret*.

The mid-Victorian era witnessed Shakespeare burlesques at the height of their frenzy and favour. Within a decade of the passage of the Theatres Regulation Act of 1843, which left Shakespeare, as Planché quipped a year later in *The Drama at Home*, free to be performed 'where'er you please / No longer pinioned by the patentees',[7] Phelps at Sadler's Wells and Kean at the Princess's Theatre embarked upon lengthy managerial careers distinguished above all by Shakespearean revivals. As Stanley Wells has calculated, 'roughly twice as many Shakespearian burlesques' were written between 1840 and 1870 as in the preceding thirty years (*Nineteenth-Century Shakespeare Burlesques*, III, p. 52). 'We have been done

---

[6] W. Davenport Adams' *A Book of Burlesque: Sketches of English Stage Travestie and Parody* (London: Henry & Co., 1891) and V. C. Clinton-Baddeley's *The Burlesque Tradition in the English Theatre after 1660* (London: Methuen & Co., Ltd, 1952) are more surveys than monographs. Some of the more extended research on Shakespeare burlesques has been undertaken by non-Anglophone scholars. See, for example, Gerhard Müller-Schwefe's *Corpus Hamleticum* (Tübingen: Francke, 1987) and the same author's anthology *Shakespeare im Narrenhaus* (Tübingen: Francke, 1990). That burlesques have been so lightly researched is itself symptomatic of the longstanding critical neglect of nineteenth-century popular drama.

[7] J. R. Planché, *The Drama at Home*, in *Plays by James Robinson Planché*, ed. Donald Roy (Cambridge: Cambridge University Press, 1986), p. 17. Under the 1843 Act, the patent theatres (Covent Garden, Drury Lane and, in the summer, the Haymarket) lost their monopoly in the production of legitimate – i.e., scripted – drama.

to death with burlesques', the *Spectator* entreated in the spring of 1853, the year in which a record-setting six Shakespearean parodies were performed in London theatres.[8] A few weeks later, a bemused *Lloyd's Weekly London Newspaper* reported that a 'Charles Kean mania [was] breaking out like a rash upon all [burlesque] actors' and so it was impossible to 'go to a theatre without hearing the continual imitation' of Kean's Macbeth.[9] No new Shakespeare burlesque was performed for almost the entire 1860s, a period marked by a pronounced decline in the frequency of memorable London productions of Shakespeare. Burlesques revived in the 1870s and 1880s, however, as a new generation of tragedians – Tommaso Salvini, Wilson Barrett and Irving – produced Shakespeare with greater frequency, thus making themselves vulnerable to burlesque ridicule.

While Shakespeare burlesques certainly parodied specific actors, productions, and methods of *mise-en-scène*, they also parodied the pomposities of official Shakespearean culture. To that extent, these plays bore witness to the nineteenth century's profoundly equivocal commitment to Bardolatry. In the wake of David Garrick's 1769 Stratford Jubilee – the founding moment of institutionalized Bardolatry – Shakespeare's iconicity seemed unassailable. The evolving forms of Shakespeare worship, both magisterial and humble, were varied indeed: not just theatrical performances, but also public readings, critical editions, biographies, essays and articles, trips to Stratford-upon-Avon, anniversary celebrations, Shakespeare societies, and a vast range of iconographic material from Charles Knight's eight-volume *Pictorial Edition of the Works of Shakespeare* (1839–42) to enamel Tercentenary buttons decorated with a 'rosy-cheeked miniature of the Bard'.[10] What Elin Diamond has observed of Tom Stoppard's *Dogg's Hamlet* (1979) and *Cahoot's Macbeth* (1979) seems equally appropriate when assessing the broad cultural interventions made by nineteenth-century Shakespeare burlesques: that such

[8] *Spectator* 30 April 1853. The six Shakespeare burlesques produced in 1853 were Barton's *Hamlet According to an Act of Parliament* (Strand 7 November 1853); Francis Talfourd's *Macbeth Somewhat Removed from the Text of Shakespeare* (Olympic 25 April 1853); Malone's *Macbeth Travestie* (Strand 18 April 1853); Talfourd's *Shylock; or, The Merchant of Venice Preserved* (Olympic 4 July 1853); a revival of Maurice Dowling's *Othello According to an Act of Parliament* (Strand September and October 1853); and a revival of Charles Selby's *Kynge Richard ye Third* (Strand October 1853).
[9] *Lloyd's Weekly London Newspaper* 8 May 1853. For example, *Bell's Weekly Messenger* noted that Hodson, in the Strand burlesque, carried a 'shellelagh' as the Irish Macbeth, a prop which seems likely to have been inspired by the stick Kean himself used when playing Macbeth (24 April 1853). Similarly, the manuscript for John E. Chalmers' *King Leer and His Darters* (Bower Saloon 1848) indicates that during the storm scene burlesque Lear should declaim in an 'imitation of Macready' (Chalmers, *King Leer and His Darters* 1848 BL Add Mss 43,001, f. 405b).
[10] 'Shakespeare-Mad', *All the Year Round* 11 (21 May 1864), p. 345.

comic plays do not simply parody the original tragedies in order to 'criticise the institutional appropriation of Shakespeare' but actively use parody to *situate* 'Shakespeare, or rather the canon... both as a cultural force and as a cultural menace'.[11] Shakespeare burlesques are testaments to both the vitality *and* the vulnerability of nineteenth-century Bardolatry.

In thinking about how burlesques expose the fragility of official Bardolatrous culture, we must remember that the theatre was but one site of Shakespearean parody in the nineteenth century. In the 1850s, the comic singer Sam Cowell, for example, performed one-man parodies of *Hamlet*, *Macbeth*, *The Merchant of Venice*, and *Richard III* in Evans's Supper Rooms in Covent Garden. James and Horatio Smith's *Rejected Addresses* (1812), a satire on the scripts submitted for production at the newly rebuilt Drury Lane, included a musical version of Macbeth's dagger soliloquy. George Cruikshank's 1835 caricature of Charles Kemble as Hamlet confronting the ghost demonstrates the satiric potential of Shakespearean iconography. And since many prominent burlesque playwrights earned their living as journalists, we need not be surprised that Shakespearean parodies regularly appeared in the nineteenth-century periodical press. Indeed, *Punch* parodied Shakespeare more than any other author, whether through caricatures, burlesque sketches, or fictive theatrical anecdotes. In the fanciful 'Ballet of Lady Macbeth', for example, the Scottish thane's hallucinatory soliloquy becomes a *pas de deux* as Lady Macbeth 'coquettishly' draws the dagger away from her husband 'whenever he attempts to grasp it'.[12] Similarly, the *Comic Almanack* predicted that the next Shakespeare Jubilee Festival would feature both the new pantomime *Harlequin Macbeth; or, the Magic Cauldron and the Walking Wood* and a grotesque 'Pas de Caliban' inserted in *The Tempest*.[13] These parodic imaginings are no mere pleasantries, for they allude to the legitimate theatre's developing obsession with producing Shakespeare as song-and-dance extravaganzas which dispensed with ever-increasing amounts of text.

More sober periodicals also featured satiric versions of Shakespeare. Published in *Bentley's Miscellany*, Thomas Ingoldsby's poem 'The Merchant of Venice' (1842) shared many of the formal features of theatrical burlesques, including sarcastic references to Shakespearean editors; colloquial depiction of characters (Portia is 'Mrs. Bassanio',

---

[11] Elin Diamond, 'Stoppard's *Dogg's Hamlet, Cahoot's Macbeth*: The Uses of Shakespeare', *Modern Drama* 29 (1986), p. 594.
[12] 'Ballet of Lady Macbeth', *Punch* 5 (July–December 1843), p. 240.
[13] *The Comic Almanack* 1844–1853 2nd ser. (London: Chatto and Windus, n.d.), p. 134.

p. 431); localizations (the Doge lives in London's Hanover Square); and the repeated use of Jewish Cockney dialect ('vat, pray', Shylock asks Antonio, '[m]ight your vorship be pleashed for to vant in my vay', p. 431).[14] Indeed, Ingoldsby's poem reads as a workable script for a miniature burlesque of *The Merchant of Venice*. Similarly, the six cartoons 'New Readings for Unconventional Tragedians' (c. 1850s), as shown in illustration 2, display Shakespearean vignettes whose impish humour would have been equally at home on the burlesque stage: Macbeth, attended by a pair of frogs, implores the Witches to 'show, show, show' while peering through a pair of binoculars at shadow puppets; Shylock literalizes his line '[m]y deeds upon my head!' (his riposte to Portia's plea for 'deeds of mercy') by carrying a stack of actual deeds and bonds on top of his head; Hamlet and Ophelia, discovering a topical meaning in 'jig maker', dance the can-can before Claudius and Gertrude; Romeo hurls himself over the wall outside Juliet's balcony, careful to avoid the embedded glass shards designed to deter thieves; Othello makes the customary pun on 'spirits'; and, in a parody of *Richard III*, the Duke ('Jockey') of Norfolk appears as an actual jockey who presents Richard (distinguished by a grotesque white rose of the House of York) with a copy of the contemporary sporting journal *Bell's Life*.[15] By no means, however, did all Shakespearean parodies evoke a sense of theatricality. F. W. Fairholt's *The Grimaldi Shakspere* (1853) is a case in point. In 1852, the Shakespeare editor J. P. Collier announced in the *Athenaeum* his discovery of an annotated 1632 Folio. As Collier conjectured, the so-called 'Perkins Folio' superseded the authority of all other Folios by virtue of its contemporaneous annotations.[16] Among the most ingenious attacks on Collier's audacious claim was *The Grimaldi Shakspere*. As its title suggests, the comic pamphlet purported to be the compilation of alterations and emendations found in the newly discovered 'Grimaldi Folio of 1816' in which the great pantomime clown had corrected the texts of Shakespeare's plays with 'true sympathetic genius'.[17] Any 'violation of sense' in Shakespeare's texts, Fairholt attested, 'was painful to the

---

[14] Thomas Ingoldsby (pseud. Revd Richard Harris Barham), 'The Merchant of Venice', *Bentley's Miscellany* 11 (1842), pp. 429–38. Shylock's speech mimics the stereotyped accent and cadence of East End Jews.
[15] The cartoon of Romeo is only too accurate. In *Romeo and Juliet Travestie*, a wounded Romeo complains that '[h]e jests at scars, who never . . . / mounted garden wall and got a scratch / From a row of broken bottles' (Andrew Halliday, *Romeo and Juliet Travestie; or, the Cup of Cold Poison*, London: Thomas Hailes Lacy, n.d., p. 17).
[16] *Athenaeum* 17 January 1852.
[17] F. W. Fairholt, *The Grimaldi Shakspere* (London: J. Russell Smith, 1853), p. 6.

2. 'New Readings for Unconventional Tragedians', c. 1850s. Hamlet appears to be played by a burlesque 'boy'. Note the long hair and ankle boots which match the pair Ophelia wears.

distinguished pantomimist who gave meaning to "Tippety Witchet"' (p. 11). As these varied examples attest, Shakespeare burlesques were but one aspect of a parodic disposition to Shakespeare which ran throughout Victorian popular culture.

While this study does not pretend to survey the stage history of nineteenth-century Shakespeare burlesques – or even to reconstruct selected productions – it does undertake to explain the principal features of burlesque dramaturgy, acting, and *mise-en-scène*. That explanation begins by specifying which plays were burlesqued.[18] To be a viable candidate for burlesque treatment, a play would have to be both well known *and* responsive to comic rewriting. As might be deduced from these criteria, *Hamlet* was the most frequently burlesqued Shakespearean play in the nineteenth century, with over a dozen versions either performed or published. Given that many burlesques parodied specific productions, frequently performed plays such as *Hamlet* and *Macbeth* generated a disproportionately high number of burlesques. As an emblem of the entire Shakespearean canon, *Hamlet* offered burlesque artists an unparalleled opportunity to mock the cult of Bardolatry. By contrast, plays rarely performed during the nineteenth century – e.g., *All's Well that Ends Well* and *Measure for Measure* – were never burlesqued.

Timeliness also played an essential part in the burlesque critique of legitimate Shakespeare. Less than six weeks after Kean played Richard III at Covent Garden in 1844, two mock versions were written, rehearsed, and performed: J. Stirling Coyne's *New Grand, Historical, Bombastical, Musical and Completely Illegitimate Tragedy to be called Richard III* (Adelphi) and Charles Selby's *Kynge Richard ye Third; or, ye Battel of Bosworth Field* (Strand). The anonymous *Salthello Ovini* (1875), as its title's transposed syllables would suggest, burlesqued Salvini's performance as Othello. Irving's 1874 performance in *Hamlet* (Lyceum) not only led to a revival of Poole's *Hamlet Travestie* (Globe) but also inspired two new burlesques: W. R. Snow's *Hamlet the Hysterical, a Delirium in Five Spasms* (Princess's 1874) and Gilbert's *Rosencrantz and Guildenstern*.[19] Similarly, Wilson Barrett's 1884

---

[18] For lists of Shakespeare burlesques performed and/or published in nineteenth-century Britain, see William Jaggard, *Shakespeare Bibliography* (Stratford-upon-Avon: The Shakespeare Press, 1911); Henry E. Jacobs and Claudia D. Johnson, *An Annotated Bibliography of Shakespearean Burlesques, Parodies, and Travesties* (New York: Garland Publishing, Inc., 1976); Allardyce Nicoll, *A History of Early Nineteenth-Century Drama 1800–1850* 2 vols. (Cambridge: Cambridge University Press, 1930) and *A History of Late Nineteenth-Century Drama 1850–1900* 2 vols. (Cambridge: Cambridge University Press, 1946); Senga Wallace Roche, 'Travesties and Burlesques of Shakespeare's Plays on the British Stage during the Nineteenth Century', unpublished Ph.D. dissertation, University of London, 1987; Jacob Bonnist Salomon, 'Dramatic Burlesques of Shakespeare in Great Britain Before 1900: A Stage History and Analysis', unpublished Ph.D. dissertation, University of Pennsylvania, 1975; and R. Farquaharson Sharp, 'Travesties of Shakespeare's Plays', *Library* 1 (June 1920), pp. 1–20.

[19] Gilbert's play, not produced until 1891, was initially serialized in *Fun* (December 1874).

Hamlet (Princess's) spawned two further burlesque versions: J. Comyns Carr's *A Fireside Hamlet* (Princes') and William Yardley's *Very Little Hamlet* (Gaiety).[20]

Familiarity alone, however, does not tell the entire story. The Shakespearean 'source text', as it were, had to be amenable to burlesque treatment. Like the seventeenth-century literary parodies from which they descended, nineteenth-century theatrical burlesques typically enacted ludicrous versions of serious events. In *Macbeth Modernised*, for example, Duncan outwits Macbeth by placing a pig's 'bladder filled with blood' in his own bed.[21] When the would-be assassin unsuspectingly thrusts his dagger through the concealed bladder, the blood spurting out of it convinces him that he has murdered Duncan. Shakespeare's tragedies provided the most advantageous material for the 'low' treatment (a pig's bladder) of 'high' subjects (regicide). *Hamlet Travestie* (1810) was quickly followed by Richard Gurney's *Romeo and Juliet Travesty* (1812) and *Othello Travestie* (1813) by 'Ibef'.[22] The burlesque 'tragedy' repertoire expanded over the ensuing half-century, with Maurice Dowling's *Othello Travestie* (1834), James Morgan's *Coriolanus; a Burlesque* (1846), the anonymous *Kynge Lear and Hys Faythfulle Foole* (1860), *Julius Caesar Travestie* (c. 1861), and Burnand's *Antony and Cleopatra* (1866). Of the English history plays, *Richard III* was the most obvious choice for burlesque treatment given the popularity of its title role with legitimate tragedians. Among the other history plays, only *King John* was burlesqued. *The Tempest* and *The Winter's Tale* appear to be the only romances turned into burlesques. Among the comedies, only *The Merchant of Venice* held any appeal as a burlesque. The principal nineteenth-century productions were E. L. Blanchard's *The Merchant of Venice (very far indeed) from the Text of Shakespeare* (1843) and Talfourd's *Shylock; or, the Merchant of Venice Preserved* (1853).[23] Shakespeare's other comedies were seldom, if ever, parodied either because they were rarely performed or because their humour already verged on the burlesque. How, after all, could anyone improve

---

[20] The burlesque qualifier 'Very Little' refers both to Shakespeare's original play – very little of which would be found in the burlesque – and to the diminutive stature of Nellie Farren, the burlesque voluptuary who played Hamlet.

[21] Anon., *Macbeth Modernised* (London: n.p., 1838), p. 14.

[22] By contrast, Shakespeare burlesques were published in French and German beginning in the late eighteenth century. See, for example, Pierre-Germain Parisau, *Richard, parodie de Richard III, en vaudevilles* (Paris, 1781) and Karl Ludwig Giesecke (pseud. Johann Georg Metzler), *Der travestirte Hamlet* (Vienna, 1798).

[23] The title of Talfourd's burlesque also contains a joke on Thomas Otway's *Venice Preserved* (1682).

upon Shakespeare's own masterful burlesque of 'Pyramus and Thisbe' in *A Midsummer Night's Dream*?[24]

By the 1840s, burlesque scripts fell into a highly consistent pattern which remained largely unchanged for the remainder of the century: rhymed couplets in either a paraphrase or parody of Shakespeare's original text (Portia's declaration that '[t]he quality of mercy is not strained, / Nor filtered as Thames water needs to be / Before it's drinkable' from Talfourd's *Shylock; or, the Merchant of Venice Preserved*[25]); the transposition of characters from 'high' to 'low' and of events from past to present (Othello becomes a modern-day street sweeper in Charles Mathews' *Othello, the Moor of Fleet Street*); the ludicrous re-enactment of classic scenes (Juliet's dog barks continually throughout the balcony scene in *Romeo and Juliet Travestie*); a pronounced theatrical bias, with an emphasis on stage business, sight gags, and special effects (Old Hamlet's rusty suit of armour in *Hamlet According to an Act of Parliament*); relentless puns (Lady Anne's play on Richard of Gloucester and 'double Gloucester' cheese in Coyne's *Richard III* burlesque); topical references to life in London, ranging from the price of butter to the Trafalgar Square riots; and soliloquies and set pieces rewritten as lyrics to familiar songs, whether popular, operatic, or even minstrel ('To be or not to be' becomes in *Hamlet Travestie* a song to the tune of 'Here we go up, up, up', with the nonsense refrain 'Ri tol de rol, &c'[26]).

Since burlesques presume the competency of their spectators, any change in the audience's exposure to Shakespeare will induce a corresponding change not only in the burlesque's appeal, but in its very intelligibility. (This is one way to explain why, despite its detractors' impassioned predictions, burlesque can never displace Shakespeare: because it cannot be understood *without* Shakespeare.) Most Victorians acquired their knowledge of Shakespeare not at school, but at the theatre. And since theatres traditionally employed a repertory system, audiences were able to witness an enormous range of productions within a single theatrical season, let alone over a lifetime of theatregoing. But the advent of the 'long run' in the 1850s changed everything. When,

---

[24] John Brougham's *A Recollection of O'Flannigan and the Fairies; or a Midsummer Night's Dream, not Shakespeare's* (c. 1856) is a fairy extravaganza which bears scant relationship to the Shakespearean comedy misleadingly invoked in its sub-title.

[25] Francis Talfourd, *Shylock; or, the Merchant of Venice Preserved* (London: Thomas Hailes Lacy, n.d.), p. 27. Burlesque playwrights generally dramatized the most familiar scenes from the most familiar plays: e.g. Hamlet's soliloquies, the balcony scene from *Romeo and Juliet*, the tent scene in *Richard III*, Lady Macbeth sleepwalking, and the trial scene from *The Merchant of Venice*.

[26] John Poole, *Hamlet Travestie: In Three Acts, with Burlesque Annotations* 2nd edn (London: J. M. Richardson, 1811), pp. 23–4.

for example, Kean's productions of *Henry VIII* (1855) and *The Winter's Tale* (1856) both ran for a hundred consecutive performances, his audience lost the opportunity to see the dozens of other plays which the actor–manager might have produced. Because of the long run's considerable economic advantages, particularly with respect to small-cast, modern-dress new plays, entrepreneurial managers gradually abandoned the repertoire of Shakespeare, melodrama, comedy, farce, and pantomime which nineteenth-century audiences had come to expect. One regrettable result of the drastically curtailed repertoire, as William Archer explained in 1886, was that 'the theatrical public of the day knows only one corner, so to speak, of Shakespeare's genius – far less than was known to the unsophisticated frequenters of Sadler's Wells twenty-five years ago. And this corner it knows superficially, unlovingly, unappreciatively.'[27] The implications for burlesque were only too obvious: as audiences became less and less familiar with Shakespeare, they became less and less capable of appreciating a burlesque on Shakespeare. As the critical capacities of their audiences gradually declined throughout the Victorian era, burlesque performances transformed themselves into eroticized 'leg pieces'. Having lost their satiric edge, Archer reported, burlesques sank to the level of 'music-hall imbecility' (*About the Theatre*, p. 22).

When burlesques still possessed a knowing audience, their popularity rested largely on topicality, novelty, and variety.[28] Even though burlesque was a staple item in the repertoire of several West End theatres, no single burlesque text became a fixed part of any theatre's repertoire. Only a handful of the most popular burlesques, such as *Hamlet Travestie*, were ever revived. The more common fate of a Shakespeare burlesque was to have a London production – lasting anywhere from a few weeks to a few months – followed by occasional productions in provincial theatres. *The Enchanted Isle* ran for ninety-three performances at the Adelphi Theatre in 1848, while J. Stirling Coyne's 1844 burlesque of *Richard III* had been withdrawn from the same theatre after only three weeks. The principal London theatres associated with burlesques, particularly at the height

---

[27] William Archer, *About the Theatre* (London: T. Fisher Unwin, 1886), p. 245.
[28] Like any theatrical form, the burlesque changed over time. John Hollingshead's account (c. 1883) of the Gaiety 'masher' who 'comes night after night, week after week, to see the burlesque' and who 'knows every line and every air in the piece' is a telling indicator of shifting audience expectations. Only at the end of the century did audiences come to think of burlesques in terms of consistency rather than variety. See 'A Theatrical Manager on the Morals of the Stage. An Interview with Mr. John Hollingshead', unidentified newspaper review, bound in the *Theatre* n.s. 2 (July–December 1883), Folger Shakespeare Library, Washington, DC.

of their mid-century popularity, were the Strand, the Olympic, and the Adelphi. Later in the century, the Gaiety continued to keep alight the sacred lamp of burlesque. Both before and after theatrical deregulation, the patent houses – Covent Garden and Drury Lane – rarely produced Shakespeare burlesques. None of the century's principal actor–managers ever staged a Shakespeare burlesque, although a young Herbert Beerbohm Tree did play a burlesque Hamlet in *A Fireside Hamlet* (1884).[29] Nor were Shakespeare burlesques performed with any regularity at East End or south London theatres. The Royal Grecian Saloon's production of R. Spry's *Macbeth, a Burlesque* (1857) and the Britannia's production of Hazelwood's *New King Richard the Third; a Burlesque Extravaganza* (1878) occupy an anomalous position in a theatrical culture slanted heavily toward working-class melodrama.

Through their slang, topical allusions, and domestication of character and situation, Shakespeare burlesques, as Stanley Wells has noted, show 'Victorian society at its most unbuttoned' (*Nineteenth-Century Shakespeare Burlesques*, I, p. viii). But there was nothing relaxed about the performances themselves. There were precious few moments of tranquillity in burlesque, as Henry Barton Baker confirmed in describing the breakdown dance, customarily performed at the end of each scene, as a 'frantic outburst of irrepressible animal spirits' in which the performers had 'no more control over their legs than the audience had over their applause'.[30] Burlesque performances, he further recalled, were always marked by a certain 'go', an irresistible 'riotous mirth' which embraced actors and audiences alike. While a good measure of the burlesque's humour was written into the script, the success of any production rested largely with the actors, who were called upon to demonstrate an impressive range of histrionic skills in performances which typically lasted between an hour and an hour-and-a-half. In his 1864 series 'Theatrical Types', published in the *Illustrated Times*, T. W. Robertson offered a stunningly comprehensive appraisal of the intense demands made upon burlesque performers. Posing as the 'Theatrical Lounger', Robertson amusingly explained that

---

[29] In Carr's sketch *A Fireside Hamlet*, Tree played a Cockney baker who begins to speak like Shakespeare's tragic hero after 'his mind is affected by Mr Wilson Barrett's performance of "Hamlet"' (*Under the Clock* 6 December 1884).

[30] H. Barton Baker, *History of the London Stage* 2nd edn (London: G. Routledge & Sons, Ltd, 1904), p. 448. Michael Booth describes a 'breakdown' dance as an 'extraordinarily lively shuffle, with vigorous and often grotesque arm and body movements'. In a 'cellar-flap' breakdown, the dancer's feet remained fixed on the same spot while the arms and torso gyrated madly (Michael Booth, *Prefaces to English Nineteenth-Century Theatre*, Manchester: Manchester University Press, 1980, p. 187).

the burlesque heroine must

> sing the most difficult of Donizetti's languid, loving melodies, as well as the inimitable Mackney's 'Oh, Rosa, how I lub you! Coodle cum!' She can warble a drawing-room ballad of the 'Daylight of the Soul' or 'Eyes melting in Gloom' school, or whistle 'When I was a-walking in Wiggleton Wale' with the shrillness and correctness of a Whitechapel bird-catcher. She is as faultless on the piano as on the bones. She can waltz, polka, dance a *pas seul* or a sailor's hornpipe, La Sylphide, or the Genu-*wine* Transatlantic Cape Cod Skedaddle, with equal grace and spirit; and as for acting, she can declaim à la [Samuel] Phelps or [Charles] Fechter; is serious, droll; and must play farce, tragedy, opera, comedy, melodrama, pantomime, ballet, change her costume, fight a combat, make love, poison herself, die, and take one encore for a song and another for a dance, in the short space of ten minutes.[31]

Notwithstanding its hyperbolic compression of all the tasks an actress might undertake in the course of a single performance, Robertson's survey vividly captures the sheer virtuosity required of burlesque stars. Marie Wilton's 1859 performance as Juliet in *Romeo and Juliet Travestie* incorporated many of the 'turns' which Robertson enumerated. During the course of the performance, Wilton drove a child's toy hoop around the stage during the ball scene; sang a version of 'Buffalo Girls' ('Oh pretty little girl, will you dance to-night – dance to-night – dance to night?') with her rival suitors Romeo and Paris; joined in a 'grotesque' ensemble dance as the orchestra played 'Pop Goes the Weasel' (scene 2, stage direction); sang 'The Old Bog Hole' with Romeo; performed a serenade from Donizetti's *Don Pasquale* as a duet with her barking dog; sneezed her way through the balcony scene; bid Romeo goodnight to the tune of 'Behold how brightly'; danced with the Friar and Romeo to the tune of 'Jemmy Rogers'; played with her doll and skipped rope while waiting for the Nurse; imitated a boxing coach as the Nurse re-enacted the fight between Romeo and Tybalt; crooned 'Villikins and his Dinah' with Capulet, Lady Capulet, and Paris; pantomimed falling asleep while reading Martin Tupper's *Proverbial Philosophy* (the burlesque's version of Juliet taking a sleeping potion); and, in the final scene, performed a minstrel show serenade with 'banjo, tambourine, and bones' (scene 6, stage direction).

While this sort of information is undeniably useful in getting a sense of how Shakespeare burlesques were staged, it cannot really evoke the 'feel' of any such performance in its full kinetic, aural, and visual dimensions. We have only to experience the tedium of reading nineteenth-century burlesque texts to realize that they scarcely convey the vitality of the

---

[31] *Illustrated Times* 23 April 1864.

performances which they appear to document. Whether in manuscripts, actors' sides, a published acting edition, or even a rare promptbook, a burlesque *script* provides only tantalizing hints of what the *Saturday Review* described as 'the grimace, the humorous inflections of voice, the quaint posturing, the graceful dance, light, sparkle, and colour' of the burlesque performer.[32] Still less can a script convey the audience's perspective. As Augustin Filon astutely noted more than a century ago, no burlesque script ever gives a 'just impression' of the sensual totality of the spectators' experience, from 'the pervading odour of the *poudre de riz*' to 'the *flonsflons* of the orchestra', and from 'the quivering of the gasaliers' to 'the dazzling electric light'.[33] There is ample justification, indeed, for Barnard Hewitt's claim that no theatrical form 'suffers so much from the passage of time' as burlesque.[34]

Of course *every* performance suffers from the 'passage of time' because it is the nature of performance to evanesce. Any performance can only ever be imperfectly preserved, whether in memory, artifacts, or documentation. Yet burlesque was the most disposable form of theatrical entertainment in the nineteenth century. The very idea of 'disposable' Shakespeare works against the preservation of souvenirs, artifacts, and documentation. Written practically overnight, rehearsed in a week, and performed for a month or two, these comic plays were attractive only as long as they remained novel. Burlesque playwrights laboured under no illusion that their works would survive as theatrical masterpieces; rather,

[32] Review of W. Davenport Adams' *A Book of Burlesque* in the *Saturday Review* 18 July 1891. In its review of George L. Fox's starring performance in T. C. DeLeon's *Hamlet Travestie*, the *New York Times* acknowledged that the 'prompter's copy' had 'little to do with the triumph of yesterday's representation' (15 February 1870).
[33] Augustin Filon, *The English Stage* (London: John Milne, 1897), p. 95.
[34] Barnard Hewitt, 'Mrs. John Wood and the Lost Art of Burlesque Acting', *Theatre Journal* 13.2 (May 1961), p. 84. It is not difficult, however, to find scripts. About fifty Shakespeare burlesques were published in the nineteenth century, and the British Library contains the manuscript versions of almost every new play submitted to the Lord Chamberlain's Office for licensing. Plays submitted prior to 1824 are in the Larpent Collection in the Huntington Library. Several dozen promptbooks are held by the Birmingham Shakespeare Library, the Folger Shakespeare Library, the Harvard Theatre Collection, and the Shakespeare Centre in Stratford-upon-Avon. Not surprisingly, promptbooks for Shakespeare burlesques are fewer in number and less heavily annotated than those for legitimate productions. The first nineteenth-century Shakespeare burlesque to be reprinted in a modern anthology was the Broughs' *The Enchanted Isle* (1848), which Michael Booth edited for his *English Plays of the Nineteenth Century* 5 vols. (Oxford: Clarendon Press, 1976), v, pp. 163–201. Stanley Wells' *Nineteenth-Century Shakespeare Burlesques* features unglossed transcriptions of thirty-three burlesques previously published in Great Britain and the United States and a prefatory essay to each volume. The only full-scale critical edition of a nineteenth-century Shakespeare burlesque is Charles Mathews' *Othello, the Moor of Fleet Street*, ed. Manfred Draudt (Tübingen: Francke, 1993). In the digital age, Chadwyck Healey's 'Editions and Adaptations of Shakespeare' includes the texts of more than one hundred adaptations, sequels, and burlesques from the seventeenth, eighteenth, and nineteenth centuries.

they laboured under the relentless pressure to turn out scripts at a rapid pace. Robson, for example, tried to obtain the original orchestral score for Talfourd's burlesque of *The Merchant of Venice*, only to be told that it had been lost.[35] Small wonder that the custodians of Victorian cultural memory have ignored theatrical burlesque when even its own practitioners were indifferent to preserving a documentary record. The dearth of primary materials documenting nineteenth-century Shakespeare burlesques makes them seem *more* lost to us than the more extensively documented legitimate Shakespearean revivals. But it only seems that way. To acknowledge that no performance can ever be fully recovered is not, however, to concede the impossibility of historical and critical inquiry. Rather, it is to recognize that any investigation of the theatrical past cannot have reconstruction as its ultimate goal. Even though I rely on the traditional materials of theatre history – promptbooks, manuscripts, acting editions, playbills, correspondence, newspaper and periodical reviews, and performance iconography – I profess no interest either in reconstructing the performance of Shakespeare burlesques or in issuing aesthetic judgments about them. I profess great interest, however, in exploring the broad discursive activity of a largely unexamined theatrical tradition.

In assessing the cultural significance of that tradition, a judicious performance historian might begin by asking, 'what is a burlesque?' The question can hardly be trivial since it has never admitted a single answer. Linda Hutcheon and Margaret Rose, among others, have amply demonstrated that the study of parody has been circumscribed by the inconsistency and insufficiency of definitions.[36] Historically, burlesque has been defined as a subset of literary or theatrical parody which inverts form and content.[37] As Joseph Addison observed in the *Spectator*, a burlesque either 'represents mean Persons in the Accoutrements of Heroes' (i.e., low to high) or 'describes great Persons acting and speaking like the basest among the People' (i.e., high to low).[38] In the first instance,

---

[35] William Farren, a letter to Frederick Robson, n.d., Fol. Y.c. 898 (10), Folger Shakespeare Library, Washington, DC.

[36] Linda Hutcheon, *A Theory of Parody: The Teachings of Twentieth-Century Art Forms* (New York and London: Methuen, 1985); Margaret Rose, *Parody/Meta-Fiction* (London: Croom Helm, 1979) and *Parody: Ancient, Modern, and Post-modern* (Cambridge: Cambridge University Press, 1993).

[37] For the sake of etymological precision, it bears remembering that parody is a Greek term (*parodia*) whose first recorded usage, in Aristotle's *Poetics*, refers to mock-epics. Burlesque, by contrast, is an early-modern term which derives from the Italian *burla*, meaning to ridicule or to joke. Travesty – meaning to dress up – is an even later term, first used to describe the mock-epic poetry produced in seventeenth-century France.

[38] *Spectator* 15 December 1711; qtd in *The Spectator*, ed. Donald F. Bond 5 vols. (Oxford: Clarendon Press, 1965), II, pp. 467–8.

the burlesque preserves the style of the original text but applies it to inappropriate characters and circumstances (e.g., a chimney sweep who speaks like Othello); in the second, the burlesque deforms the style of the original text but retains its characters and circumstances (e.g., an Othello who speaks like a chimney sweep). This definition boasts staying power. In 1871, Charles Cowden-Clarke explained that a theatrical burlesque either 'elevat[es] a daily occurrence ... into a situation of classic dignity' or 'invest[s] subjects or events of "great pith and moment" in the costume and dialect of vulgar life'.[39] Twentieth-century critics argued much the same. Simon Trussler, John Jump, and Simon Dentith all maintain that the high treatment of low subjects constitutes a 'classic' burlesque while a low treatment of high subjects is better termed a 'travesty' (or 'low' burlesque).[40] According to such definitions, most nineteenth-century Shakespeare burlesques should be considered travesties since, to borrow Trussler's definitional terms, they 'vulgaris[e]' an 'elevated or classical theme' (*Burlesque Plays*, p. ix). While fine distinctions between 'burlesque' and 'travesty' carry their own logic, they do not conform to nineteenth-century theatrical practice. As theatre historians know only too well, the terms 'burlesque', 'travesty', and even 'extravaganza' were used interchangeably by playwrights, actor–managers, critics, and spectators alike. A cursory survey of the titles of Shakespeare parodies – *Hamlet Travestie*, *Macbeth: a Burlesque*, *New King Richard the Third; a Burlesque Extravaganza*, and *Othello Travestie, an Operatic Burlesque Burletta* – reveals that the nineteenth-century stage did not insist upon precise definitions of theatrical forms and styles. While for the sake of convenience I use the term 'burlesque' throughout this work, I do not thereby exclude certain kinds of plays and performances. Whether they were originally labelled burlesques, travesties, extravaganzas (or some combination thereof), the plays under discussion in this book all present themselves as comic misquotations of Shakespeare.

Instead of relying on generic categories which attempt to impose a retrospective order on unruly theatrical practices, we would do better to focus on the essential activities of burlesque as a sustained, self-conscious comic interpretation of a specific text. In other words, let us concentrate less on the formal properties which Shakespeare burlesques 'possess' and more on the critical work which they actually 'do'. The specific,

---

[39] Charles Cowden-Clarke, 'On the Comic Writers of England. VII. – Burlesque Writers', *Gentleman's Magazine* n.s. 5th 7 (June–December 1871), p. 557.

[40] Simon Trussler, ed., *Burlesque Plays of the Eighteenth Century* (Oxford: Oxford University Press, 1969); John Jump, *Burlesque* (London: Methuen, 1972); and Simon Dentith, *Parody* (London and New York: Routledge, 2000).

almost technical questions we might ask about a Shakespeare burlesque (e.g., 'what does a burlesque Lady Macbeth do in the sleepwalking scene?') are useful only to the extent that they lead us to pose more searching questions about the play's metacritical dynamics (e.g., 'what does it mean that burlesque Lady Macbeth becomes Irish – she croons "tooral looral" – in the sleepwalking scene?'). This shift in definition – from form to function – recalls the theoretical principle which the Russian Formalists first articulated: that parody 'refunctions' canonical literary forms once they have become rigid or mechanistic. Although it appears counter-intuitive, parody in fact preserves the continuity of literary traditions by endowing familiar (indeed, overly familiar) texts with new capabilities. Because parody comically distorts both an original text and readers' expectations of that text, readers always understand a parody by reference to its original. Parody is an exemplary instance of intertextuality. This is what Mikhail Bakhtin means by the dialogism of parody: 'another's speech in another's language'.[41] Burlesque, like other forms of parody, is necessarily ambivalent toward its sources, whose value it at once both affirms and denies.

While much attention has been focused on parody's role in postmodern aesthetics, particularly with regard to pastiche and hybridization, we must be careful not to label the Victorian burlesque postmodern *avant la lettre*. To be sure, burlesques employ strategies customarily identified with postmodernism, including the denial of authorial power, the decentring of texts, the repudiation of the Romantic notion that works of art are 'originals', and, correspondingly, an emphasis on the artist's ceaseless reworking of found materials. In the case of Shakespeare burlesques, we might well think of the entire Shakespearean canon as 'found' material. Even so, attending to the burlesque's specific historical context reveals that it enacts a distinctively modernist criticism. However much it attacks dominant cultural practices, the Shakespeare burlesque always implies – indeed, sustains – a nostalgia for a culture which would no longer need to be attacked if only it were properly reformed. Yet as we shall see, it is the burlesque's bitter irony never to bring into being the culture which it can only imagine.

Throughout the nineteenth century, burlesques came under attack for being 'sensational vulgarities'[42] which consisted of nothing better than 'lame metres, cockney rhymes, inane puns and senseless "topical"

---

[41] Mikhail Bakhtin, 'Discourse in the Novel', in *The Dialogic Imagination*, ed. Michael Holquist and trans. Caryl Emerson and Michael Holquist (Austin: The University of Texas Press, 1981), p. 324.
[42] R. H. Horne, 'The Burlesque and the Beautiful', *Contemporary Review* 18 (1871), p. 400.

allusions'.[43] W. B. Donne, the Examiner of Plays (1857–74), likened burlesque to an 'impure flesh-fly' which 'battens upon the imagination of Shakespeare' only to eat away at his genius.[44] In a more sustained denunciation, George Eliot asserted that Shakespeare burlesques had 'debas[ed] the moral currency' and 'lower[ed] the value of every inspiring fact and tradition'.[45] She feared that future generations of Englishmen would come to know Shakespeare only through burlesques, while the original master-texts would 'be reduced to a mere *memoria technica* of the improver's puns' (p. 96). In Eliot's nightmarish prophecy:

> [a] bottle-nosed Lear will come on with a monstrous corpulence from which he will frantically dance himself free during the midnight storm; Rosalind and Celia will join in a grotesque ballet with shepherds and shepherdesses; Ophelia in fleshings and a voluminous brevity of grenadine will dance through the mad scene, finishing with the famous 'attitude of the scissors' in the arms of Laertes ... [These are] premonitory signs of a hideous millennium, in which the lion will have to lie down with the lascivious monkey that his soul naturally abhors. (Eliot, 'Debasing the Moral Currency', p. 96)

As suggested by Eliot's image of the 'lion' laying down 'with the lascivious monkey', nineteenth-century remarks on the perceived demerits of burlesque turned on reductive oppositions between 'high' and 'low' culture in which the burlesque could only be a debauched version of a classic original. Twentieth-century critics generally followed a similar line of reasoning. Most recently, Jonathan Bate maintained that, for all their 'comic and ironic sharpness', plays like *Hamlet Travestie* are 'mean and limited' when 'set beside the magnanimity and breadth of vision' of Shakespeare's original works.[46]

On the face of it, all these critics are right. Shakespeare burlesques are not great plays (at least not in the way that Shakespeare's originals are great). Their language, characters, and situations do not appear complex. Still less do they invite a compelling range of interpretation. Yet such pronouncements, though seemingly logical, actually conceal a flawed premise: that Shakespeare burlesques should be read as 'rival' versions of

---

[43] William Archer, *English Dramatists of To-Day* (London: Sampson Low, 1882), p. 113. To be sure, not all critics were hostile. Cowden-Clarke, for example, praised the 'genuine humour, and wit' of *Hamlet Travestie* ('Comic Writers. VII', *Gentleman's Magazine*, p. 572).

[44] W. B. Donne, 'Dramatic Register for 1853', *Quarterly Review* 95 (June 1854), p. 87. As he flatly declared to Charles Kean, 'I abominate Burlesques' (Donne, a letter to Charles Kean, 19 March [185-], Theatre Museum, London).

[45] George Eliot, 'Debasing the Moral Currency', in *Impressions of Theophrastus Such* (1879; Edinburgh and London: William Blackwood and Sons, 1901), p. 97.

[46] Jonathan Bate, *Shakespearean Constitutions* (Oxford: Clarendon Press, 1989), p. 126.

Shakespeare and judged accordingly. Everything we know about parody, however, tells us that we cannot read Shakespeare burlesques simply as mock versions of Shakespeare's plays. Certainly, these plays are mocking; but they are neither redactions, adaptations, nor renderings – not even false renderings – of Shakespearean originals.[47] While an adaptation *is* the play which it adapts, a burlesque *represents* the play it burlesques. For over a century and a half, performances of John Dryden and William Davenant's *The Enchanted Island* (1667) counted as performances of *The Tempest*. By contrast, performances of *Hamlet Travestie* have never counted as performances of *Hamlet*. Of course someone who has neither read nor seen Shakespeare's original play could mistake *Hamlet Travestie* for *Hamlet*. But that does not make *Hamlet Travestie* any less a burlesque.

Shakespeare burlesques are *not* Shakespeare because they do not iterate – but rather interpret – their precursory texts.[48] What David Z. Saltz has written of Heiner Müller's *Hamletmachine* (1977) applies equally well to any nineteenth-century burlesque of *Hamlet*: that it 'spins a dense web of allusions to Shakespeare's play, and even more, to the mythologies that have accrued around the play over the centuries, and to the ideological implications of those mythologies'.[49] The hostility which most critics have shown toward nineteenth-century burlesques results, I believe, from a fundamentally misguided strategy of interpretation and not from any inherent unworthiness of the plays themselves. This is not to say that no Shakespeare burlesque is bad. Of course some are. But it is to say that a bad Shakespeare burlesque is bad in a way that has not been generally appreciated. Much of the criticism written about nineteenth-century Shakespeare burlesques over the past 150 years can be likened, in an image worthy of burlesque, to blaming a cat for being the wrong kind of dog.[50]

---

[47] Daniel Fischlin and Mark Fortier, in their anthology *Adaptations of Shakespeare* (London: Routledge, 2000), fail to distinguish between burlesque and adaptation, thus listing both David Garrick's 1772 radically altered version of *Hamlet* and John Poole's *Hamlet Travestie* under the overly inclusive category of *Hamlet* 'adaptations' (p. 319).

[48] The Reduced Shakespeare Company does not imply – in its name – that its performances will burlesque Shakespeare, even though many aspects of their performances do. Even a 'reduced' version of a Shakespearean play can count as a performance of that play, just as Kenneth Branagh's film version of *Love's Labour's Lost* (2000) counts as a version of Shakespeare's comedy even though it retained only half of Shakespeare's text.

[49] David Z. Saltz, 'When is the Play the Thing? – Analytic Aesthetics and Dramatic Theory', *Theatre Research International* 20.3 (Autumn 1995), p. 267.

[50] The principal exceptions are the prefatory essays in Wells' 1977 anthology and his series of articles written in the early 1960s. See his 'Burlesques of Charles Kean's *The Winter's Tale*', *Theatre Notebook* 16 (1962), pp. 78–83; 'Shakespeare in Planché's Extravaganzas', *Shakespeare Survey* 16 (1963), pp. 103–17; and 'Shakespearian Burlesques', *Shakespeare Quarterly* 16 (1965), pp. 49–61.

The popularity of burlesques in the nineteenth century recalls a similar, though not identical, taste for theatrical parody in the Elizabethan and Jacobean era. Although Shakespeare and his contemporaries did not produce burlesques in the nineteenth-century sense – that is, self-conscious comic critiques of particular texts – they nonetheless delighted in writing parodic allusions, dialogue, and scenes. In surveying the early modern uses of dramatic satire, we might first cite Shakespeare's own plays which feature varying degrees of parody. Hamlet mocks extravagant acting styles in his famous speech to the players while Ancient Pistol, in *2 Henry IV*, burlesques Marlowe and other university wits. In his two memorable scenes of theatrical burlesque from *A Midsummer Night's Dream* and *Love's Labour's Lost*, Shakespeare ridicules traditions not of literature, but of performance: the rude mechanicals' bungled attempt to stage 'Pyramus and Thisbe' and the embarrassingly inept succession of tableaux in 'The Pageant of Nine Worthies' hastily arranged by the 'pedant, the braggart, the hedge-priest, / the fool, and the boy' (*Love's Labour's Lost*, 5.2.537–8). Shakespeare may have burlesqued himself since 'Pyramus and Thisbe' reads as a botched version of his own love tragedy, *Romeo and Juliet*. As Peter Holland astutely notes, Bottom's endlessly repeated cries of 'O' recall 'the Nurse's lament over the "dead" body of Juliet'.[51] Victorian burlesque playwrights were only too quick to cite Shakespearean precedents in defending their work from charges of vulgarity and impropriety.

Dramatists other than Shakespeare often wrote burlesque allusions into their plays as a means of attacking their rivals. In *The Poetaster*, Ben Jonson ridicules Thomas Dekker (among others) while Dekker, in turn, mocks Jonson in his *Satiromastix*. The burlesque entertainment *The Return from Parnassus*, staged by Cambridge students in 1601, parodies 'sweet Mr Shakespeare'. *The Puritaine, or The Widdow of Watling-Streete* (1607), 'written by W. S'. – and thus included in the Third and Fourth Folios – reads like nothing so much as a burlesque of *Hamlet*, complete with a grieving widow and her graceless son. More notable, however, is the play's transposition of *Hamlet*'s characters and events from a medieval Danish court to contemporary bourgeois London. A similar domestication of plot and character was virtually axiomatic for nineteenth-century burlesque authors. The one Jacobean play which approaches a modern burlesque sensibility is Beaumont and Fletcher's *The Knight of the Burning Pestle*, which burlesques such city comedies as Thomas Heywood's *The*

---

[51] Peter Holland, ed., *A Midsummer Night's Dream* (Oxford: Clarendon Press, 1994), p. 89.

Four Prentises of London. In its play-within-a-play conceit, a Grocer and his wife repeatedly interrupt the performance of a drama called *The London Merchant* and insist that their son, Rafe, play the eponymous knight, a role of their own devising. The play's function is not merely satiric, as Lee Bliss explains, but also 'metadramatic', heightening the audience's 'consciousness of plays as artistic mechanisms, [and] contrived structures that rely on learned conventions and a whole set of social assumptions about the nature of the theatre itself'.[52] It is precisely the 'metadramatic' qualities of nineteenth-century Shakespeare burlesques which allow them to function not merely as idle mockeries, but as searching critiques of Shakespeare's cultural worth. To that extent, the Victorian comic stage looks back to early-modern instances of theatricality and the 'knowingness' of theatre audiences.

In terms of Shakespeare's theatrical legacy, we must be careful to distinguish between abbreviations and burlesques. During the Commonwealth, itinerant acting troupes performed abridged versions of comic scenes taken mainly from popular, full-length plays originally performed before the Puritans closed the theatres in 1642. These playlets, known as drolls, included at least three Shakespearean scenes: 'The Bouncing Knight' (*1 Henry IV*), 'The Grave-makers' (*Hamlet*), and 'Bottom the Weaver' (*A Midsummer Night's Dream*). Played in halls, taverns, and 'Mountebancks Stages', the drolls functioned not as satires, but as rough-and-ready renditions of favourite scenes from pre-Commonwealth plays.[53] Far from denigrating or even critiquing traditions of playwriting, drolls kept those traditions alive at a time when public playhouses remained shut.

For all their theatrical immediacy, Shakespeare burlesques nonetheless find their origins in poetry. The French satirist Paul Scarron inaugurated the comic genre of the 'mock-epic' with his *Virgile Travestie en vers Burlesques* (1648–53), a profaned classical text whose regal and aristocratic characters were transformed into stereotypes of the contemporary *bourgeoisie*. To employ the apt metaphor of travesty, we might say that Scarron's poems constituted a 'dressing down' of Virgilian heroes. In both Charles Cotton's translation of Scarron (1664–5) and Samuel Butler's *Hudibras* (1663), English burlesque authors found a poetic device which could be

---

[52] Lee Bliss, 'Pastiche, Burlesque, Tragicomedy', in *The Cambridge Companion to English Renaissance Drama*, ed. A. R. Braunmuller and Michael Hattaway (Cambridge: Cambridge University Press, 1990), p. 243.

[53] The reference to 'Mountebancks Stages' appears on the title page of the anthology *The Wits; or, Sport upon Sport* (London, 1673). An earlier volume, similarly titled, was published in 1662.

easily translated into a theatrical vocabulary. Yet unlike George Villiers' *The Rehearsal* (1671), which satirized the entire genre of heroic drama, Shakespeare burlesques always focused upon specific plays and productions. Through a combination of the debased treatment of exalted characters as found in burlesque poetry and the self-conscious theatricality of plays like *The Rehearsal*, Shakespeare burlesques emerged as a distinctive theatrical form in the 1670s. The sometime milliner Thomas Duffet penned the earliest of them: a farcical version of Elkanah Settle's *The Empress of Morocco* (1673) which includes an epilogue parodying the witches in *Macbeth*, and *The Mock-Tempest* (1674). Both plays were staged by the King's Men.

Under the terms of the letters patent granted by Charles II, only two companies – the Duke's Men and the King's Men – were permitted to stage plays in London. In 1672, after the Theatre Royal was destroyed by fire, the King's Men had to perform in a converted tennis court. The Duke's Men, led by Davenant, performed at Dorset Garden, where they enjoyed vastly superior resources in a new playhouse equipped to support the perspective scenery, elaborate settings, and stage machinery formerly associated exclusively with theatre at court. Perhaps making a virtue of a necessity, the King's Men quickly realized that if they could not duplicate their rival company's technical wizardry, they could at least parody it. And so they did, most likely in the autumn of 1673 with the 'Epilogue Spoken by Hecate and three Witches' from Duffet's *The Empress of Morocco*. The epilogue burlesques the elaborate production of the witches' scenes in Davenant's adaptation of *Macbeth* then being performed by the Duke's Men in a production which John Downes famously described as 'being drest in all it's [*sic*] Finery, as new Cloath's, new Scenes, Machines, as flyings for the Witches; with all the Singing and Dancing in it'.[54] Mocking scenic effects produced behind 'Painted Tiffany' to 'blind and amuse the Senses', Duffet's epilogue flatters itself as being more theatrically honest than Davenant's semi-operatic spectacle because its own 'Thunder and lightning is [*sic*] discover'd ... openly, by the most excellent way of Mustard-bowl and Salt-Peter'.[55] In this burlesque vignette, Thunder and Lightning – characters played by actors – appear as absurd emblems of the full scenic effects which the production knew it could not achieve.

[54] John Downes, *Roscius Anglicanus, or an Historical Review of the Stage* (London, 1708), p. 33. '[I]t being all Excellently perform'd, being in the nature of an Opera, it Recompenc'd double the Expence.'

[55] Thomas Duffet, *Epilogue. Being a new Fancy after the old, and most surprising way of Macbeth, Perform'd with new and costly machines* (London, 1674), p. 30. Through the word 'surprising', Duffet characterizes Davenant's spectacle as a deviation in need of correction.

Hecate's homespun 'Glorious Charriot' was nothing more than a 'large Wicker Basket'. Aware that he could not attract spectators who were easily seduced by the charms of stage machinery, Duffet congratulates his audience on its refined sensibility:

> Those that adore the Ghosts and Devils yonder,
> The Powder Lightning and the Mustard Thunder;
> Who though they can't of Plot and Language prattle,
> Can mew like Cats, and roar like Drum in battle.
> ... Those we shall hardly please.
>
> (p. 42)

An insistent pride dwells within the burlesque's refusal to embrace scenic illusionism. Indeed, the King's Men never bothered to burlesque the more ordinary productions staged by their competitor. And it is precisely this refusal to surrender to spectacle which allows Duffet's epilogue to trumpet itself, however disingenuously, as a *more* legitimate version of Shakespeare than the Dorset Garden *Macbeth*, which owed much of its success to intricate, behind-the-scenes technology. To be sure, scorn for elaborate stage effects was hardly unique to the King's Men. John Dryden, a year earlier, also attacked Davenant's *Macbeth* in his 'Prologue and Epilogue to the University of Oxon.' Anticipating Duffet's parody, Dryden decried the stage effects produced by mechanical scenery:

> But when all fail'd, to strike the Stage quite Dumb,
> Those wicked Engines call'd Machines are come.
> Thunder and Lightning now for Wit are Play'd
> And shortly Scenes in *Lapland* will be Lay'd.[56]

Even after moving to expanded quarters in 1674, the King's Men produced Duffet's *The Mock-Tempest* and *Psyche Debauch'd* (1675). These additional productions confirm that the King's Men did not stage burlesques *faute de mieux*. As Gerald Langbaine recorded, the 'Design' of *The Mock-Tempest* was 'to draw the Town from the Duke's Theatre, who for a considerable time had frequented the admirable revis'd Comedy

---

[56] John Dryden, 'Prologue and Epilogue to the University of Oxon.' (1673), in *The Works of John Dryden*, ed. Edward Niles Hooker and H. T. Swedenberg, Jr, *et al.* 20 vols. (Berkeley and Los Angeles: University of California Press, 1956), I, p. 148, lines 21–4. Dryden's piece was written for a performance of Ben Jonson's *The Silent Woman [Epicoene]* at Oxford in July 1673. Also that same year, an anonymous writer lamented in a theatrical epilogue that 'Nonsense shall wear the gay disguise of Rhime, / And though not understood, shall sweetly chime: / Now empty shows must want of sense supply, / Angels shall dance, and *Macbeths* Witches fly: / You shall have storms, thunder & lightning too / . . . . Damn'd Plays shall be adorn'd with mighty Scenes / And Fustian shall be spoke in huge Machines' (Anon., Epilogue to *The Ordinary*, in *A Collection of Poems Written upon several Occasions By several Persons*, London, 1673, p. 167).

called *The Tempest*[57] – that is, Thomas Shadwell's semi-operatic version of Dryden and Davenant's *The Enchanted Island*. Theatrical rivalry is written into Duffet's script. In the opening scene, Duffet infamously reimagines the tempest-tossed ship as a London brothel besieged by apprentices who 'clime the Walls like Cats' (*The Mock-Tempest*, p. 5). The burlesque thus begins not with howling winds and crashing waves, as specified in the Dryden–Davenant text, but with 'breaking Doors', 'breaking Windowes', and the apprentices' cries of 'a Whore a Whore' (stage directions, p. 1).[58] Like Thunder and Lightning in the *Macbeth* parody, the apprentices function as comic personifications of scenic effects – in this instance, the surging waves which overtake Alonzo's ship. In a parody of the 'shower of Fire' from *The Enchanted Island* which descends upon the sailors as their ship sinks,[59] Duffet's burlesque calls for a shower of 'Fire, Apples, [and] Nuts' during the fight between the 'Rabble' apprentices and the 'Wenches' (*The Mock-Tempest*, stage direction, p. 9). Later in the play, Prospero commands Ariel to arrange for 'two great Baboons' to be 'let down with ropes' to snatch the banquet set for Alonzo and his comrades. Ariel protests – with satiric reference to the Duke's Men – that 'Sir *Punchanello* did that at the Play-house.'[60] Prospero then whispers an alternative plan into Ariel's ear, thus alerting the audience that a parody of the Dorset Garden production lay in store. In the eventual banquet scene, Gonzalo and Antonio are 'snatch'd up into the Air' by two 'Devils' while Alonzo 'sinks with the Table out of sight' (pp. 42, 41). Shortly after divulging to Ariel alone his plan for the disappearing banquet, Prospero fears that the Duke's Men may yet mimic his designs. '[M]ake hast [*sic*]', he warns, 'least the Conjurers of to'ther [*sic*] House steal the Invention – thou know'st they snatch at all Ingenious tricks' (pp. 32–3).

When Dryden retrospectively attacked Duffet's burlesques in 1683, he did not focus on their parody of theatrical spectacle since he himself was equally suspicious of intricate scenery. Reserving his invective for

---

[57] Gerald Langbaine, *An Account of the English Dramatick Poets* (Oxford, 1691), pp. 177–8. The reference to 'the Town' tells us something about the elevated social status of the audience at the Duke's Theatre, which included Samuel Pepys. Langbaine dismissed Duffet as 'a Wit of the third Rate' (p. 177).

[58] The apprentices' call is no doubt a pun on the sailors' cry 'ahoy, ahoy'.

[59] John Dryden and William Davenant, *The Tempest, or the Enchanted Island. A Comedy* (London, 1674). 'And when the Ship is sinking, the whole House is darken'd, and a shower of Fire falls upon 'em [the sailors]. This is accompanied with Lightning, and several Claps of Thunder, to the end of the Storm' (stage directions, 1.1.20–2).

[60] Thomas Duffet, *The Mock-Tempest: or The Enchanted Castle. Acted at the Theatre Royal* (London, 1675), p. 32.

the burlesque's deplorable desecration of poetic beauty, he scornfully observed that:

> The dull Burlesque appear'd with impudence,
> And pleas'd by Novelty, in Spite of Sence.
> All, except trivial points, grew out of date;
> *Parnassus* spoke the cant of *Belinsgate*:
> Boundless and Mad, disorder'd Rhyme was seen;
> Disguis'd *Apollo* chang'd to *Harlequin*.
> This Plague, which first in Country Towns began,
> Cities and Kingdoms quickly over-ran;
> The dullest Scriblers some Admirers found,
> And the *Mock-Tempest* was a while renown'd:
> But this low stuff the Town at last despised,
> And scorn'd the Folly that they once had pris'd.[61]

Montague Summers cited this diatribe against 'dull Burlesque' as evidence that Duffet's plays were ineffectual even in their original context.[62] Surely the opposite view is more persuasive: Dryden's indictment of *The Mock-Tempest* a decade after its first performance tells us that 'dull Burlesque' remained quite sharp. Indeed, Duffet's plays anticipated the principal features of nineteenth-century Shakespeare burlesques: first, that the object of their satire is not so much a Shakespearean text (although it is comically rewritten) as a specific *performance* of a text; and second, that the burlesque defends Shakespeare when he comes under attack – at least in the opinion of burlesque playwrights – from latter-day theatrical iconoclasts.[63] From its inception, then, the burlesque sought not merely to criticize contemporary Shakespearean performances but to *correct* them. An act of theatrical reform which aggressively compensated for the deficiencies of other people's productions, the burlesque became part of the very performance history upon which it first had cast its reproachful eye. In honouring Shakespeare, the burlesque really honoured itself as the poet's rightful heir and only legitimate descendant, effectively displacing – indeed, bastardizing – all other competing versions and performances of the Bard.

---

[61] John Dryden, 'The Art of Poetry. Written in French by the Sieur de Boileau, Made English', lines 81–92 (1683; *Works*, II, pp. 126–7).
[62] Montague Summers, Introduction, *The Rehearsal* (Stratford-upon-Avon: The Shakespeare Head Press, 1914), p. xxi.
[63] Arthur Murphy's *Hamlet, with Alterations* (1772) was written as a satire upon David Garrick's adaptation of *Hamlet* which he first produced at Drury Lane in December 1772. Never performed, Murphy's parody was posthumously published in Jesse Foot's *The Life of Arthur Murphy* (London: J. Faulder, 1811).

This book aims at a wide audience of Shakespeareans, performance historians, and Victorianists. Like *Shakespeare's Victorian Stage*, my study of the relation between theatrical and historical culture in mid-Victorian Britain, this book moves around and across disciplinary boundaries. Since the subject matter is relatively unfamiliar, a certain amount of summative material is necessary to acquaint many readers with some of the performances, personalities, and events under discussion. For the sake of convenience, much of this information has been covered in this introduction, whose broader purpose is to establish the parameters of the historical material out of which the book's arguments arises.

The first chapter examines the linguistic conventions of Shakespeare burlesques, focusing not only on topicalities, localizations, and puns, but also on the inevitable revisions made to any burlesque script whether in the course of its original run, a provincial tour, or a revival. Like all forms of parody, burlesques make 'elite' language our own, but always on the condition that such redirected language can never be fully our own. While the burlesques studied in this book rendered Shakespeare proximate through colloquial and contemporized language, the price to be paid for that proximity was nonsense. This is the always already breached promise of burlesque: the seductive prospect of greatness made familiar; the disconcerting reality of the familiar made absurd. It was not so much that Shakespeare burlesques were bereft of meaning as that they articulated meaning in unexpected ways.

The second chapter looks at some of the ways in which burlesque performances theorized their relationship to so-called 'legitimate' Shakespearean culture. The popularity of Shakespeare burlesques throughout the Victorian era undoubtedly tells us that the sanctity of Shakespeare as cultural and national icon was under siege. But not from where we would expect. For the threat to Shakespeare was posed not by the burlesque, so its proponents claimed, but rather by self-righteous Bardolators, pedantic literary critics, mediocre performers, and sensationalizing actor–managers. The burlesque claimed to perform not Shakespeare's debasement, but the ironic restoration of his compromised authority. In so doing, the burlesque empowered itself to define and to enforce standards of Shakespearean correctness. As an explicitly metatheatrical form, burlesques acted out the very issue of what constituted 'the authority of Shakespeare in the action of performance'.[64]

---

[64] W. B. Worthen, *Shakespeare and the Authority of Performance* (Cambridge: Cambridge University Press, 1997), p. 3.

The Shakespeare burlesque's authoritative claims meant nothing apart from the specific interpretive practices of its audience. Any discussion of the burlesque's critical disposition toward Bardolatry therefore must address the broad social dynamic of the performance itself, with a particular emphasis on audience composition, knowledge, and experience. The third chapter thus extends beyond the confines of the playhouse (but without deserting it) to investigate how the burlesque critiqued the middle-class cult of respectability from its privileged position within Bohemian 'fast' culture. Analysis of the burlesque's 'worldliness' culminates in the final chapter with an exploration of how these comic plays imagined different political realities. In so doing, the burlesque used Shakespeare as the means – and not the object – of its parody. Through close readings of burlesques of *Coriolanus*, *King John*, and *The Tempest*, I argue in the final chapter that theatrical parodies were neither inherently progressive nor inherently conservative. A more accurate appraisal would be that burlesques drew upon Shakespeare's cultural capital to realize theatrically a range of political possibilities.[65]

In explaining how nineteenth-century theatrical burlesques situated Shakespeare within discourses on cultural patrimony, respectability, and political reform, this book shares the object of much recent criticism: to offer historically specific accounts of post-Renaissance Shakespearean appropriations. This interdisciplinary field might be termed 'Shakespeare *after* Shakespeare'.[66] Along with other works in this continually expanding field, this book regards performance as a cultural production and not as an isolated aesthetic artifact which needs only to be fully described or even meticulously contextualized in order to be understood. Because this work scrutinizes material which is manifestly 'not Shakespeare', it cannot be read as a straightforward work of Shakespeare performance history. It can, however, be read as a work on the dissemination of Shakespeare within nineteenth-century popular culture. Like

---

[65] Politics was not the only external issue which Shakespeare burlesques confronted. Such plays frequently trafficked in ethnic and racial stereotypes, with Macbeth converted into a 'stage Irishman', Shylock appearing as a Jewish rag merchant from London's East End, and Othello as an Ethiopian serenader from a minstrel show. Precisely because of their representation of race, some nineteenth-century *Othello* burlesques have received careful study. See, for example, Joyce Green MacDonald's 'Acting Black: *Othello*, *Othello* Burlesques, and the Performance of Blackness', *Theatre Journal* 46 (1994), pp. 133–46.

[66] See, for example, Jonathan Bate, *Shakespearean Constitutions: Politics, Theatre, Criticism 1730–1830* (Oxford: Clarendon Press, 1989); Michael D. Bristol, *Big-time Shakespeare* (London and New York: Routledge, 1996); Richard Burt and Lynda E. Boose, eds., *Shakespeare, the Movie: Popularizing the Plays on Film, TV, and Video* (London and New York: Routledge, 1997); and Barbara Hodgdon, *The Shakespeare Trade: Performances and Appropriations* (Philadelphia: University of Pennsylvania Press, 1998).

much recent scholarship on the sociology of nineteenth-century theatre and drama, this work does not fail to situate performance within a dense network of cultural practices.[67] But neither does it fail to attend to the structure and content of the plays themselves as vital parts of an overall performance event. This book is thus partly a genre study because it conducts close readings of dramatic texts. And yet it is not possible to study burlesques purely as ahistorical textual artifacts precisely because burlesques necessarily implicate themselves in other texts and other performances. In consequence, anyone watching (or reading) a burlesque will immediately move beyond it to consider the specific cultural values which the burlesque confronts and problematizes. It is impossible to stay inside such a script because, in fact, it has no inside; the burlesque is always outside itself. And it is precisely in virtue of what lies 'outside' Shakespeare burlesques that they furnish us with uniquely compelling material for historical and critical investigation.

---

[67] See, for example, Jim Davis and Victor Emeljanow, 'New Views of a Cheap Theatre: Reconstructing the Nineteenth-Century Theatre Audience', *Theatre Survey* 39.2 (1998), pp. 53–72; Tracy C. Davis, *The Economics of the British Stage 1800–1914* (Cambridge: Cambridge University Press, 2000); Richard Foulkes, *Church and Stage in Victorian England* (Cambridge: Cambridge University Press, 1997); Jane Moody, *Illegitimate Theatre in London, 1770–1840* (Cambridge: Cambridge University Press, 2000); and Kerry Powell, *Women and Victorian Theatre* (Cambridge: Cambridge University Press, 1997).

CHAPTER I

'Vile beyond endurance': the language of burlesque

Gilbert Abbott à Beckett's *King John (with the Benefit of the Act)* premiered at the St James's Theatre on 16 October 1837. In his burlesque of the tyrannous monarch, the comedian Henry Hall wore an ermine trimmed robe, a chain mail tunic, and a breast plate with a spike in the centre (illustration 3). This pseudo-medieval garb sneeringly alludes to the vogue for historically accurate stage dress which began, not coincidentally, with J. R. Planché and Charles Kemble's production of *King John* (Covent Garden 1823), the first Shakespearean revival to feature costumes of antiquarian propriety. Hall's helmet (in the shape of a chimney cowl) also ingeniously features a bird-topped weather vane, complete with four spindles labelled 'N', 'E', 'W', and 'S'. The sartorial flourish is ludicrous since weathercocks belong on spires and not on the heads of royalty.[1] The sources of its humour are several. In its blatant contrast with Hall's vaguely antiquarian costume, the weather vane mocks the legitimate theatre's increasing obsession with historically correct stage accessories. The costume indeed guarantees accuracy – not historical, but meteorological. Additionally, the costume encodes a burlesque of dramatic character. The four letters on John's weather vane stand not for geographical directions but, as Walter Hamilton relates, for the satiric epithet 'Naughty English Wrongful Sovereign'.[2] The acronym thus functions as a joke on the character's villainy.

More suggestively, the ornamental headpiece expresses the provisional and mutable nature of theatrical performance. Like the weather vane which continually turns in the wind, never pointing for long in any one direction, so, too, the Shakespeare burlesque never comes to rest at

---

[1] An illustration in Charles Selby's *Kynge Richard ye Third* shows Lady Anne wearing a similar headpiece, described as a 'moveable weather arrow with N.S.E.W., made of pasteboard and gold paper' (London: Thomas Hailes Lacy, n.d., pp. 4, 5).

[2] Walter Hamilton, ed., *Parodies of the Works of English and American Authors* 6 vols. London: Reeves and Turner, 1885.

3. Henry Hall as burlesque King John in Gilbert Abbott à Beckett's *King John (with the Benefit of the Act)*, St James's Theatre, London, 1837.

a single point, never affixes itself to a single, invariable meaning. This ingenious comic metaphor confirms Robert Allen's recent assertion that there is 'no moment' when a burlesque 'speaks with the voice of moral and authorial omniscience' (*Horrible Prettiness*, pp. 27, 28). One of the principal ways in which burlesque performance remains continually open, continually resistant to the ascription of meaning, is through its own language. The weather vane's four letters 'N', 'E', 'W', 'S' tell us that the unpredictability of burlesque – its newness – begins in language, even before the undecidability of theatrical performance comes into play. As the *King John* burlesque vividly announces, burlesque speech is always already a redirection, always already a whirlwind. Performance only intensifies, then, the conundrum that begins in the language of burlesque nonsense. While it is the nature of *all* burlesques to disable themselves through language, such disability is most forcefully enacted in Shakespeare burlesques since their 'source texts' are themselves repositories of sanctified meanings. The nonsense locutions of the Shakespeare burlesque act as a reified negation: the palpable collapse of a once familiar, once sensible Shakespearean canon. Like the crazy weather vane atop a chimney cowl which purports to be an appropriate costume for a twelfth-century English king, the inanities of Shakespeare burlesques obstruct their own meaning, rendering them 'not simply improbable', as the critic E. S. Dallas observed, but also 'impossible and incomprehensible' (*Blackwood's Magazine* 79 Feb. 1856, p. 229). The acknowledged incomprehensions of burlesque language – its topicalities, puns, and revisions – do not obstruct or impede the spectator from accessing an otherwise intelligible performance text; rather, those incomprehensions enable spectators to undertake interpretive acts. The bafflement of meaning thus provides the burlesque with its own critical metalanguage, enabling it to move beyond what would seem to be an interpretive stalemate and toward acts of cultural engagement.

Shakespeare burlesques gleefully trafficked in topicalities, with characters, events, and scenic locations regularly contemporized to conform to the audience's knowledge, if not necessarily to its own experience. A few examples will suffice to demonstrate the burlesque's fluency in what the *Theatrical Times* called 'the town-talk of the day'.[3] The most pronounced localization was that Shakespearean characters were transformed into

---

[3] Review of *The Judgment of Paris; or, the Pas de Pippins*, by Charles Selby, Adelphi Theatre, London, *Theatrical Times* 22 August 1846.

ordinary Londoners, a strategy of social demotion which recalls the classic definition of literary burlesque as the low treatment of a serious subject. In Blanchard's *The Merchant of Venice (very far indeed) from the Text of Shakespeare*, the merchant Antonio becomes a fishmonger, the money-lending Shylock a neighbourhood pawnbroker, Gratiano a footman in plush breeches, and the noble Portia a buxom tapstress.[4] London environs were frequently substituted for Shakespeare's historical and foreign locales. In Burnand' *The Rise and Fall of Richard III* (1868), Lord Stanley resides in the facetiously described suburban 'village' of Seven Dials, an area of St Giles' parish in central London then notorious for squalor and homicide.[5] Even when burlesque characters retained their noble or regal status, they nonetheless spoke with anachronistic references to contemporary urban culture. Thus, in Coyne's burlesque of *Richard III*, Buckingham swears to the Lord Mayor (falsely, as it turns out) that the respectable Richard never visits the 'Cider Cellars', a notorious late-night drinking club in the Strand.[6] A travesty King Lear rages in the midst of a storm that he can easily knock out 'the Benica Boy' because he has 'learned the uppercut from our Champion Sayers'.[7] The allusion here is to the 1860 bare-knuckle prizefight between the American John Heenan ('the Benica Boy') and the victorious Englishman Tom Sayers. In *Hamlet According to an Act of Parliament* (1853), Bernardo takes advantage of the ghost's midnight visitation to mock the contemporary vogue for seances or 'spirit rapping'.[8]

Shakespeare burlesques frequently alluded to the contemporary theatrical scene, with satiric references to actors, theatre repertoires, and even the Lord Chamberlain's licensing authority. In *A Thin Slice of Ham Let!*, the sceptical hero likens his father's spectre to the stage 'ghost' which John Henry Pepper conjured upon the stage of the Royal Polytechnic. 'It may be a trick / From the Polytechnic', he warns Horatio; '[j]ust a spectre of Pepper's invoking' (Wells, *Nineteenth-Century Shakespeare Burlesques*, IV, p. 59).[9] Among the literary and theatrical ghosts which Pepper depicted

[4] E. L. Blanchard, *The Merchant of Venice (very far indeed) from the Text of Shakespeare. A Burlesque Operatic Extravaganza in One Act* 1843 British Library Add Mss 42,968 fols. 688–700.
[5] F. C. Burnand, *The Rise and Fall of Richard III; or, a New Front to an Old Dickey* (London: Phillips, n.d.), stage direction, p. 15.
[6] J. Stirling Coyne, *New Grand, Historical, Bombastical, Musical and Completely Illegitimate Tragedy to be Called 'Richard III'* 1844 British Library Add Mss 42,973, f. 9b.
[7] Anon., *Kynge Lear and Hys Faythfulle Foole. Burlesque in One Act* 1860 British Library Add Mss 52,994 C, f. 8.
[8] Barton, *Hamlet According to an Act of Parliament* 1853 British Library Add Mss 52,943 M, f. 7.
[9] In Pepper's trick, the image of a person standing beneath the stage was projected through a series of mirrors onto a large sheet of glass slotted into the stage floor and held up by imperceptible

4. 'Hamlet; a *ballet d'action* in the court of Denmark, into which are introduced some strange figures and awful frights. For characters, see small bill of great William', c. 1850s. The ghost of Old Hamlet is played by 'Pepper's Ghost', a popular magic trick in the mid nineteenth century which created the theatrical illusion of a ghost through an ingenious placement of mirrors and plate glass. Note the anachronistic umbrellas, which identify Horatio and Marcellus as Victorian 'gents'.

during his entertainments at the Polytechnic was, indeed, the ghost of Old Hamlet. A nineteenth-century cartoon, depicted in illustration 4, exploits the comic potential of Pepper's Ghost by imagining it as part of a *Hamlet* burlesque. Appearing in double to indicate movement upon catching sight of his father's ghost, Hamlet calmly scratches his chin. By contrast, the terrified Horatio and Marcellus (whose hair stands

wires. From the audience's perspective, the resulting projection appeared to be an incorporeal presence. Because 'Pepper's Ghost' was only a reflection, a stage actor could seem to pierce it with a knife or even to walk through it. When the gas lamps placed beneath the stage were turned on and off, the ghost seemed to materialize and disintegrate.

on end) cower behind an anachronistic umbrella, the property of choice in Victorian burlesque. The translucent ghost consists of a carved pumpkin head atop a suit of armour. The papers scattered on the floor – 'Pepper and Dirks', 'Plate Glass', and 'Spirit Medi[um]' – quite explicitly instruct us to read the ghost as a spirit conjured up by the magician Pepper (and his collaborator Henry Dirks) through the clever use of unseen mirrors and plate glass.

In *Romeo and Juliet Travestie*, the young lovers catch head colds while standing in the night air during the balcony scene and thus find themselves swearing to 'the boon, the inconstant boon' (p. 18). Apart from butchering the most famous love scene in English drama (an irreverence compounded by fits of sneezing), the characters' nasal intonations also mocked Charles Kean's speech impediment which made 'm' sound like 'b'. Hamlet's speech to the players in *Hamlet! The Ravin' Prince of Denmark!!* (1866) becomes an address to the audience in which the burlesque tragic hero ironically laments the decline of tragedy and the rise of 'sickly' sensation melodrama (Wells, *Nineteenth-Century Shakespeare Burlesques*, IV, p. 111). 'O for some Bard to consecrate the scene', Hamlet importunes, '[a]nd bid the Drama be what she hath been!' Maurice Dowling's *Romeo and Juliet, as the Law Directs* (Strand 1837) alludes not only to the patent theatres' longstanding monopoly, but also to the Strand's ongoing legal battles with the Lord Chamberlain over violations of the Licensing Act of 1737. Until 1843, minor theatres like the Strand were restricted to the production of burlettas in which scripted dialogue was supplemented by extensive musical accompaniment, singing, and dancing. In the opening scene of Dowling's play, Sampson and Gregory clarify the extent to which they are legally permitted to rely on their script:

SAMPSON: ... Is this a lawful thing? What shall I say?
GREGORY: Don't say at all, but sing.
SAMPSON: Is that the law? May I say words that teaze?
GREGORY: So that you sing it, say whate'er you please.[10]

Recognizing a duty to melodize their speech, the pair immediately launch into a duet to the tune of 'Sampson and Balthazar'. Their preceding banter exposes the law's inane emphasis on form over content: Shakespeare's words (at least his unalloyed words) could not be performed outside

---

[10] Maurice Dowling, *Romeo and Juliet, as the Law Directs. An Operatic Burlesque Burletta* (London: J. Duncombe & Co., n.d.), p. 5.

a patent theatre yet the most ribald puns could be sung with impunity from the stage of the Strand.

The scant scholarly attention which these comic plays have received can be traced in part to the enduring perception – erroneous, as I shall argue – that burlesque humour depends primarily upon comprehending long outdated topical allusions, puns, and slang. For many students of nineteenth-century popular drama, burlesques do not warrant serious attention because over the intervening years they have become unintelligible. Consider, for example, James Ellis' assertion in his 1983 survey of Victorian burlesques of *Hamlet* that while topicalities guarantee a burlesque's short-term notoriety, they also render it 'utterly inaccessible' to later generations.[11] Ellis certainly has a point. Many of the local references in these plays elude general comprehension. In order to decode them, modern readers will need to research nineteenth-century social and cultural history. Similarly, colloquialisms such as 'tol lol' (tolerably well), 'shindy' (a spree), and 'like bricks' (with gusto) which initially gave the burlesque its arresting immediacy – Shakespeare's characters speaking in the idiom of modern Londoners – now send exasperated readers to J. C. Hotten's *A Dictionary of Modern Slang, Cant, and Vulgar Words* (1859). The very language which first made Shakespeare burlesques so breathlessly up-to-the-minute now makes those same plays so hopelessly out-of-date. Of course every theatrical era dates itself, and no doubt audience members will exchange bewildered looks during some far distant revival of the Reduced Shakespeare Company's *The Compleat Works of Wllm Shkspr (abridged)* (1994) when the actors refer to 'Donahue, Geraldo, and Oprah Jessy Raphael [*sic*]' and a 'Southern California white trash surfer dude'.[12]

But let us not accept defeat too easily. While it is undeniably true that many of the local references in Shakespeare burlesques are no longer intelligible in the twenty-first century, it is equally true that those same references were never completely intelligible to anyone except their immediate, target audience – and, even then, not in all cases. In other words, nineteenth-century burlesques began to date even in the nineteenth century. In *A Book of Burlesque* (1891), W. Davenport Adams acknowledged that *Hamlet Travestie* made for 'dreary reading' eighty years after its initial publication (p. 123). In 1883, the author T. F. Dillon-Croker wrote to his

---

[11] James Ellis, 'The Counterfeit Presentment: Nineteenth-Century Burlesques of *Hamlet*', *Nineteenth-Century Theatre Research* 11.1 (Summer 1983), pp. 29–50.
[12] Jess Borgeson, Adam Long, and Daniel Singer, *The Compleat Works of Wllm Shkspr (abridged)* (New York: Applause Books, 1994), pp. 5, 32.

friend Walter Hamilton, suggesting that he include a reference to *King John (with the Benefit of the Act)* in his forthcoming collection of parodies and burlesques even though 'at the present day [the burlesque] sounds very insipid, if not, irreverent fooling'.[13] Of course à Beckett's burlesque was not even a memory for Dillon-Croker, who was only six when it premiered. His interest in the *King John* burlesque was thus purely antiquarian; the play was a 'curious' relic which preserved a 'style of composition that amused an audience nearly fifty years ago'. For Augustin Filon, burlesques deteriorated at an even more accelerated rate. Reading in middle age a burlesque one adored as a youth, he confessed, was like cutting through a 'thicket of allusions which had become enigmas' (*The English Stage*, p. 95). Topical allusions were no longer amusing, he lamented, because they were no longer 'intelligible'.

Retrospective accounts of the burlesque's fading appeal do not, however, tell the whole story. For it is demonstrably the case that burlesques were not uniformly intelligible even when they were first performed. After undergoing the 'penitential study' of reading several burlesque texts to learn if he had missed any 'clever writing' which had been injuriously 'gabbled' by the performers, William Archer concluded that because the writing was so bad, the performers had done him an unwitting favour by turning the impoverished dialogue into gibberish through their strong Cockney accents (*English Dramatists*, p. 113). In a more measured account, the *Illustrated London News* reported that 'the jokes were so thick' in Selby's *Kynge Richard ye Third*, that 'the hearers had not time to reflect on the worth of one before the wit of another flashed forth'.[14]

All these accounts reveal that the topicalities of Shakespeare burlesques, even for their original audiences, have *never* been fully intelligible. The audience's awareness of its own inability to 'recognize' the play has always been part of the burlesque experience. Thus, our own inapprehension of such topicalities does not depart from, but actually conforms to (without precisely duplicating), a continuing pattern of spectating and reading. Certainly, it is now perplexing to read a nineteenth-century Shakespeare burlesque. But it was equally perplexing for members of the original audiences, if only because actors 'gabbled' the jokes, playwrights crammed too many topical allusions into the text, or audiences themselves did not possess the requisite knowledge to catch all the local references. Indeed, spectators from the provinces (to say nothing of those

---

[13] T. F. Dillon-Croker, a letter to Walter Hamilton, November 1883, qtd in Hamilton, *Parodies*, II, p. 199.

[14] *Illustrated London News* 2 March 1844.

from outside Britain) were far less likely to be acquainted with details of metropolitan life than were the burlesque's 'native' audience. There was no original moment of spectatorial mastery which later generations of critics must struggle heroically to recover. It is liberating, indeed, to realize that topicalities – the very feature which was supposed to make burlesque Shakespeare *more* accessible than legitimate Shakespeare – puzzled even some of the original audience members. It is liberating because it allows us to escape from the burden of our perceived ignorance. We need not be intimidated by seemingly irretrievable topicalities to the point where we forsake the plays entirely. Instead, we can recognize that ignorance – both ours and the original audience's – is the constitutive condition of burlesque spectating.[15] Here is a paradox, indeed. On the one hand, topicalities enact the seductive fantasy of a transparent text completely available to its immediate audience (and, subsequently, to earnest scholar–detectives). To be sure, some topical references were indeed understood by some spectators. (It would be ludicrous to argue that audiences understood nothing.) On the other hand, topicalities, because they were self-disintegrating, asserted that no text was ever completely transparent and that no spectator (or scholar) was ever a perfect interpreter.

The fundamentally equivocal nature of burlesque topicalities is not just a self-congratulatory academic conceit but a critical perspective articulated from within Shakespeare burlesques themselves. *Hamlet! The Ravin' Prince of Denmark!!* (1866) offers a vivid example of familiarity which cannot be trusted. Ophelia recounts to her father that Hamlet wore

> [n]o shoes at all, and only half a stocking,
> Burst into the nursery without ever knocking;
> Then seized the infant by its little throttle,
> And drank the dead king's health in its milk-bottle!
> (Wells, *Nineteenth-Century Shakespeare Burlesques*, IV, p. 98)

The sight of a prince who '[d]escend[s] to such familiarity' only convinces Ophelia that 'there's no trusting to appearances'. The familiarity of the 'ravin'' prince Hamlet stands metonymically for burlesque's own descent into familiarity through localizations and topical allusions. But

---

[15] The gaps in the original audience's comprehension need hardly strike us as exceptional. The twenty-seven-line, high-speed, backward version of *Hamlet* which concludes the Reduced Shakespeare Company's performance subverts its audience's desire to take in that performance moment by moment (see Borgeson *et al.*, *Compleat Works*, pp. 107–9). And yet audiences applaud this *tour de force* precisely because of the actors' heroic efforts not to abbreviate *Hamlet* but to render this most familiar of all Shakespearean plays both familiar *and* elusive; perceived, but not understood.

just as Ophelia disavows seemingly familiar appearances, so, too, the audience must disavow a seemingly familiar performance. In this moment, the Shakespeare burlesque signals its own disabling intentions, its own self-generated occlusion of meaning under the ultimately false guise of recognition and remembrance. Similarly, the 'counterfeit presentments' in *Hamlet the Hysterical: A Delirium in Five Spasms!!!* are represented by 'two large empty picture-frames'.[16] The absent portraits clearly mock Irving's virtual placement of the portraits along the invisible fourth wall between the actors and the audience, thus suggesting that the images might exist only in Hamlet's mind. The burlesque, in its contorted staging, does not support the ambiguous implication of the Lyceum production, but rather depicts a lack of implication which it reifies through picture frames which frame only an absence. Since those frames function, moreover, as an icon of the proscenium stage on which they appear, we can read the stage image as an assertion of the performance's own renunciatory stance: the refusal to mark out a set of meanings which derive mimetically from a Shakespearean antecedent. *Hamlet the Hysterical* offers not 'counterfeit presentments', but no presentment at all.

To get a better sense of how burlesque topicalities mystify more than they clarify, we might look at how topicalities function in Shakespeare's original plays (without, however, implying that burlesques function as miniature versions of supposedly greater plays). In *Puzzling Shakespeare*, Leah Marcus argues that localizations in Shakespearean texts actively resist the hermeneutic compulsions of readers. 'To attempt topical readings of Shakespearean drama', she contends, 'is not at all to find reassuring patterns. It is more like entering a murky labyrinth [*sic*] without signposts or exits.'[17] In 'old' historicist criticism, decoding topical references was the key which unlocked a text's hidden, but nonetheless fixed, meaning. Only in the final, decisive act of decoding would that fixed meaning become fully apparent. Turning this positivist method on its head, Marcus contends that Shakespearean topicalities do not provide access to uniform meaning (which, she claims, was never there in the first place) but rather thwart our attempts to regularize meaning. We might claim, similarly, that the localizations of Shakespeare burlesques do not adorn an immanent master-text which we can understand only by decoding all its localizations; rather, the topicalities *are* the burlesque itself. Fragmentary,

---

[16] *Under the Clock* 29 November 1884.
[17] Leah Marcus, *Puzzling Shakespeare: Local Reading and its Discontents* (Berkeley: University of California Press, 1988), p. xi. Marcus clearly means 'maze' instead of 'labyrinth'. It is impossible to get lost in a labyrinth since there is only ever one path to follow.

unstable, and hostile to the ascription of unitary meaning, burlesque topicalities provide only the illusion of certain meaning. In actuality, they disperse meaning by implicating the play in an extensive network of references and cross-references. Some impassioned editor might well produce an exhaustively glossed edition of a nineteenth-century Shakespeare burlesque, an edition whose rising tide of footnotes threatens to capsize a vulnerable, exposed textual artifact. But meticulous annotations will not – indeed cannot – restore a burlesque's original meaning by clarifying all its references, solving all its puzzles, and answering all its riddles. To decode all the codes will never put us in possession of the burlesque itself. Rather, the burlesque will always dispossess us.

My claims for the critical functions of nineteenth-century burlesque topicalities would not have been made by most nineteenth-century theatrical observers. But it is precisely because Shakespeare burlesques are now remote that the singularity of meaning which has always lain at the heart of the burlesque experience has become even more pronounced. Because the plays' local meanings are no longer available to us (at least not in the way they once seemed to be) we stand better prepared to realize that these plays do not transmit meaning so much as they confound the possibility of meaning. When localizations are no longer local and when allusions no longer allude, we can see how those textual features offer something more than socio-historical sign posting. My intention here is not to assume a condescending superiority in relation to the burlesque's original readers and spectators, but only to clarify the opportunities for critical awareness which historical dispossession ironically affords. What critics routinely lament as the 'utter inaccessibility' of burlesque turns out to be, upon reflection, the precise point of access. Not to a lost, yet recoupable, meaning; but to the ways in which burlesques problematize the very notion of meaning. By thwarting our efforts to decode topical references, the modern experience of reading discloses, however obliquely, the historical experience of burlesque spectating.

It might be objected that while both modern readers and original spectators equally misunderstand the topicalities of Shakespeare burlesques, such misunderstandings are not constitutive, but simply accidental. That is, we in the twenty-first century do not possess sufficient knowledge of daily life in nineteenth-century Britain to decode the topical allusions, but there is nothing to prevent us from acquiring such knowledge. Similarly, there was no reason why original audience members could not have understood all the topical references if only the actors' diction were clearer, pacing were slower, and volume greater. Such a view presumes that the burlesque was itself a pre-existing coherent entity whose coherence would be fully available to audiences and readers alike if only the optimum conditions could be achieved. That premise, I believe, is false. Incomprehension is a built-in feature of burlesques and has never been – then or now – merely the unfortunate result of circumstances which might otherwise be ameliorated. And the most incontrovertible example of the burlesque's blockage of its own meaning is the quibbling pun – the 'fatal *Cleopatra*', in Samuel Johnson's damning description, for which Shakespeare 'lost the world, and was content to lose it'.[18]

Audaciously, a pun makes a word's sound the basis for its meaning. If two words sound alike, then they also must mean alike. The classic pun thus consists of two evident homophones with divergent, irreconcilable meanings (e.g., 'heir' and 'air'). John F. Poole's *Romeo and Juliet; or, the Beautiful Blonde who Dyed for Love*, for example, puns on the homophones 'dyed' and 'died'. Puns render meaning absurd by divorcing the word as verbal object – the phoneme – from the word as sign. While Jonathan Swift disparaged it as the '*Fundum*' or 'Bottom' of language,[19] the reviled, indecorous pun has come into its own in the post-structural age, when the waywardness of language itself has been the subject of relentless critical investigation. Puns offer a 'model of language', Jonathan Culler has argued, characterized by 'looseness', 'unpredictability', and the 'mutability of meaning'.[20] Far from being inconsequential, the pun reveals a fundamental aspect of language which we might prefer to keep hidden: that meaning is never identical to itself. In a sense which Swift certainly did not intend, the pun truly is the 'fundum' – or foundation – of language. Since Shakespeare's own wordplay has received particular scholarly attention in recent years, it seems appropriate that wordplay in Shakespeare burlesques also be reappraised.[21] Such reappraisal entails

---

[18] Samuel Johnson, 'Preface to Shakespeare' (1765; London: 1778), p. 19. 'A quibble, poor and barren as it is, gave him such delight, that he was content to purchase it, by the sacrifice of reason, propriety, and truth.'

[19] Jonathan Swift, 'A Modest Defence of Punning', in *Prose Works*, ed. Herbert Davis 12 vols. (Oxford: Basil Blackwell, 1957), IV, p. 205.

[20] Jonathan Culler, 'The Call of the Phoneme', in *On Puns: The Foundation of Letters*, ed. Jonathan Culler (Oxford: Basil Blackwell, 1988), p. 14.

[21] See, for example, Patricia Parker's *Shakespeare from the Margins: Language, Culture, Context* (Chicago: University of Chicago Press, 1996). Nineteenth-century critics were hardly unaware of Shakespearean wordplay. The German scholar Hermann Ulrici, for example, observed that Shakespeare's own 'verbal play', despite having been 'declared unnatural and disagreeable', nonetheless reveals the 'inadequacy of human cognition and knowledge, [for] which language is the expression' (*Shakspeare's Dramatic Art*, trans. A. J. W. Morrison, London: Chapman Brothers, 1846, pp. 163–4).

illuminating the ways in which burlesques function as a performative meta-language. What Patricia Parker has written of Shakespearean wordplay is equally germane to the wordplay of Shakespeare burlesques: that it neither disfigures nor ornaments an otherwise hallowed language but rather constitutes a form of 'discourse *as* discourse' (*Shakespeare from the Margins*, p. 3).

The most common form of burlesque pun juxtaposes either simple homophones or confected homophonic phrases. In *Macbeth Somewhat Removed from the Text of Shakespeare*, Macbeth learns that Fleance, who was carrying a torch to light Banquo's way, escaped from the murderers. '[T]he young *torcher*', he groans, 'lives to *torture* me'.[22] The pun cleverly serves a deeper self-referential function by acknowledging its own status as word 'torture'. Later in the play, after Macbeth learns that he shall not be troubled until 'Birnam Wood be come to Dunsinane', the murderous sovereign gleefully declares that he would be a '*dunce-inane*' were he to renounce the throne (p. 31). In a slightly more complicated pun which depends upon reversing word sequence, Macbeth curses '*Birnam Wood!* – would any one *would burn 'em!*' (p. 35). Similarly, in *Shylock; or, the Merchant of Venice Preserved*, Shylock transposes Antonio's off-hand comment ''Tis but a spree, Jew' into 'But a *jeu d'esprit*' (p. 6).[23]

Whether in soliloquies or dialogue, puns were typically arranged in sequences. Such extended punning carried a cumulative effect in performance whereby each successive pun was more excruciating than the last. The audience thus experienced an ecstatic agony as the performance repeatedly carried itself to – and then retreated from – the brink of semantic collapse. The virtuosity of burlesque performers lay in their ability first to intercept a word before it landed on its accustomed meaning and then to redirect it toward an entirely different meaning. Here is a brief example from the opening scene of *Perdita*, just after Polixenes announces his impending departure for Sicily:

HERMIONE: Nay I am sure your Majesty but jokes –
 You only talk of starting, for the hoax.
POLIXENES: Start for the Oaks? Not so; my heart it grieves,
 Speaking of trees, that we must take our leaves,
 And trunks, and make our bows. To follow suit
 With these vile puns, we should now be *en route*.[24]

---

[22] Francis Talfourd, *Macbeth Somewhat Removed from the Text of Shakespeare* (1847; London: Thomas Hailes Lacy, n.d.), p. 25.
[23] Puns were underlined in both manuscript and published versions of nineteenth-century burlesques so that readers would not overlook instances of wordplay better suited to auditors.
[24] William Brough, *Perdita; or, the Royal Milkmaid* (London: Thomas Hailes Lacy, n.d.), p. 8.

Hermione blithely rejects Polixenes' decision to return home, gently insisting that the Sicilian king only teases her, that his declaration was but a 'hoax'. In the Cockney dialect which Mrs Buckingham White spoke as burlesque Hermione, the organic initial '/h/' in 'hoax' would have been suppressed, making the word sound like 'oax'. Hermione says 'hoax'; but Polixenes hears 'oaks'. This is a perfect pun. Yet it is also a topical allusion since the Oaks was an annual horse race for three-year-old fillies at Epsom Downs. Polixenes' interrogative 'Start for the Oaks?' is thus not only a distortion of Hermione's statement, but also a slang expression from horse racing. The allusion flits by, however, as the more conventional meaning of 'oaks' becomes the basis for a series of painfully obvious arboreal puns: leaves, trunks, bows, and *en route*.[25] Distancing himself from his 'vile puns', Polixenes assumes an ironic stance toward language for which he is not responsible; language which he does not speak, but rather which speaks *him*.[26]

Characters also traded puns, as in the fast-paced wooing scene from Burnand's *The Rise and Fall of Richard III*:

RICHARD: I see that you a passion for me foster.
ANNE: Passion for you! *High, mighty, double Gloster*.
RICHARD: Oh, call me double Gloster, if you please,
As long as I, in your eyes, am the cheese.
ANNE: A cheese! Why then I cut you.
RICHARD: I've the daring
To ask you to consider this cheese *paring*.
ANNE: You are hump-backed.
RICHARD: Oh, hump-bug!
ANNE: And knock knee'd.
RICHARD: A friend *in-knee'd*, maam, is a friend in deed. (p. 10)

The wordplay embedded in this snappy dialogue poses little difficulty: the single word 'Gloster' refers both to Richard, Duke of Gloster, and to a type of cheese; 'to be the cheese' is a figurative expression meaning to be the best or most in fashion; the passing pun on 'I' and 'eyes' is only too obvious; to 'cut' means both to slice and, in Victorian slang, to ignore someone; 'paring' functions as a pun on the gerunds for 'to pare' and 'to pair', meaning both to slice up and to couple; 'hump-backed'

---

[25] The colloquial expression to 'take [one's] trunk' meant to depart, with 'trunk' as a synecdoche for the entire body.
[26] In *Macbeth Somewhat Removed from the Text of Shakespeare*, Rosse fails to 'twig' – i.e. apprehend – Duncan's pun on 'air' and 'hare', and thus laughs (under the king's compulsion) at words whose double meaning eludes him (p. 15).

is easily converted into 'hump-bug', allowing Richard to dismiss the description of his deformity by pronouncing it in a different way and thereby endowing it with a different meaning; and the volley of puns concludes with a twist on the homophones 'knee'd' and 'need'.

Yet to explicate burlesque puns is to be false to the experience of burlesque performance. Contemporary theatrical accounts confirm that the puns of Shakespeare burlesques – like their topicalities – regularly failed to register with audiences. Thus, the *Morning Advertiser* suggested that the audience for *King Queer! and his Daughters Three* (1855) did not appreciate the puns because the Strand's ensemble had not yet perfected its comic timing. '[M]any of the puns, after a few nights' performance', the newspaper reassuringly predicted, 'will tell with good effect'.[27] Halliday complained that '[h]alf of the puns' in a burlesque performance were 'lost upon the audience owing to [their] obscurity and the rapidity with which they follow upon each other's heels'.[28] *The Times* observed that the puns in *Shylock; or, the Merchant of Venice Preserved* 'were sometimes too recondite for the heedless auditory'.[29] Of that same production, E. S. Dallas scornfully decreed that 'the system of punning has been carried to the limit of endurance'.[30] 'Let any one read the following address of Gratiano to Nerissa', Dallas challenged the readers of *Blackwood's Magazine*, 'and attempt if he can to make any meaning out of the puns' (p. 211).

Here are Gratiano's puns to which Dallas so vehemently objected:

> The pangs of Cupid, I the first time knows 'em
> His bows and arrows pierced my harrow-ed bo-sum
> Let's off to Night – there's no chance of dis*kivery*.
> With me dear, *put up*, & don't *stand at livery*.
> Blush not that I'm a flunkey I implores;
> Let not my *plushes* be the cause of *yours*.
> *You* to the eyes – but, though more difficulter,
> *I* to the knees plush as the *knee plush* ultra.[31]

The opening couplet turns 'bows and arrows' into 'harrow-ed bo-sum', its lingual transposition. The Cockney dialect in which the cast performed (as in the example from *Perdita*) would have resulted in the '/h/'

---

[27] *Morning Advertiser* 10 April 1855.
[28] Andrew Halliday, 'Burlesques', *Cornhill Magazine* 4 (August 1861), p. 176.
[29] *The Times* 6 July 1853. The double emphasis on aurality – 'heedless auditory' – is only too appropriate.
[30] E. S. Dallas, 'The Drama', *Blackwood's Magazine* 79 (February 1856), p. 211.
[31] Francis Talfourd, *Shylock; or, the Merchant of Venice Preserved; a Burlesque in One Act* 1853 British Library Add Mss 52,941 I, f. 12.

of 'harrow-ed' being dropped, thus making the word sound like 'arrowed'. The second couplet is a bit more dense. 'Discovery' is vulgarly mispronounced as 'diskivery' to accommodate the rhyme. 'Put up' carries the double meaning of 'to tolerate' and, in slang usage, 'to plan a robbery'. The play on words is apt, indeed, since Gratiano beseeches Nerissa to accept him *and* proposes to steal her away from her mistress Portia's home. His proposal is a kind of theft. '[S]tand at livery' refers both to the footman's uniform which Gratiano wears – his livery – and to the thief's injunction 'stand and deliver', thus continuing the image of Gratiano's criminality. The final four lines become more convoluted still. Gratiano deftly turns 'blushes' into 'plushes' – that is, a footman's knee breeches. He implores Nerissa not to be embarrassed that he is only a servant, begging her not to let his 'plushes' be the cause of her 'blushes'. The concluding image contrasts Nerissa, who blushes up 'to [her] eyes' at her suitor's humble status, with Gratiano, who 'plushes' up to his knees – that is, he wears a flunkey's knee breeches. For good measure, the final couplet also contains a fleeting pun on 'eyes' and 'I'. The declaration of love ends with a Gallic flourish in which the lowly suitor boldly exalts himself as the 'knee plush [*ne plus*] ultra'. Though intricate, Gratiano's puns are not indecipherable – at least not for patient readers. But during the performance at the Olympic Theatre, as Dallas observed, the puns were not fully apprehended by the audience.

In a more churlish assessment, Dallas derides Talfourd's script as a 'meaningless clatter of words' whose composition required 'little more skill than [that needed] to clash the cymbals in the orchestra' (*Blackwood's Magazine* 79 Feb. 1856, p. 211). That assessment is partly right and partly wrong. As for the burlesque playwright's skill, Dallas certainly underestimates the virtuosity of Talfourd's excruciatingly sustained wordplay. Much discernment lies behind the playwright's deft manipulation of language. Dallas seems on safer ground, however, when he characterizes the puns as a 'meaningless clatter of words'. If, indeed, the puns are 'meaningless' (it seems more accurate, however, to think of them as intelligible individually, yet incomprehensible in the aggregate), then it is all the more curious that Dallas does not include Nerissa's evasive rejoinder in the passage of dialogue which he quotes at length. 'I scarce know what to say', she flatly replies to Gratiano's heartfelt, punning plea (BL Add Mss 52,941 I, f. 12). Perhaps Dallas fails to cite Nerissa's pithy response precisely because it candidly acknowledges – from within the burlesque performance itself – just how overwhelming puns can be. So overwhelming, in fact, that even the characters charged with speaking them are stunned into silence. Within the logic of the dramatic narrative, Nerissa remains silent because she is overcome with emotion. Nerissa scarcely knows what to say because she scarcely knows what she has heard. And here the character's reaction simulates the audience's reaction, or at least the audience's implied reaction. Like Nerissa, who cannot counter Gratiano's puns with any meaningful language of her own, the audience cannot hold in check the performance's own language. Relinquishing the hope of comprehending what has been spoken on the stage, the audience must accept that it, too, 'scarce know[s] what to say' in the face of such unmeaning.

Let us not, however, mistakenly believe that the unmeaning of a burlesque's puns constitutes a defect, any more than does the obscurity of its topical allusions. In fact, just the opposite is true. The performance aspires not to the self-congratulatory titters of spectators pleased with their own ability to 'get' the joke (though such tittering there may be) but rather to the silence of spectators for whom the language of burlesque no longer signifies in a comprehensible manner. Dallas was right to ask whether anyone could derive meaning from *Shylock*'s puns; but he was wrong to pose the question as an indictment of burlesque. Rather, the pun is most ingenious when it possesses the least meaning. To explain a pun is to restore confidence in signification. But confidence in signification is precisely what the pun erodes. Exegesis does not 'improve' the pun by laying bare its divided meaning; in fact, exegesis arrests the pun.

Where do such observations leave us? With the counter-intuitive view that a bad pun is the surest sign of a good burlesque. The puns of a Shakespeare burlesque cannot be reintegrated into a normative view of the original text. The ferocity with which some nineteenth-century theatrical observers condemned puns attests not to the degradation of burlesque, but to its exaltation. The Shakespeare burlesque was most splendidly itself when its word torture was at its most horrific. For all his stubborn unwillingness to make peace with puns, even Dallas begrudgingly concluded in his essay from *Blackwood's Magazine* that '[a] pun is on a small scale what parody is on a large. Accept the burlesque drama wholesale, and there is no reason why one should object to the quibbling [i.e., punning] in detail. It is consistent throughout' (p. 212). It is only fitting, then, to look upon the Shakespeare burlesque as a kind of gigantic pun on the entire Shakespearean canon – one which renders its meaning absurd. But the story does not end at the impasse of meaning. For while burlesque puns do not necessarily enhance our understanding of their source text, they do enhance our understanding of the source text's claims on canonicity and authority. Just as Shakespearean wordplay 'expose[s] the very orthodoxies and ideologies [of] the plays themselves' (Parker, *Shakespeare from the Margins*, p. 114), burlesque wordplay exposes the ideologies of Shakespearean authorship. We can see this exposition most clearly by studying the revisions made to Poole's *Hamlet Travestie* for an 1870 revival at the Park Theater, Brooklyn.

The burlesque's principal asset – its spirited timeliness – was also its principal liability. Even the freshest topicality quickly staled, leaving the burlesque with no recourse but to 'update' itself through continual revisions and interpolations. Indeed, both puns and topical allusions are particularly vulnerable to change over time since they frequently derive from a slang lexicon. If the virtue of legitimate Shakespeare was durability, then the virtue of burlesque Shakespeare was novelty. Tragedians placed themselves within genealogies of acting traditions (e.g., the Garrick 'school', the Kemble 'religion') while spectators carefully took note of the same, well-established acting 'points' in successive productions of individual plays. But it would be ludicrous to suppose that anything like a sedimented tradition of burlesque acting could exist. Apart from new jokes in the script, a burlesque production could be refreshed by inserting a song newly popularized by opera singers, minstrel show serenaders, or street balladeers; imitating the idiosyncrasies of an eminent actor then performing in a nearby legitimate theatre; satirizing the stage business in a current 'hit' production; or introducing the latest dance craze at the end of a deeply tragic scene. As Marie Wilton recalled in her memoirs, the Strand's audience quickly detected changes to a burlesque performance.[32] Yet Wilton misread her audience, wrongly concluding that they were disappointed by the changes and would have preferred a reliably 'fixed' production. But fixity runs counter to burlesque logic. For any burlesque audience, the successive changes introduced in the performance *were* the performance precisely because those changes branded the performance as custom-made. Every production was different because every audience was different.

Because many of the burlesque's ever-changing novelties were left unscripted, it is difficult to compile a detailed record of how productions evolved over time. The stage-manager's promptbook remains the performance historian's most valuable tool not for verifying the actuality of a performance, but for disclosing its insistently protean nature. Far from

---

[32] Marie Bancroft and Squire Bancroft, *The Bancrofts: Recollections of Sixty Years* (London: J. Murray, 1909), p. 18.

reifying the performance, the promptbook actually articulates the burlesque's deconstructive logic. Burlesque texts offered themselves not as inviolable scripts meant to be spoken upon the stage, but as opportunities for endless revisions, deletions, substitutions, and additions. Given that the burlesque's injunction might be 'always contemporize', we ought not to be surprised that burlesque scripts were invariably altered to suit the local circumstances of their production. Thus, the *Daily News*, reviewing an 1874 revival of *Hamlet Travestie*, noted the 'new songs, hornpipes, and jigs' which were added to the production, as well as the 'allusions to current events' which were 'thickly interspersed throughout the dialogue'.[33] A 'fixed' burlesque script was a contradiction in terms. When we read a burlesque text, even in manuscript, we are not reading anything approximating what was said, heard, or enacted in different theatrical stagings of that text.

To get a more specific sense of how the Shakespeare burlesque embraced its own provisionality, let us examine the promptbook for Mrs F. B. Conway's 1870 revival of *Hamlet Travestie* at the Park Theater, Brooklyn, a production which starred Edward Lamb as Hamlet and John Moore as Claudius.[34] For any theatrical producer in the late nineteenth century who wanted to burlesque *Hamlet*, the unlikeliest choice was *Hamlet Travestie*.[35] While the play had been popular earlier in the century, it seems not to have been performed in New York since John Brougham's revival at the Chatham Theatre twenty-five years earlier. Not only was the play sixty years old (irredeemably antique for a theatrical form which prided itself on novelty), but it contained few topicalities and even fewer directions for stage business. In settling on *Hamlet Travestie*, the Park Theater had no choice but to substantially alter Poole's original text so that it would meet its new audience's expectations. As the densely annotated promptbook confirms, an extract from which is shown in illustration 5, some of Poole's original scenes were omitted while the remainder were combined, heavily cut, and then supplemented with new dialogue, comic business, and topical references – all of which amply justified the

---

[33] *Daily News*; qtd in Globe Theatre advertisement, 1 December 1874. Since there had not been a London production of *Hamlet Travestie* for nearly sixty years, the reviewer was clearly comparing the Globe Theatre's performance with the published text of Poole's play.

[34] John Poole, *Hamlet Travestie*, Folger promptbook H38, Folger Shakespeare Library, Washington, DC. The promptbook includes actors' 'sides' for the various roles as well as a complete script. The full script was later used by Stuart Robson for an 1876 production, perhaps also occasioned by Edwin Booth's revival of *Hamlet* in New York that same year.

[35] Of the five *Hamlet* burlesques staged in New York City in 1870 – all inspired by Booth's acclaimed production – only that performed by Mrs Conway's company used Poole's *Hamlet Travestie*.

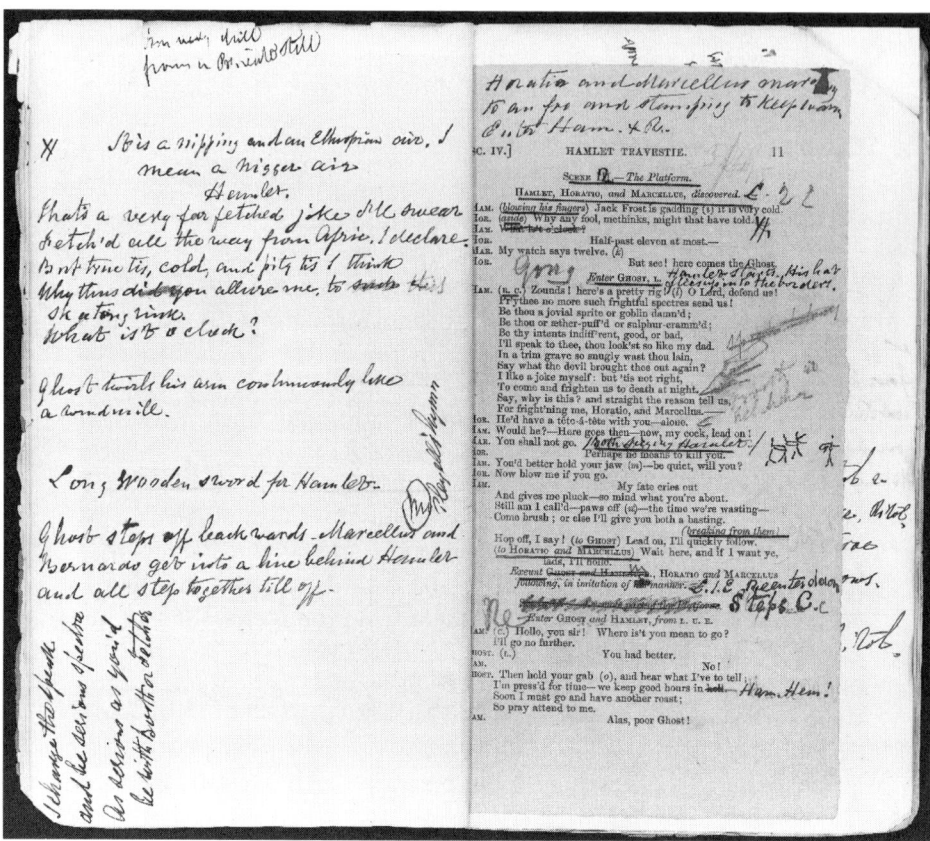

5. Extract from the promptbook for Mrs F. B. Conways's production of John Poole's *Hamlet Travestie*, Park Theater, Brooklyn, 1870. Note the stick figures accompanying the inserted stage direction 'Both [Horatio and Marcellus] siezing [*sic*] Hamlet' and the ghost's stage business of 'twirl[ing] his arms continuously like a windmill'.

playbill's description of the production as a 'Latitudinarian and Reconstructed version of *Hamlet*'.[36]

References to life in New York appear in nearly every scene. As Hamlet waits in the 'nipping' air for the ghost's predicted appearance, he likens the battlements of Elsinore to a 'skating rink' (*Hamlet Travestie*, Fol. promptbook H38, f. 11) – referring, perhaps, to the frozen lake in Central Park on which New Yorkers had been able to ice skate during the winters since 1859. In the closet scene, Hamlet alludes to prominent figures within New York's judicial system as he craftily advises

[36] Playbill, *Hamlet Travestie*, Park Theater, Brooklyn, 1870, bound in Folger promptbook H38, Folger Shakespeare Library, Washington, DC.

Gertrude to stay well beyond the law's reach. 'Mother your crimes have not the least alloy', he starkly explains; '[y]ou'd better hold aloof from just Judge Troy / Attorney Morris too, you'd better dodge / Or in states [*sic*] prison, you long time will lodge' (f. 25).[37] Other changes reflect how the conventions of burlesque performance had developed over the sixty years since *Hamlet Travestie* was first published. Poole's original text, for example, ends with Horatio's anguished remark (the role of Fortinbras having been elided) that the 'dead bodies strew'd about like cattle, / Were better suited to the field of battle' (*Hamlet Travestie*, p. 70). Hamlet, Claudius, Gertrude, and Laertes lie on the stage, with Horatio leading a dead march as the curtain falls. Burlesques of Shakespearean tragedy written later in the nineteenth century, however, avoided such sombre endings by miraculously restoring dead characters to life.[38] By 1870 audiences fully expected a burlesque tragedy to close with a rousing song-and-dance number performed by the entire company. And this is precisely how the Park Theater's production ended. The ghost of Old Hamlet enters immediately after Hamlet's death, declaring

> Zounds. What a scene of slaughter's here!
> But I'll soon change it never fear.
> One touch of my most mighty magic
> Shall to gay Comic change, this dismal tragic.
> (*Hamlet Travestie*, Fol. promptbook H38, f. 35)

The ghost restores everyone to life (except himself) and the formerly dead either raise themselves from the stage floor or, in the case of Polonius and Ophelia, enter from the wings. The ghost then beats the newly resurrected characters with a stick and the entire performance concludes with a company dance.

Among the numerous sections of Poole's text which did not survive Mrs Conway's scrutiny are the gravediggers' scene and Hamlet's speech to the players. Most nineteenth-century parodies of *Hamlet* omit the gravediggers, most likely on the quite sensible presumption that because their scene was already comic it was necessarily impervious to burlesque treatment. The excision of Hamlet's discourse on acting is, however, a rather different matter. In Poole's text, Hamlet ridicules nine contemporary London performers. This much at least is true to Shakespeare's

---

[37] These lines replace Poole's original – and contrasting – dialogue in which Hamlet urges Gertrude to '[c]onfess [her] sins this instant to the vicar; / Repent what's past, and don't do so again' (*Hamlet Travestie*, p. 43).

[38] Tony Pastor's production of John F. Poole's *Romeo and Juliet; or, the Beautiful Blonde who Dyed for Love* (1869) concluded with Romeo, Juliet, Mercutio, Tybalt, and Paris performing a minstrel show 'Walk Around' (Poole, *Romeo and Juliet*, script 2, p. 35, Tony Pastor Collection, Harry Ransom Humanities Research Center, The University of Texas at Austin).

Hamlet, who ridicules the antics of 'robustious periwig-pated' players (*Hamlet*, 3.2.9). But as we would expect in the topsy-turvy world of burlesque, Hamlet's advice to the players is turned upside down. Singing to the tune of *Liberty-Hall*, Poole's burlesque Hamlet implores the players to 'mumble' as if their mouths were 'full of plums', to 'saw the air' into 'slices', and to 'strut, bellow, and rant' during the quiet moments of a play (*Hamlet Travestie*, pp. 28, 29). The ridiculed actors are indicated in the text only by their initials, as in contemporary scandal sheets or gossip columns. With respect to tragic acting, Hamlet advises that

> in speeches which, teeming with passion, require
> All an E- - - - -'s spirit, a K- - - - -'s own fire,
> If you'd hope H- - - - - S- - - - - to equal in fame,
> You, like him, must be lifeless, insipid, and tame.
> (p. 29)

The unnamed actors are Robert Elliston, John Philip Kemble, and his nephew Henry Siddons.

No doubt the audience assembled for the 1811 premiere of *Hamlet Travestie* was only too well acquainted with the actors being satirized. But a Brooklyn audience in America's Gilded Age was unlikely to know much about London theatrical celebrities in the final years of the Regency. Mrs Conway, quite prudently, chose not to perform a scene which her audience almost certainly would not have understood.[39] Yet why did she not simply substitute the names of contemporary actors – Edwin Booth, Charles Fechter, or even the ageing Edwin Forrest – for the ones in Poole's text? One answer, I suggest, lies in an observation made earlier in this chapter with respect to puns: that the wordplay of Shakespeare burlesques raises questions about Shakespearean authorship and authenticity. The Park Theater production of *Hamlet Travestie* does not satirize actors whom its audience would know precisely because the production does not think of itself as an affront to the dignity of legitimate Shakespeareans.

This missed opportunity for topical parody becomes even more curious, given that theatrical topicalities appear earlier in the performance when Hamlet commands the spectre to be as 'serious' with him as it would 'be with Booth or Fetcher [*sic*]' (*Hamlet Travestie*, Fol. promptbook H38, f. 11). The metatheatricality of the allusion enables us to read

[39] Lacy's acting edition of *Hamlet Travestie* provides in a gloss the full names of the actors whom Poole had indicated only by initials on the clear presumption that not even British readers would comprehend forty-year-old theatrical allusions (Poole, *Hamlet Travestie*, 1811; London: Thomas Hailes Lacy, *c*. 1850, p. 19).

burlesque Hamlet's directive to be placed on a par with gentlemanly tragedians as the burlesque performance's own insistent desire to be placed on a par with legitimate productions of Shakespeare. The apocryphal story that Shakespeare played the ghost only underscores the scene's metatheatricality, turning Hamlet's appeal to the ghost into the burlesque's unmediated appeal to Shakespeare himself. The production's strategic deletion and insertion of topical references tell us that its serious nonsense had little to do with the easily won laughter of mimicry and a great deal to do with the thoughtful laughter of more searching parody.

The scene in which Hamlet encounters the ghost offers further insights into how the seeming inanities of this revised burlesque script repeatedly problematize the burlesque's legitimacy in relation to Shakespeare's *Hamlet*. Upon first seeing the ghost, burlesque Hamlet 'starts', thus exhibiting his fright through a sudden and violent bodily reaction (*Hamlet Travestie*, Fol. promptbook H38, f. 11). The stage direction is entirely unremarkable. Although Fechter did replace the stylized stage representation of terror with the more colloquial gesture of clutching Horatio (an informality which engendered much criticism), both Booth and Forrest continued to rely on the time-honoured start. But the stage business which accompanied Edward Lamb's start in *Hamlet Travestie* looked back to David Garrick, the most famous Hamlet of the preceding century. By all accounts, what made Garrick's reaction to the ghost particularly vivid was that his hat tumbled to the stage floor and his hair appeared to stand on end. The latter effect was allegedly due to his wearing a mechanized wig. In the Park Theater's burlesque version of the scene, the terrified hero's hat 'flies up into the borders' (f. 11). What a deliciously comic moment this must have been, when Hamlet's hat did not fall down but rather flew upward and out of sight, disappearing into the recesses behind the proscenium arch. More than a metonym for Hamlet's own fear, more than a visual exclamation point to his line 'O Lord, defend us! / Prythee no more such frightful spectres send us!' (f. 11), the fugitive hat appears more frightened than Hamlet himself. It is not so much that the actor playing burlesque Hamlet follows the codified rules for the correct display of emotions as that he wears a mechanical hat which emotes on his behalf. Here is tragic acting displaced from man-as-machine (the actor who acts mechanistically) to machine-as-man (the mechanism which acts like an actor).

But just what is being mocked in this canny reversal of histrionic effect? While the sight gag certainly trades on the audience's knowledge of Garrick's legendary mechanized wig, the famed actor himself is not the parodic object. After all, he had been dead for nearly a century. Rather, the mockery comments on the burlesque's capacity to deliver the heightened emotional impact which this celebrated moment from *Hamlet* requires. Yet the commentary is itself necessarily equivocal. On the one hand, the burlesque suggests that its representation of Hamlet's fright is *more* powerful than that found in conventional performances. If Garrick's mechanical wig is good, then a mechanical hat is better; and a disappearing hat best of all. The hat functions as a site of intensified, even unbearable, emotion. So unbearable that the hat must quit the scene. On the other hand, the mechanized hat is a fraud since there is no art – but only artifice – in its emotive effect. The technical 'trick' sneers at the tragedian's art, turning the virtuosic display of the passions into a mere stunt. Like Garrick caught between the muses of Tragedy and Comedy in Sir Joshua Reynolds' 1765 painting, the burlesque is caught between legitimacy and imposture, an equivocation sublimely symbolized by Hamlet's wayward hat.

A final example will reveal the concentrated metatheatricality of the Park Theater production. The scene in question corresponds to the moment in Shakespeare's text when Hamlet, concluding the soliloquy 'To be, or not to be', catches sight of Ophelia (*Hamlet* 3.1.90–150). Spurning the gifts she has come to return, Hamlet instead lectures Ophelia on the 'power of beauty' to turn 'honesty' into a 'bawd' (3.1.111–12). In *Hamlet Travestie*, Poole condenses most of Hamlet's ravings into new lyrics for the song 'Mr. Mug'. '[L]et your honesty discourse not with your beauty', Hamlet sings in a near-Shakespearean paraphrase (Poole, *Hamlet Travestie*, p. 25). In the song's final verse, burlesque Hamlet declares to Ophelia, again in a close paraphrase, that 'Heav'n gave you one face, and to make another is not right' (p. 26). In adapting this scene from Poole's text, Mrs Conway not only introduced topical allusions into Hamlet's caustic remarks on face-painting but also inserted those lines in the 'To be, or not to be' soliloquy. The second half of Hamlet's immortal speech thus becomes a comic refrain on the opposition between beauty and honesty. Here are burlesque Hamlet's new thoughts when torn between his love for the 'gushing' Ophelia and his agonizing knowledge of her treacherously 'false heart':

> Who could not love a gushing girl like that
> With Hempen Chignon and a sailor's hat?
> But who can tell how much of her is there
> Or what she's purchased at a Fancy fair
> False heels – False calves – False color for the face

> False palpitaters to give the bosom grace
> For want of shape. The pannier is a blind
> False hearts in front – and false behinds – behind.
> (*Hamlet Travestie*, Fol. promptbook H38, f. 17)

Recalling that burlesque language is always directed away from its ostensible source, we can ponder the surplus meanings released in Hamlet's vivid description of the 'gushing' Ophelia. We might observe, for example, that while Shakespeare's Hamlet speaks only of cosmetics, burlesque Hamlet questions the sincerity of Ophelia's entire appearance. It is not so much that burlesque Ophelia's beauty is false – the elaborate scaffolding of her hair, the 'false behind' of her bustle, and the 'false heart' palpitating underneath her shapeless bosom – as that her beauty is 'purchased'. In the burlesque, Hamlet regards Ophelia not merely as a stylish conniving woman, but as a produced stage persona. Through the combined arts of the perruquier, the cosmetician, and the couturière, Ophelia performs herself for Hamlet. In this astute reconfiguration of Poole's original text, Hamlet itemizes Ophelia's appearance and wardrobe immediately before she enters the scene. The audience thus receives Hamlet's equivocal comments on self-presentation as instructions for interpreting what will soon follow. Hamlet, in other words, 'prompts' the audience to look at Ophelia from a metatheatrical perspective. Her act of self-travesty stands metonymically, then, for the more expansive travesty of the performance itself – the travesty of 'dressing up' as *Hamlet*.

But dressing up as *Hamlet* is not the same thing as being *Hamlet*. Just as burlesque Hamlet places no confidence in Ophelia's 'purchased' appearance, *Hamlet Travestie* places no confidence in itself as a token of *Hamlet*. The performance does indeed ask to be treated as 'serious[ly]' as a performance starring 'Booth or Fetcher [*sic*]'; but it does not ask to *become* such a performance – or even to be mistaken for it. Indeed, *Hamlet Travestie* pleads to be placed on an equal footing with *Hamlet* precisely because it does not stand in a clear mimetic relationship to Shakespeare's original play. *Hamlet Travestie* is not *Hamlet*. It is not a copy of *Hamlet*. It is not even a 'counterfeit presentment' of *Hamlet*. Indeed, the perverse virtue of the burlesque is to recognize its own failure, its own boundedness within the nonsensical. As I hope this chapter has shown through its survey of topicalities, puns, and revisions, the language of burlesque – an elaborate misquotation, if you will – always performs its own insufficiency. Failing to instantiate a fixed meaning (the scribbles and scrawls in the *Hamlet Travestie* promptbook tell us that much), the burlesque instead arrives at an evasion of meaning.

Yet this evasion entails less a foreclosure of interpretation than an engagement with a different sort of interpretation. For while the burlesque holds no value according to the standard of Shakespearean authenticity (which, at any rate, is an imaginary standard), it holds substantial value as a means for thinking through that standard's ideological premises. The burlesque, in short, contests an *idea* of Shakespeare. Just as the weather vane from *King John (with the Benefit of the Act)* described at the beginning of this chapter theorized the nature of burlesque performance *and* satirized the vogue for historical accuracy in Shakespearean revivals, the materiality of burlesque language cannot remain detached from its broader cultural significance. In the next chapter, then, the focus shifts from the internal operation of burlesque language to the burlesque's social dynamic within the nineteenth-century cult of Bardolatry. Whether in Hamlet's mechanized hat or Ophelia's hempen chignon, form *is* function in the Shakespeare burlesque.

CHAPTER 2

Shakespeare's surrogates

'The business of burlesquing Shakespeare', W. Davenport Adams argued at the close of the nineteenth century, had never been conducted in a 'wholesale or intentionally irreverent spirit' (*A Book of Burlesque*, p. 122). At the mid-century height of Victorian burlesques, the *Morning Advertiser* rebuked those who dismissed burlesques as 'impertinent degradations' of Shakespeare's plays with the rejoinder that the 'mighty original . . . only rises to the memory with greater force, as it is recollected through the mummery and nonsense of its merry parody'.[1] Poole, more than forty years earlier, had argued in the preface to *Hamlet Travestie* that 'instead of derogating from the value or reputation of its subject', a burlesque may be considered 'no inadequate test of its merit' (p. ix). Of that same text, the *Monthly Review* enthused that 'Shakespeare himself' would have 'delighted in this very comic travestie'.[2] And no less an authority than William Hazlitt, in his 'Lectures on the English Comic Writers' (1819), cautioned against the 'common mistake' of supposing 'that parodies degrade, or imply a stigma on the subject; on the contrary, they in general imply something serious or sacred in the originals'.[3] The nineteenth-century burlesque thus maintained an unwavering critical perspective: far from being an insult to Shakespeare's poetic genius, the burlesque expressed such undoubted loyalty to the playwright that he himself could not have withheld his mirthful assent.

In *Hamlet Travestie*, the nineteenth-century burlesque tradition begins by vigorously asserting its fidelity to Shakespeare himself. The most winning aspect of Poole's burlesque, as its original critics affirmed, was not the text itself (a bland, full-length Shakespearean paraphrase) but its richly comic versions of the critical notes, glosses, and emendations provided by Samuel Johnson, George Steevens, and Edmund Malone in their

---

[1] *Morning Advertiser* 5 July 1853. [2] *Monthly Review* November 1810, p. 325.
[3] William Hazlitt, 'On Wit and Humour', in *The Complete Works of William Hazlitt*, ed. P. P. Howe (London: J. M. Dent and Sons Ltd, 1931), VI, p. 23.

monumental editions of Shakespeare. Mocking eighteenth-century editorial conventions, *Hamlet Travestie*'s facetious endnotes purport to define obscure words, reconcile contradictions between folio and quarto texts, and establish Shakespeare's sources. Poole asserted that his parody of Shakespeare criticism required neither 'apology' nor 'extenuation' because all admirers of the Bard – and who, he presumed, would read the burlesque *but* an admirer – must feel 'indignant at finding his sense perverted and his meaning obscured, by the false lights, and the fanciful and arbitrary illustrations of Black-letter Critics and Honey-Catching Commentators' (*Hamlet Travestie*, p. viii). On behalf of those whose devotion to Shakespeare remained undiminished, Poole undertook to out-Herod Herod, declaring that 'it had been well if some able satirist had exposed and punished their folly, their affectation, and their arrogance'. Jealous, then, of its own privileged relationship with the simple and plain-speaking national poet, the burlesque disavowed the haughty exhortations of 'every pedant in Black-letter lore'. In its criticism of Shakespeare's editors lies the burlesque's continuing desire, inherited from Duffet, to safeguard Shakespeare from pedants who 'assumed the prerogative of an *authorized* pollutor of his text' (p. ix).[4]

The opprobrium cast upon 'authorized pollutor[s]' need hardly surprise us because, from a strategic perspective, the burlesque stood to gain little from criticizing Shakespeare's plays. As remarked in the last chapter, the pun, for all its topicality, betokened the burlesque's Shakespearean pedigree since it recalled the poet's own wordplay. More pointedly still, Shakespeare burlesques never failed to exploit – for their own purposes – Shakespeare's gift for burlesque. Planché's extravaganza *Love and Fortune* (1859), for example, alludes to *A Midsummer Night's Dream* when Love dissuades Fortune from being 'horribly afraid' of Shakespeare with the emboldening reminder that 'pleasant Will' himself had 'shed a glory round things most grotesque / [And] wrote for Grecian clowns the best burlesque'.[5] In *Romeo and Juliet Travestie*, the poet's sudden appearance – in the guise of an animated version of the statue in Westminster Abbey sculpted by Louis-François Roubilliac – allows the burlesque to speak directly to the Bard himself. Reinforcing the apparent incongruity that burlesque is the form which Shakespeare must take if 'Shakespeare' is to survive at all, the Nurse astutely notes that the burlesque which has

---

[4] Similarly, Selby's *Kynge Richard ye Third* – a self-proclaimed 'familiar alteration of the celebrated history' – slyly mocked actor–managers who continued to use Colley Cibber's outdated adaptation by referring to its own 'copious alterations, additions, and omissions' (pp. 1, 2).

[5] J. R. Planché, *Love and Fortune*, in *The Extravaganzas of J. R. Planché, 1825–1871* 5 vols. (London: Samuel French, 1879), v, p. 203.

angered the playwright is itself of Shakespearean provenance. 'You wrote burlesques yourself, and well you know it', she remonstrates with considerable justification (Halliday, *Romeo and Juliet Travestie*, p. 39). Caught, then, in a literary imposture, the figure of Shakespeare literally 'descends' from his elevated stage position, acknowledging that his hypocritical outrage has failed to mask his own complicity with the burlesque. The Nurse then gloats that she 'had him there', and so acts out her own superiority for having explained to Shakespeare just what being Shakespearean means. The Shakespeare who appears within the burlesque performance is not a workaday dramatist but the cultural icon memorialized in Westminster Abbey. This crucial scene, which the *Era* denounced as an 'indignity' to the poet's genius,[6] begins with Shakespeare as the forbiddingly monumental reification of culture itself yet ends with Shakespeare as a site of open contestation – the duly chastened statue compelled to abandon its accustomed pedestal.

However much burlesques strategically cited their origins in Shakespearean dramaturgy and affirmed their desire to preserve its 'sense' and 'meaning' (Poole, *Hamlet Travestie*, p. viii), they never claimed to be reproductions of Shakespeare's plays. The burlesque's relationship to its sources or origins was always characterized by ambivalence, as when the Olympic Theatre tellingly announced its impending production of 'not Shakespeare's but Talfourd's *Macbeth*'.[7] The burlesque's ambivalence toward an original Shakespeare was dramatized in various ways: as a confused theatrical genealogy, the correction of a defective original script, the failure to cite an original text, and, indeed, a complete departure from an original text. Ambivalence represents not the burlesque's failure, but its essential disposition. The burlesque's critical value lies not in cannibalizing the canonical object of its satire (Donne was wrong to liken burlesque to an 'impure flesh fly') but in always placing itself in critical counterpoint to any notion whatsoever of canonicity. The burlesque critique of Shakespeare is corrective without being destructive, reformist without being vicious.

To get a sense of how Shakespeare burlesques enact their ambivalence, let us explore in some detail the fundamental irony of burlesque acting. The play-within-the-play scene from *Rosencrantz and Guildenstern* provides an interpretive guide to the ironic posture of burlesque performance. While rehearsing *Gonzago*, the five-act tragedy written years before by

---

[6] *Era* 6 November 1859.
[7] Playbill, *Macbeth Somewhat Removed from the Text of Shakespeare*, Olympic Theatre, London, 11 April 1853 (Olympic Theatre production file, Theatre Museum, London).

the young Claudius, Hamlet concludes that the play must actually be a burlesque because it contains much 'pedantical bombast and windy obtrusive rhetorick'.[8] As Hamlet later explains to Claudius, the burlesque actor – unlike the tragedian – should 'mark, label, and underscore' his 'antik speeches', thereby signalling to the audience that his character remains 'alive to [the] absurdity' of the scene and enabling the actor to 'take part with his audience against himself'. Hamlet thus urges the players to forego the clichéd burlesque conventions of 'huge red noses', 'extravagant monstrous wigs', and men dressed as women because such contrivances wrongly assume that an audience cannot 'recognize a joke' on its own.

Hamlet's censure can hardly be idle since burlesques routinely indulged in precisely this sort of inflated comic expression. Banquo wore a 'false nose' in the banquet scene from *Macbeth Modernised* (p. 25). Edwin Yarnold played Lady Macbeth *en travestie* at the Strand. And in Robert Craig's *Hamlet; or, Wearing of the Black* (Arch Street Theater, Philadelphia, 1866), Ophelia carried a basket filled not with flowers, but with celery and pickles (Fol. D.a. 68, f. 29). But Gilbert's Hamlet would have none of this grotesquerie. A burlesque performer, he flatly declares, must deliver his absurd lines as if 'under protest' (*Rosencrantz and Guildenstern*, p. 98). The true comicality of burlesque humour lies not in exaggerated appearance or stage properties, but in the ironic stance of the performance itself – one of underlying sobriety which leaves its audience in a state of interpretive perplexity. The most successful burlesques, V. C. Clinton-Baddeley remarked, 'support an elaborate pretence of not being funny at all' (*Burlesque Tradition*, p. 10).

For a striking example of burlesque irony, let us compare the 'counterfeit presentments' of two memorable Hamlets: Edwin Booth and George L. Fox (illustrations 6 and 7). Both photographs date from around 1870, the year when New York theatregoers could choose between Booth's acclaimed revival of *Hamlet* and Fox's starring performance in T. C. DeLeon's *Hamlet Travestie*. The carefully posed studio photographs clearly reference the same moment in performance: Hamlet immersed in reading, just before Polonius' approach. Upon first glance, the images probably strike us as surprisingly similar. Both Hamlets read an appropriately antique book and wear a vaguely medieval black tunic with striped sleeves, white cuffs, and a contrasting hooded cloak (most of Booth's cloak is thrown over his shoulder). The sartorial likeness is no mere accident

---

[8] W. S. Gilbert, *Rosencrantz and Guildenstern*, in *Original Plays by W. S Gilbert* (London: Chatto and Windus, 1903), p. 86.

6. Edwin Booth as Hamlet, *c*. 1870. The 'accepted Hamlet of the American stage' (*New York Herald* 6 January 1870), he played the role at the Booth Theater, New York, at the same time George L. Fox played a burlesque Hamlet at the Olympic Theater. Compare with Fox's Hamlet in illustration 7.

for, as the *New York Herald* affirmed, Fox's costume 'follow[ed] the fashion set by Mr. Booth'.[9] Nor is there anything grotesque about Fox's appearance, pose, or expression. As a burlesque Hamlet, he might wear an extravagant costume, sport a red nose, carry a ridiculously over-sized (or under-sized) book, or even sing and dance. But he does none of that.

All these similarities notwithstanding, Fox's Hamlet still remains distinct from its legitimate counterpart. The distinction lies, however, not in Hamlet's action or appearance, but in his *attitude*. Booth is meditative, but focused. His left hand firmly grasps his book, holding it close to his body. The tragedian relates to his surroundings by leaning into the reading

[9] *New York Herald* 25 October 1877.

7. George L. Fox as burlesque Hamlet in T. C. DeLeon's *Hamlet Travestie*, Olympic Theater, New York, 1870. Compare with Edwin Booth's Hamlet in illustration 6. Booth and his wife attended a performance of *Hamlet Travestie*. When Fox entered reading a newspaper, Mrs Booth allegedly turned to her husband, asking 'are you here, or is that you on the stage?'

table, comfortably resting his weight on his right elbow. By contrast, Fox appears not to be reading at all. The comedian holds his book gingerly, at a reassuringly safe distance. The thumb and the first two fingers of his left hand support the entire weight of the book, while the right hand barely touches it. He sits awkwardly, feet splayed, contorting himself to face the adjacent table. Even then, his left arm hangs uncomfortably over the side of the chair. His eyes are downcast, the gaze detached. It is difficult to believe this Hamlet is actually reading a particular passage in the book. Indeed, his eyebrows are raised quizzically, as if he rejects the action which he has been assigned to perform. Anticipating, as it were, Gilbert's directive, Fox's performance is ironic because it looks as if it were conducted 'under protest'. The comedian remains ambivalent – the tell-tale arched eyebrows – toward the action which he will not enact, but only indicate.[10] So detached was Fox's performance that 'not even once', the *New York Herald* reported, 'did a smile attempt to play around the corners of his handsome mouth' (25 October 1877).[11]

Of course such ambivalence was not merely the actor's stylistic overlay, but rather was embedded in the burlesque script. Talfourd's *Macbeth Somewhat Removed from the Text of Shakespeare* is a case in point. Through its pun on 'removed', the play enacts the problematics of theatrical genealogy: the burlesque is at once distanced from the original tragedy and yet bound to it through familial ties. The Olympic playbill, as shown in illustration 8, spatializes the ambivalence between Talfourd's burlesque and Shakespeare's original play. The crucial qualifier 'somewhat removed' is compressed between the much more prominent (and potentially misleading) descriptors 'Macbeth' and 'From the Text of Shakespeare'. A reader who only glances at the playbill might wrongly assume that it advertises a production of Shakespeare's *Macbeth*. I am not arguing that the playbill was designed to trick the Olympic's audience; but I am arguing that the playbill deliberately articulates the problematic of Shakespearean authenticity which the burlesque itself enacts. Talfourd's play meditated upon its own disputed legitimacy, disclosing its own unstable position of being 'somewhat removed' within Shakespeare's extended theatrical family. What Macbeth, fearful of murdering his sovereign, says of his relationship to Duncan – the king is his 'kinsman, in a sort of way; / (How many times removed, I cannot say;)' (p. 17) – is comparable to the imprecise relationship between the burlesque and the tragedy enacted through the performance itself: an affinity that is simultaneously an alienation.

Yet how much further can Talfourd's parallel take us? If the burlesque is removed from Shakespeare in the same way (i.e., genealogically) that Macbeth is removed from Duncan, are we then invited to believe that the burlesque's designs are similarly murderous? Is the burlesque now an

---

[10] In *Perdita*, for example, the Chorus temporarily quits the stage to accommodate a tableau of Phoebus depicting the passing of sixteen years, leaving the audience responsible for overseeing the transition: 'I'll leave them [i.e., the figures in the tableau] to it; / P'raps you'll keep the count the while, and see they do it' (p. 18).

[11] The production did not lack for moments of hilarity, such as the frenzied chorus of 'Shoo fly' incited by Claudius' angered interruption of the players' dumbshow. See Yvonne Shafer, 'George L. Fox and the *Hamlet* Travesty', *Theatre Studies* 24/25 (1977–9), p. 91.

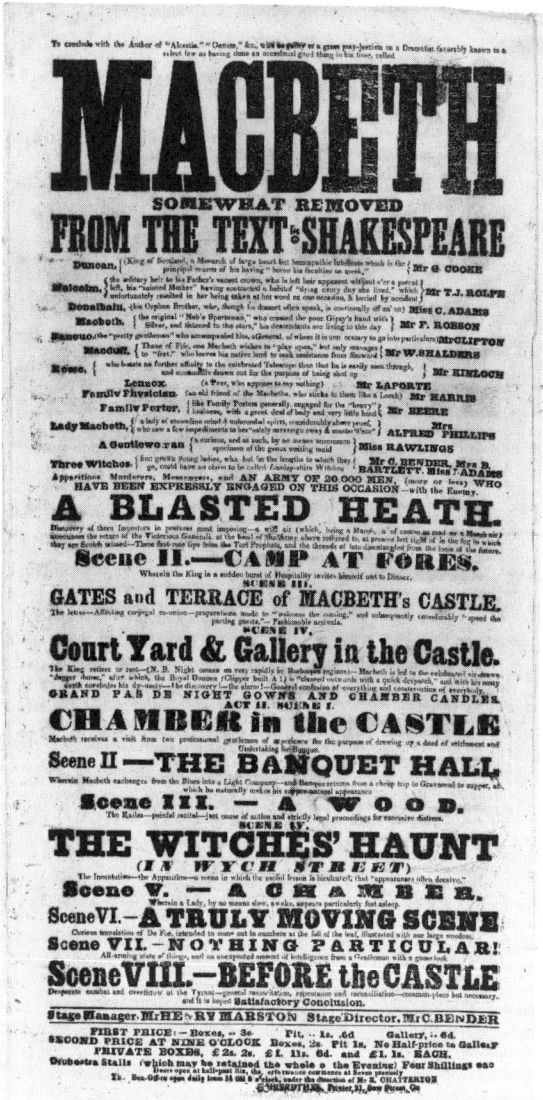

8. Playbill, Francis Talfourd's *Macbeth Somewhat Removed from the Text of Shakespeare*, Olympic Theatre, London, 1853. Note the punning description, in the fine print above the title, of the burlesque as a 'gross play-jeerism on a Dramatist favorably known to a select few as having done an occasional good thing in his time'. Note also the pun on 'THE WITCHES' HAUNT' and the Olympic's location 'IN WYCH STREET' (scene 4).

instrument of Bardicide? Surely this cannot be, since the explicit target of the play's jocular invective is not Shakespeare but Charles Kean – the very man who *does* usurp Shakespeare's authority, so we are asked to believe, by sacrificing the text to antiquarian splendour and supernatural stage effects. When produced at the Olympic Theatre in April 1853, Talfourd's burlesque explicitly satirized the historical accessories and ghostly effects of Kean's concurrent production of *Macbeth* through such sight gags as armour made of 'pot lids'[12] and the appearance of Banquo's ghost not from within a pillar, as in Kean's staging of the banquet scene, but from within an anachronistic 'clock case'.[13]

This burlesque's duty, then, is not to overthrow Shakespeare but to overthrow Kean's unfounded claims of legitimacy, thereby restoring the rightful order of succession in the House of Shakespeare. In consequence, Kean himself now becomes Macbeth, the expropriator of authority, while the burlesque takes on the avenging role of Malcolm. Indeed, the burlesque ranges so far in its quest to recognize Shakespeare's authority that it must conclude with a most un-Shakespearean moment in order to reclaim that authority. As Macduff prepares to crown Malcolm, the unexpectedly alive Duncan enters the scene nodding and winking. In a quasi-Napoleonic gesture, he replaces the crown on his own head. Malcolm, Macduff, and the other noblemen 'fall back in astonishment' as Duncan declares that he shall once again wear the crown 'if it's all the same to you' (Talfourd, *Macbeth Somewhat Removed*, p. 36). Macbeth, dead all the while on the stage floor, now suddenly sits up, looks around, and abdicates his throne (posthumously, as it were): 'at [Duncan's] feet I lay my regal diadem / Without regret, nor wish again that I had 'em' (p. 37). Duncan's peaceful return to power, hailed even by the usurping 'ex-Monarch' (as Macduff topically terms the penitent Macbeth) who at first wished him dead, not only signals that the burlesque itself harbours no selfish designs on Shakespeare's authority, but also warns that actor–managers such as Kean should behave with a due regard for that authority.

For all the sharp wit of its theatrical topicalities, this *Macbeth* burlesque operates on a comparatively predictable, indeed almost mechanical, allegory in which the textual narrative of usurpation and regicide stands in for the broader cultural narrative of the 'true' Shakespeare's usurpation and regicide in the legitimate Victorian theatre. Of course this reception narrative is just that – a story which the burlesque tells about

---

[12] *Observer* 1 May 1853.   [13] *Bell's Life in London* 1 May 1853.

itself – and not an impartial adjudication of the burlesque's cultural worthiness. Other comic plays offered a more involved, but no less prejudicial, assessment of the productive interactions between Shakespeare and burlesque. One such interaction, vividly dramatized in the final scene of *Romeo and Juliet Travestie*, was for the burlesque to defend Shakespeare from himself. Alarmed by the angered poet's sudden appearance, all the characters – including Romeo, Juliet, and Mercutio restored to life as minstrel show serenaders – immediately fall silent. As Romeo quickly perceives, Shakespeare's 'noble tragedy [has] turned to fun; / And he don't like it' (Halliday, *Romeo and Juliet Travestie*, p. 38). To soften Shakespeare's heart, and reconcile him to the burlesque's presumably justified distortions of his original play, Romeo concedes that the acting ensemble has 'not been behavin'' / With that respect' deserved by the 'illustrious Swan of Avon'. Yet he further advises that

> ... if we essayed your play
> As you did write it – the boxes and the pit
> Would say we could not act the play a bit.
> And so that *with* us, not *at* us they may laugh
> We've winnowed your fine corn into *chaff*.
> (pp. 38–9)

As Romeo freely confesses, the burlesque amends the original, yet defective, Shakespearean text by rendering it more theatrically effective for a contemporary audience. Romeo's decision to 'update' the tragedy – by incorporating aspects of minstrelsy, for example – is the decision inevitably faced whenever classic plays are restaged. Actors and directors in the nineteenth century no less than today are always trying to make Shakespeare speak across time. Yet there is a particular tension within nineteenth-century burlesque amendments to Shakespeare. The only means of making *Romeo and Juliet* acceptable to a mid-Victorian audience, the burlesque asserted, was to coarsen the playwright's refined sensibilities; to winnow the poet's corn into the clown's chaff. The burlesque preserved Shakespeare by denying Shakespeare.

Shakespeare burlesques recalled their origins with similar ambivalence when characters had to recite well-known speeches or soliloquies. Unlike direct quotations which provide evidence in support of an argument, burlesque quotations do not serve a normative function. Far from reinforcing Shakespeare's originary authority, such quotations foreground their own ambivalence because they reveal, as Margaret Rose has maintained, both the 'discrepancy' and the 'contingency' between parodies and their precursory texts (*Meta-Fiction*, p. 50). In *Hamlet! The Ravin' Prince of Denmark!!*, the 'To be or not to be' soliloquy remains deliberately unfinished:

> 'To be or not to be, that is the question',
> Oh dear! I'm suffering from the indigestion!
> 'Whether 'tis nobler in the mind to suffer
> The slings and arrows of' – a paltry duffer;
> 'Or to take arms, and by opposing end them' –
> These rhymes are very poor, I can't amend them –
> To sleep away the pain of too much grub;
> 'To sleep – perchance to dream – aye, there's the rub'.
> Than this no 'consummation' could be betterer,
> 'For who would bear the whips and scorns', *et cetera* –
> I really can't go on, for people say
> This is the noblest passage of the play!
> (Wells, *Nineteenth-Century Shakespeare Burlesques*, IV, p. 107)

Hamlet manages to recite only a handful of Shakespeare's lines – interspersed with his own nonsensical images and complaints about the poet's failure to use rhyming couplets – before giving up entirely, gesturing vaguely toward the lines left unspoken with an all-inclusive '*et cetera*'. Hamlet's objection to Shakespeare's 'very poor' rhymes refers to the burlesque convention of rhymed couplets. Quite simply, the burlesque hero does not know how to speak in blank verse; moreover, he cannot understand why Shakespeare wrote it in the first place. The more intriguing aspect of Hamlet's aborted citation is its justification. 'I really can't go on', he protests, 'for people say / This is the noblest passage of the play'. Hamlet refuses to 'go on' not because he has failed to learn his part but because he has learned it only too well. What overwhelms him is not the poetry itself (though from his perspective it could stand some revision) but the status accorded to that poetry. In response to the oppressive familiarity of 'To be or not to be', an exasperated Hamlet refuses to quote it fully and accurately. Interruption – and, finally, cessation – are the burlesque's distinctive answer to the pressures induced by Shakespeare's canonicity. The play leaves us with the impression that 'ravin'' Hamlet might indeed be able to complete the soliloquy if only 'people' were not obsessed by the 'noblest passage of the play'. In Hamlet's refusal to speak we can see quite clearly how the burlesque continually shifts its focus from Shakespeare's texts as dramatic masterpieces to Shakespeare's texts as objects of canonization. Through its acts of lexical equivocation the burlesque understands these texts not as isolated literary artifacts, but as the foundation for entrenched – yet contested – cultural practices.

Rosencrantz and Guildenstern also features a sustained, elaborate use of comic misquotation which relies not only on inaccuracy and interruption, but also on omission, transposition, deferral, substitution, and literalization – in short, the full panoply of burlesque linguistic contortions. As Hamlet 'gloomily' roams throughout Elsinore, Gertrude does not bid Rosencrantz and Guildenstern to discern the cause of her son's erratic behaviour, as she does in Shakespeare's original, but to prevent him from soliloquizing (Gilbert, *Rosencrantz and Guildenstern*, p. 81). 'Anticipate his points', the travesty queen commands, so that her son will be left with 'nought to say'. Indeed, no sooner does a dejected Hamlet, throwing himself into a chair, utter 'To be – or not to be' than Rosencrantz immediately rejoins 'Yes – that's the question.' As Hamlet struggles to recite Shakespeare's words, his companions obstruct him at every turn. At one point they offer Hamlet a choice of weapons – dagger or revolver – for his contemplated suicide. 'Oh, sirs, this interruption likes us not', he pleads, 'I pray you give it up' (p. 82). At length, Hamlet forces the meddlesome pair offstage, angrily declaring that '[t]hree persons can't soliloquize at once!' Yet he soon recalls Rosencrantz, daring him to play the flute. To Hamlet's astonishment, his companion blithely proceeds to play 'eight bars of hornpipe' (p. 83) – thus nicely reversing the moment in Shakespeare's play when Hamlet taunts Guildenstern who *cannot* play the recorder. A proficient flautist, Gilbert's Rosencrantz provides the *coup de grâce* to a scene which leaves a dispirited Hamlet bemoaning that '[e]verything goes wrong'.

Yet Hamlet eventually does manage to deliver his speech, only not within anyone's hearing. For as Ophelia and Rosencrantz converse downstage, Hamlet remains upstage where he is seen – but not heard – by both the other characters and the audience. Only when Ophelia breaks off does anyone realize that Hamlet has been soliloquizing *sotto voce* all the while. As she crosses upstage, we hear Hamlet say 'And lose the name of action!' – the fragmentary *final* line of the soliloquy which he has been desperate to deliver all along (Gilbert, *Rosencrantz and Guildenstern*, p. 83). The audience thus intercepts Hamlet at the most frustrating moment possible: too late to have overheard anything but the last line of his immortal soliloquy, but not so late as to have missed it entirely. Gertrude's victory is complete. Hamlet truly has 'nothing to say', at least not to us. The suddenly audible last line betokens not the entire soliloquy but the 'nothing' which has passed before us. Far from resanctifying the Shakespearean original through authoritative quotation, the burlesque uses comic misquotation to silence its original text in the actuality of performance. In Gilbert's dramaturgy of the disavowed, *Rosencrantz and Guildenstern* invokes *Hamlet* only as a palpable absence: something that should be *there*, on the stage, yet is not.[14]

At other times, the burlesque wanted not to disavow Shakespeare but to ensure his guiding presence. Consider, for example, the scene from DeLeon's *Hamlet Travestie* when Hamlet and the ghost, played respectively by George L. Fox and Mrs Edward Wright, chatter amiably while warming themselves at an open fire. The image is instantly ludicrous since a ghost, being incorporeal, cannot be sensitive to temperature. At length a rooster crows offstage, signalling the ghost's necessary departure at daybreak. Hamlet and the ghost ignore the repeated crowing and remain deep in conversation, even as daylight overtakes the scene. Eventually, an enormous rooster, impatient for the day – and the play – to progress, appears on stage, taps the unsuspecting ghost on the shoulder, and crows loudly in his ear while sternly pointing to the wings. Under compulsion, the ghost finally quits the stage.[15] This is a moment of high hilarity, with the ghost's parting command 'remember me' carrying a new urgency in light of his being overpowered by a stentorian chanticleer. Yet there is more to this scene of the reluctant ghost urged to his diurnal rest than the absurd literalization of a sound effect. It is not just Old Hamlet who pleads for remembrance here but also Mrs Edward Wright, for her performance risks being eclipsed by a supernumerary outfitted as a rooster. At a metatheatrical level, the moment characterizes the ambivalent relation between *Hamlet Travestie* and *Hamlet*. Just when it is about to stray too far from Shakespeare's original tragedy, the burlesque disciplines itself through the heroic measure of the rooster's commanding appearance. The burlesque thus prevents itself from drifting further and further away from its origins. The performance breathes a sigh of relief as Old Hamlet finally disappears into the wings, allowing a new day to dawn and the next scene to begin. Through the absurdly over-sized rooster, the burlesque playfully tests – and enforces – the limits of its own Shakespearean boundaries.

Over the course of the nineteenth century, burlesques became increasingly detached from their ostensible source texts. To describe a performance as a 'burlesque' had become misleading, the *Gentleman's*

---

[14] Gilbert's play is exceptional since almost all nineteenth-century burlesques of *Hamlet* transformed the soliloquy into either a popular song or a treatise on an entirely different topic. Only *Hamlet! The Ravin' Prince of Denmark!!* anticipates the irony of Gilbert's *Rosencrantz and Guildenstern* by giving the famed soliloquy in fits and starts.

[15] For an account of the scene, see Laurence Senelick, *The Age and Stage of George L. Fox: 1825–1877* (Hanover, NH: University Press of New England, 1988), p. 161.

Magazine complained in 1872, because in too many performances 'nothing is burlesqued'.[16] All too often, the magazine continued, such a performance 'intends to entertain by mumming simply. It does not mean to "burlesque" a story in the strict sense of the term' (p. 563). A prime example of a burlesque in which 'nothing is burlesqued' was Burnand's *Ariel* (Gaiety 1883). In the months preceding the opening of Burnand's play – nominally a burlesque of *The Tempest* – the *Daily News* published a series of letters debating the propriety of Shakespeare burlesques.[17] One of the paper's readers, a Mr W. Kennedy of Hampstead, the north London suburb, denounced the Gaiety's plans to stage 'degrad[ed]' burlesques of *The Tempest* and *Hamlet* (qtd in Hamilton, *Parodies*, II, p. 144). Adopting an extreme position, Kennedy argued that '[w]e had better consider ourselves no longer the same nation, and cease to pride ourselves on having produced the foremost man in all literature when we descend to this [burlesque] without protest'. In the face of such intemperate rhetoric, John Hollingshead, the Gaiety's manager, mounted a quick but decidedly low-key defence. *Ariel* initiated no surprise attack on the national poet, the manager carefully explained, but represented only the latest offering of a well-established theatrical tradition exemplified by 'Messrs. F. Talfourd, Andrew Halliday, [and] Robert Brough in the fabled "palmy-days" of the drama'.

Despite its measured tone, Hollingshead's defence of *Ariel* was entirely disingenuous. As Burnand's own correspondence reveals, the Gaiety's manager blatantly misrepresented the style of the play. This much we know from the dramatist himself, who wrote to Moy Thomas, theatre critic of the *Daily News*, that he was 'distinctly not burlesquing Shakespeare's *Tempest*', at least not in the way that his plays *Dora* and *Diplunacy* respectively burlesqued Sardou's *Fédora* and the Prince of Wales' production of *Diplomacy*.[18] Burnand, in an earlier letter to Thomas, distinguished a traditional Shakespeare burlesque – which gives an 'absurd turn' to the poet's 'lines and sentiments' – from a new-fangled

[16] 'Players of Our Day. Burlesque Actors and Actresses', *Gentleman's Magazine* n.s. 9 (July–December 1872), p. 560.
[17] Seven letters to the *Daily News* occasioned by the Gaiety's impending production of *Ariel* are reprinted in Hamilton, *Parodies*, II, pp. 144–6.
[18] F. C. Burnand, a letter to Moy Thomas, 24 August 1883, Folger Y.c. 372 (1a–d), Folger Shakespeare Library, Washington, DC. The letter was printed in the *Daily News* three days later. Burnand's *Our Own Antony and Cleopatra* (Gaiety 1873) anticipated *Ariel* in being only loosely connected with a performance of Shakespeare's original play. So little did the Gaiety's burlesque have to do with contemporary theatrical culture that it opened *before* a Drury Lane revival of *Antony and Cleopatra*, prompting *The Times* to remark that 'Time was about to reverse his course' (10 September 1873).

burlesque 'version' like *Ariel*, which 'is really an extravaganza'.[19] While Hollingshead wanted to align Burnand's fairy spectacle with Shakespeare burlesques written in the 1840s and 1850s, its author knew that his play did not share the sharp aggressivity of those earlier parodies or, indeed, of his own earlier burlesques.

Indeed, the manuscript for *Ariel* confirms how vigorously the play departs from its Shakespearean origins. Prospero, to his embarrassment, discovers that he cannot conjure up a storm at sea to wreck Gonzago's ship because he has lost his book of magic. The lost book is no mere tome, but a script – a promptbook – 'filled with every modern stage direction / For *"getting up The Tempest"* to perfection!'[20] Reading the pun in its theatrical sense of 'getting up' (that is, producing) a play, we can see that *Ariel* exploits the self-reflexivity of burlesque not to strengthen its ties to Shakespeare but to sever them. As Prospero's irretrievable book suggests, *Ariel* no longer possesses the ability to be like – to 'get up' – *The Tempest*. For at least one reviewer, the play in performance was true to its word. The critic from *Dramatic Notes* complained, with particular reference to Nellie Farren's performance as Ariel, that, except for

> the name borrowed from Shakespeare's *Tempest*, no one would have known there was any connection between the burlesque and the poet's enchanting creation. There was certainly nothing even distantly Shakespearian in Miss Farren. She was herself, and nothing more – the same Nelly [*sic*] Farren that she has been times out of number, with scanty clothing, *décolleté* dresses, and a big hat; she might have been Aladdin as much as Ariel.[21]

Of course Nellie Farren did not deserve all the blame. The fairies were equally culpable, having to deliver such insipidities as 'this is the place to spend a happy day' (Burnand, *Ariel*, BL Add Mss 53,301 J, f. 9).[22] In terms of the flimsy plot, the fairies attendant upon Ariel were warbling schoolgirls under the avuncular tutelage of Dr Prospero. But this was not at all how they appeared. The fairies, as depicted in illustration 9, seem to be neither cheerful pupils nor exotic sprites. Rather, they look like just what they are: world-weary chorines performing in yet another 'leg piece' for the ogling 'mashers' who crammed the Gaiety's stalls. There is nothing distinctively Shakespearean about the women in the

---

[19] F. C. Burnand, a letter to Moy Thomas, August 1883; qtd in Hamilton, *Parodies*, II, pp. 144–5.
[20] F. C. Burnand, *Ariel, a Burlesque Fairy Drama in Three Acts and Four Tableaux* 1883 British Library Add Mss 53,301 J, f. 25.
[21] *Dramatic Notes* October 1883, p. 49.
[22] The fairies in *Ariel* more closely resemble the fairies attendant upon the Queen in Gilbert and Sullivan's *Iolanthe*, then enjoying a run of over 300 performances at the Savoy.

9. Chorus of fairies from F. C. Burnand's *Ariel*, Gaiety Theatre, London, 1883. The fairies, pupils in Dr Prospero's school, enter singing '[w]e are elves O yes' (British Library Add Mss 53,301 J, f. 5). They exercise their powers of '[i]n-vi-si-bi-li-ty' over Prospero, who is unable to see them until he follows the instructions in his book '[S]ome receipts for Parlour Magic, or / The Conjuror's digest of Magic Lore' (f. 6).

photograph, nothing that might distinguish them from the innumerable other chorines erotically depicted in late-Victorian *cartes de visite*.

An eminent man of letters offered a more encouraging appraisal of the Gaiety production. No less an authority than F. J. Furnivall confessed, in an open letter to Hollingshead, that he had 'enjoyed the pretty music, dresses, and dances, and the brightness of the whole play'.[23] Enlarging his claim for the production's appeal, the founder of the New Shakspere Society assured the Gaiety's manager that 'Shakespeare himself' would have 'enjoy[ed] the evening' and that no 'lover' of the poet could be 'hurt at the performance' (p. 154). That one of the chief apostles of Victorian Bardolatry attended a Shakespeare burlesque is unexpected; that he publicly endorsed it is astonishing. Yet exactly what did Furnivall endorse? He did not hold Shakespeare burlesques in great esteem, for only three years later he denounced Duffet, author of *The Mock-Tempest*, as a 'vulgar beast'.[24] If Furnivall 'enjoyed' *Ariel* it was not because that play burlesqued Shakespeare but because it had precious little to do with Shakespeare. Furnivall applauded precisely what *Dramatic Notes* had criticized: that *Ariel* was not even 'distantly Shakespearian'. While he could never sanction a performance which actually criticized the cult of Bardolatry, Furnivall could unreservedly praise one which failed to engage in any critical activity whatsoever. Far from being progressive, his claim that 'no lover' of Shakespeare could take offence at *Ariel* is ultimately conservative because it implies that the only good burlesque is a squandered one.

With its etiolated critical powers, *Ariel* surely represents the burlesque genre in its late-Victorian decline. Earlier in the century, Shakespeare burlesques had styled themselves as the vehicle, however seemingly ludicrous, for a triumphal reinstatement of Shakespearean loyalties at the precise moment when those loyalties seemed imperilled by legitimate culture. In getting a sense of how burlesques enacted their sardonic assault upon Bardolatry, let us first remind ourselves of the massive edifice of Shakespeare worship which dominated the nineteenth-century cultural landscape. Examples of Shakespearean laudation are not difficult

---

[23] F. J. Furnivall, a letter to John Hollingshead, 5 December 1883, qtd in John Hollingshead, *My Lifetime* 2 vols. (London: Sampson Low, Marston and Co., 1895), II, p. 154.

[24] F. J. Furnivall, ed., *Some 300 Fresh Allusions to Shakspere from 1594 to 1694 A.D.* New Shakspere Society Publications 4th ser., 3 (London: Trübner, 1886), p. 245. The anonymous contributor of an allusive passage from *The Mock-Tempest* commented that '[a]s pearls before swine, so were Shakspere's plays in the eyes of the hog Duffet. Not content with degrading *Macbeth*, he went on to turn *The Tempest* – thro its Davenant-adaptation – into a bawdy burlesque' (p. 242).

to find. In his 1849 sonnet 'Shakespeare', Matthew Arnold imagined the poet as '[o]ut-topping knowledge'.[25] Thomas Carlyle provided one of the century's most passionate correlations of Shakespeare and national identity in his essay 'The Poet as Hero' (1840). Notwithstanding his disdain for the Elizabethan theatre as a social institution, Carlyle unashamedly worshipped the poet–hero.[26] The essay is remarkable for articulating an imperial *pax Shakespeareana* in its bold description of 'King Shakespeare' whom 'no time or chance, Parliament or combination of Parliaments, can dethrone'. Less heroically, the *Dublin University Magazine* affirmed in 1852 that Shakespeare was 'impressed on every heart which feels and owns the kindred sympathy of nature'.[27]

Such panegyrics only concealed, however, what was for some critics the fundamentally hypocritical nature of Shakespeare worship. An 1833 article from the *Westminster Review* is enlightening. While a devotion to Shakespeare foretold the financial ruin of actor–managers, the journal explained, that devotion was nonetheless a 'respectable humbug' without which no legitimate theatre could establish a solid reputation.[28] Indeed, a theatre's illegitimate, but vastly more popular, offerings effectively subsidized its moral obligation to keep up 'the civil list of that most expensive and incomprehensible personage the legitimate drama'. Like other 'revered' objects, Shakespeare was 'never spoken of but with respect' yet was 'always treated with the utmost practical contempt'. As Donne observed with reference to the national poet, '[t]here is scarcely anything that people will not say in defence of an established idol while they neglect its worship themselves'.[29] The starting point, then, for understanding the burlesque critique of Bardolatry is the recognition that to revere Shakespeare has always been to neglect Shakespeare. Indeed, complaints that the officially sanctioned rites of Shakespeare worship fail to honour the playwright date back at least to Samuel Foote's stinging observation that Garrick's 1769 Stratford Jubilee consisted of 'an ode without poetry, music without melody, dinners without victuals, and lodgings without beds'.[30]

[25] Matthew Arnold, 'Shakespeare', in *Matthew Arnold: Prose and Poetry*, ed. Archibald L. Bouton (New York: Charles Scribner's Sons, 1927), p. 438.
[26] Thomas Carlyle, *On Heroes, Hero-Worship, and the Heroic in History* (London: James Fraser, 1841), p. 130.
[27] J. W. C[alcraft], 'More Improvements in the Text of Shakespeare', *Dublin University Magazine* 41 (March 1853), p. 373. Calcraft worked for Kean at the Princess's Theatre and, under the name J. W. Cole, wrote *The Life and Theatrical Times of Charles Kean, F.S.A.* (1859).
[28] *Westminster Review* 18 (1833), p. 35.
[29] W. B. Donne, 'Poets and Players', *Fraser's Magazine* 44 (November 1851), p. 512.
[30] Qtd in 'The Confessions of William Shakespeare', *New Monthly Magazine* 44 (1835), p. 54.

And so we must set alongside the pious testimonials of Matthew Arnold and Thomas Carlyle the equally committed, yet seemingly irreverent, testimonials of those observers for whom too many sins had been committed in the name of the Bard. 'Shakespeare Clubs and Shakespeare Jubilees', the *New Monthly Magazine* despairingly observed, 'vulgarize genius by reducing it to the level of the stomach' and succeed only in 'sav[ing] people the trouble of thinking precisely why and how they should admire [Shakespeare]'.[31] The cover drawing from an 1848 issue of the *Theatrical Journal*, shown in illustration 10, depicts 'poor Billy Shakespeare' asking alms of Tom Thumb, 'the only *great actor* of consequence now-a-days that seems to have any regard for the works of our immortal bard'.[32] In this telling caricature, the national poet becomes the ward of a P. T. Barnum's protégé. An iconic Shakespeare, in the background, bears mute witness to an affront to his own dignity. The sketch is hardly idiosyncratic. Three years later, a 'French Critic in London' similarly observed in *Fraser's Magazine* that 'the people who most talk about [Shakespeare] are the least able to appreciate him, and for the most part, know him only by report'.[33] In the year of the Great Exhibition, Shakespeare was no more than an 'empty prattle'. Donne berated his fellow journalists who 'pompously take on themselves the office of patrons and protectors of Shakspeare, [and] assume that they are the sole people who truly appreciate his merits' (*Fraser's Magazine* Nov. 1851, p. 517). Nor did he show any mercy to the theatres themselves, attacking egotistical actor–managers who believed themselves to be Shakespeare's 'sole priests'.[34] It was 'monstrous', Donne railed, that Londoners could approach Shakespeare only through the 'interventions' of sacerdotal theatrical managers.

For all his abhorrence of burlesque, Donne's tirade against the impieties of Shakespeare worship ironically coincides with the burlesque's own mission to expose the hypocrisy of the stewards of official Shakespearean culture. The *Punch* cartoon 'Shakspeare and the Pigmies' (illustration 11) captures the essence of the burlesque critique. Led by

---

[31] *New Monthly Magazine* 44 (1835), p. 54. [32] *Theatrical Journal* 12 October 1848.
[33] *Fraser's Magazine* 44 (November 1851), p. 501.
[34] Phelps allowed his name to appear on an edition of Shakespeare's plays even though he undertook none of the promised editorial duties. After reviewing the edition fraudulently published under his name, Phelps regretted that he had 'not had time' to prepare the 'notes' and expressed to the publisher his 'remorse for having committed forgery' and for not acknowledging the 'real editor' (Phelps, a letter, 22 January 1852, bound in Clement Scott, *The Drama of Yesterday and To-Day*, London: George Suckling, 1901, extra-illustrated vol. VI, Harry Ransom Humanities Research Center, The University of Texas at Austin, Austin, Texas).

10. Shakespeare begging from Tom Thumb, *Theatrical Journal*, October 1848. The cartoon accompanied an article defending 'the legitimate drama' and 'upholding the stage in all its purity of purpose'. The background Shakespeare is an animated version of the statue by Louis-François Roubilliac in Westminster Abbey.

W. Hepworth Dixon, editor of the *Athenaeum*, the immodest gentlemen of the National Shakspere Committee busy themselves preparing for the 1864 Tercentenary, utterly unaware that Shakespeare's steadfast, dignified genius dwarfs their puny, self-serving efforts.[35] The colossal sculpture is practically Arnoldian in its rectitude: 'We ask and ask – Thou smilest and art still'.[36] In *Punch*'s acerbic view, these erstwhile Bardolators do not so much worship as deface Shakespeare. The committee's minuscule members paste self-promoting billboards at the base of the monument and, worse still, scrawl their names on its surface. Shakespeare, mercifully, cannot see the offences committed in his name since he is blind. In the face of such defilement, the burlesque appears – at least to its proponents – not as wantonly destructive, but prudently restorative. And thus it was only too appropriate that the low comedians Paul Bedford and

[35] *Punch* 30 January 1864.
[36] 'Shakespeare', in *The Poetical Works of Matthew Arnold*, ed. C. B. Tinker and H. F. Lowry (London: Oxford University Press, 1963), p. 2.

11. 'Shakspeare and the Pigmies', *Punch*, 30 January 1864. The National Shakspere Committee proposed to place a statue of Shakespeare in Green Park. Note the figure on a ladder, who is supposed to be the *Athenaeum*'s editor W. Hepworth Dixon, scrawling 'ATHENÆVM' next to Shakespeare's own writings.

J. L. Toole – who had performed in burlesques of *The Tempest* and *The Winter's Tale* – spoke at a Shakespeare Tercentenary Concert at the Agricultural Hall in Islington and that the Gaiety Theatre raised £450 from its 1876 'Shakespeare Memorial Benefit' to help fund the construction of the Memorial Theatre in Stratford-upon-Avon.[37]

Coyne's *This House to be Sold: (The Property of the Late William Shakspeare) Inquire Within* (Adelphi 1847) demonstrates particularly well the burlesque's strangely conservative and cozy relationship to Shakespeare. Coyne's play took its cue, as the *Literary Gazette* noted, from the recent 'sale of Shakespeare's [father's] house'.[38] This *pièce de circonstance* thus begins with Shakespeare evicted, a topic whose satiric potential attracted the interest of Albert Smith's comic magazine the *Man in the Moon*. The cartoon 'Shakspeare Packing up his Goods' (illustration 12) depicts the poet on the point of being turned out into the streets of Stratford-upon-Avon, cut off from the tourist trade which provides his 'sole support'. Picking up where the caricature leaves off, *This House to be Sold* imagines the fate of Shakespeare's birthplace after the auction has been concluded.

Who acquires the 'dilapidated, but heart-stirring premises', as the play's real-estate agent describes the house in Henley Street?[39] Not the Shakespeare Club of Stratford-upon-Avon, eager though it was to 'preserve everything connected with [the playwright's] mortal remains from further disrespect',[40] but Chatterton Chopkins, an entrepreneurial Cockney 'gent' who buys the house sight unseen and promptly paints 'Chopkins, Late Shakespeare' above the entrance to his newly purchased place of business. So much for respecting Shakespeare's 'mortal remains'. In Chopkins – the son of a London pig butcher – Coyne gives theatrical shape to middle-class fears about unrestricted access to Shakespearean culture. The flashpoint for those fears, as detailed in the contemporary periodical press, was indeed the sale of the Stratford birthplace. *This*

---

[37] Paul Bedford, *Recollections and Wanderings of Paul Bedford* (London: Strand, 1867), p. 121; Hollingshead, *My Lifetime*, II, p. 131.

[38] *Literary Gazette* 11 September 1847. Under Benjamin Webster's management, the Adelphi revived *This House to be Sold* to coincide with the Tercentenary. Starring J. L. Toole as Chopkins, the production enjoyed a lengthy run of 123 performances.

[39] J. Stirling Coyne, *This House to be Sold: (The Property of the Late William Shakspeare) Inquire Within* (London: National Acting Drama Office, 1847), p. 3. In the manuscript submitted to the Lord Chamberlain, the line reads 'dilapidated but interesting premises' (BL Add Mss 43,005, f. 892), a description which Coyne took directly from the Stratford historian R. B. Wheler. See Wheler's *Historical and Descriptive Account of the Birth-place of Shakespeare* (Stratford-upon-Avon: James Ward, 1824), p. 3.

[40] 'Monuments of Shakespeare', *Gentleman's Magazine* 157 (July 1835), p. 77.

12. 'Shakspeare Packing up his Goods', *Man in the Moon*, 1847. 'I had been happy', Shakespeare laments, 'if the General Thumb, / Barnum and all, had bought up the old house / In which I ne'er was born'.

House to be Sold realizes the 'profanation most horrible' which Dixon had predicted in the pages of the *People's Journal*: that Shakespeare's birthplace would fall into the hands of a philistine whose vulgar economic capital enabled him to acquire *tout d'un coup* the symbolic centre of the nation's cultural heritage.[41] '[L]ike any other goods and chattels', Dixon warned, Shakespeare's house would go to the highest bidder,

[41] Hepworth Dixon, 'Shakspeare's House at Stratford-upon-Avon in 1847', *People's Journal* 4 (1847), p. 52. Dixon urged the government to renounce its 'continued apathy' on a 'matter so nearly associated with our veneration and our hopes' while Harriet Martineau, writing in the same issue, dreamed of a mass 'penny subscription' to secure the birthplace as the 'property of the nation forever' (pp. 51, 79). Those calls for direct intervention, whether parliamentary or grassroots, went unheeded.

'whether he be a Jew or a Gentile, the agent of a Yankee speculator, or the deputy of a reverent people'. Or a butcher's son who fancies himself a gentleman. For anyone who had succumbed to 'domusmania', as *Bentley's Miscellany* termed the public's frenzied response to the auction, the historical precedents for Coyne's theatrical fantasia were only too disturbing.[42]

Bound up with the comedy's seemingly reactionary defence of Shakespearean culture is its own social prejudice. Chopkins' flagrant misuse of cultural capital represents but one aspect of the more general problem, so the play suggests, that shop assistants, clerks, petty tradesmen, and other members of the lower middle class were acquiring social aspirations. Disdainful of those who occupied the fringes of respectability, the middle class directed its prejudice most vehemently against the 'gent'. In Peter Bailey's apt description, the early-Victorian 'gent' appeared to polite society as a 'rude untutored man' who 'by combination of chance and cultivation' simulated gentility in dress and behaviour.[43] The simulations were never successful, however, and the 'gent' was constantly ridiculed in the periodical press and on metropolitan stages throughout the 1830s and 1840s. It is no coincidence that Chopkins sings 'I'm a Gent' only after spending his first night in Shakespeare's house (BL Add Mss 43,005, f. 898). In bestowing upon Chopkins a precise socio-economic identity, the song brands him as the play's – and, potentially, the audience's – object of ridicule: the vulgarian who uses Shakespeare to buy his way into the middle class. The lyric 'I'm a gent – I'm a gent – I'm a gent ready-made' attests to Chopkins' belief that gentility was a character trait which could be purchased and then simply put on, like a set of clothes off the rack. In light of the social stereotypes which Chopkins embodies, the imagined fate of Shakespeare's birthplace remains troubling indeed. The new owner emerges not as 'the deputy of a reverent people', but a rank impostor. Driven by an 'ambition above hogs', Chopkins had vowed to 'distinguish [him]self in the world' (f. 893). Having failed to become 'notorious' (f. 894) as a novelist, a dandy, and an amateur actor, he saw in Shakespeare one last 'glorious opportunity' to gain the notoriety which so far had eluded him. Shakespeare thus represents Chopkins' last hope of acquiring a 'ready-made' reputation.

---

[42] 'Hoax of the Shakspeare Birth-House; and the Relic Trade at Stratford-upon-Avon', *Bentley's Miscellany* 23 (1848), p. 279.
[43] Peter Bailey, *Popular Culture and Performance in the Victorian City* (Cambridge: Cambridge University Press, 1998), p. 57.

'I feel I'm half a Shakespeare already', Chopkins confidently exclaims upon first entering the birthplace (f. 895).[44]

Yet just what does it mean to feel 'half a Shakespeare'? In the classic posture of humbug, Chopkins pays tribute to the poet by remaining ignorant of him. The new occupant of Shakespeare's birthplace has never before set eyes upon it, and knows nothing of its history. Preposterously, he asks the caretaker whether she herself once nursed the infant Shakespeare. Nor does Chopkins possess much knowledge about the plays themselves, whether in literary or theatrical contexts. Apart from clichéd references to *Richard III* and Shakespeare's infamously meagre box-office returns (fols. 898, 900), Chopkins does not allude to specific productions, performers, or dramatic characters. Indeed, he fails to recognize Shakespeare when the poet visits him in the night. As shown in illustration 13, a startled Chopkins half-rises out of bed at the sudden appearance of Shakespeare's ghost. Chopkins needs only to glance at the bust on the opposite side of the room to discern the identity of the spectral form standing in the middle of the bedchamber. But the Cockney 'gent' (note that his sartorial signifiers – the tall silk hat and walking stick – remain discreetly within the picture frame) is not given to studying cultural monuments. And so the resemblance passes unnoticed. As a classic cultural philistine, Chopkins desires Shakespeare instrumentally – that is, for his use-value only. He does not recognize Shakespeare because he does not have to. It is sufficient for his purposes that others do so.

After his surprise encounter with Shakespeare, the parvenu finds himself transformed. Chopkins' own dream of a 'grand tableau' in honour of the 'immortal' playwright forestalls the profanity of having a hog butcher's son become, in his own boast, 'the legitimate successor of the Bard of Avon' (fols., 899, 894). Upon waking, he decides to abandon his lawyer's scheme of charging five shillings per person to view the birthplace (more than twice the price of admission to the pit of a West End theatre) and resolves instead to 'make a present of it to the nation'. Chopkins went to his bed a commercial speculator but rose from

---

[44] Butchery provides an ironic credibility to Chopkins' genealogical claim. In the late eighteenth century, Shakespeare's great-great-grandson, a descendant of the Hart family, allegedly set up a butcher's shop in the Stratford birthplace. Chopkins *père* was himself a 'pork butcher' (f. 893). Coyne's image of the shingle inscribed 'Chopkins, Late Shakespeare' likely derived from Wheler's history, which records that the enterprising butcher placed a sign on the front of the house which read 'William Shakespeare was Born in this House. / N.B. – A horse and taxed cart to Let' (*Birthplace of Shakspeare*, p. 10 n. 11). Perhaps embedded in all of this is a sly allusion to the Baconian authorship controversy.

13. Illustration from J. Stirling Coyne's *This House to be Sold: (The Property of the Late William Shakspeare) Inquire Within*, 1847, The Harvard Theatre Collection, The Houghton Library. 'Now Sir, what do you mean by this conduct', Chatterton Chopkins asks Shakespeare's ghost; 'I repeat, sir, this is my house' (British Library Add Mss 43,005, f. 899).

it a philanthropic Bardolator. Only by giving the house to the nation, as his friend Tiffin affirms, will Chopkins at last 'nobly link [his] name with the Poet's – and merit the gratitude of a people in bestowing upon them the dwelling in which the divine bard was born and nurtured' (f. 916).[45] Through his benefaction, Chopkins rekindles the extinguished Shakespearean flame for both the common good *and* individual advantage. The birthplace is spared the fate of being turned into a profit-driven, impersonal 'business' (*People's Journal* 4 1847, p. 52), and Chopkins can lay legitimate claim to being a gentleman. The virtuous circle is now complete. By staging such a gratifying resolution to the crisis of who owns Shakespeare – and who *ought* to – *This House to be Sold* performs its own willing Shakespearean subjection (or infantilization, we might say, since the diminutive 'Chopkins' has a childish ring to it). Subjection does not, however, exclude a degree of self-congratulation. Coyne's burlesque fancies itself uniquely able to restore Shakespeare to the nation, even if only through the purified impulses of a Cockney 'small substitute for the great Bard' (f. 897).

One of the highlights of *This House to be Sold* was its burlesque pageant of 'The Bard and his Children' in which Shakespeare's leading characters bemoan that they can no longer find work on the legitimate stage. As the playbill summarizes the plight of Shakespearean drama, the poet's 'Old Characters' must search for 'New Callings' (illustration 14).[46] Othello, for example, declares his intention to forsake Venice and 'play banjo' with the 'Eighty-opium Sar'naders' (BL Add Mss 43,005, f. 904). As he explains in the accent and idiom of an Ethiopian Serenader in a minstrel show, the British public 'lub de Moor' but 'pay de nigger'. Shakespeare, for his part, confesses – in a line which received sympathetic applause – that he cannot secure a 'roof to cover [his] head' unless he plays 'the walking gentleman in the fore leg of an Elephant at Drury Lane' (f. 911).[47] In such moments, Coyne's play reiterated one of the most enduring complaints issued in the nineteenth century about the legitimate stage: that it failed to show proper respect

---

[45] Coyne's play uncannily foreshadowed the actual turn of events since the birthplace was sold at auction to the Shakespeare House Committee, a private philanthropic organization formed expressly to prevent private speculators – like Chatterton Chopkins – from acquiring the historic premises. The Committee, whose donors included Macready and Charles Dickens, then gave the house to the government which, in turn, agreed to maintain it in perpetuity.
[46] Playbill, *This House to be Sold*, Adelphi Theatre, London, 10 September 1847 (Adelphi Theatre production file, Theatre Museum, London).
[47] The reference to the applause is from a review in the *Theatrical Times* 18 September 1847.

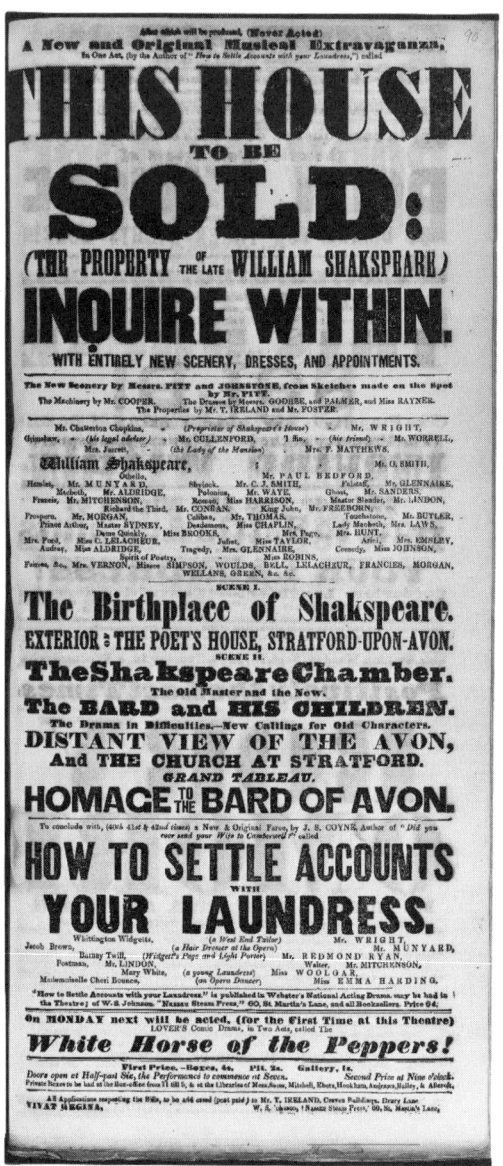

14. Playbill, *This House to be Sold*, Adelphi Theatre, London, 1847. The lay-out of the playbill resembles an auction circular, and so invites the Adelphi's audience to 'inquire within' about the premises to be sold. In a reversal of customary practice, the one-act burlesque precedes the full-length farce *How to Settle Accounts with your Laundress*.

for Shakespeare as the nation's supreme dramatist.[48] Other burlesques elaborated upon this complaint through highly pointed parodies of bombastic acting, theatrical editing, spectacular *mise-en-scène*, and the vogue for historically correct sets, costumes, and properties. Let us now examine in some detail the specific burlesque practices which, as the *Era* observed in its review of an 1854 burlesque of *Richard III*, 'throw a somewhat powerful stigma upon the "legitimate"'.[49]

Burlesques frequently ridiculed what Robertson described as the 'sepulchral' and 'solemn' manners of eminent tragedians who, in their stately comportment, 'resembled animated statues'.[50] In H. J. Byron's *The Rival Othellos* (1861), the lead characters impersonated G. V. Brooke and Charles Fechter, the rival Othellos of their day. (In the Strand's 1874 revival, the two tragedians impersonated were Irving and Salvini.[51]) The comedian J. S. Clarke parodied Brooke's 'ponderous recitation and violent carriage'.[52] The mimicry was 'as good as a criticism on Mr. Brooke', the *Illustrated London News* affirmed, and '[i]t would be well for the actor himself if he could profit by it'. As the newspaper approvingly noted, burlesques had 'gone far to modify the taste of modern audiences'. Once spectators heard the 'exaggerated utterance of burlesque dialogue', they would grow sceptical of stultified recitations of 'old Elizabethan blank-verse'. Adducing evidence for this claim, the *Illustrated London News* reported that 'two aristocratic young men' could not stop laughing during one of Charles Kean's performances because the actor made Shakespeare sound 'so like the diction of burlesque'.

Theatrical parody thus exercised not a pernicious, but a salutary influence over legitimate acting because it helped to exclude 'bombast' from the representation of Shakespeare's characters.[53] The consequent preference for 'tame' and 'colloquial' characterizations – a direct reference to Fechter's casual style – derived in good measure, so it was proposed,

---

[48] Coyne's particular emphasis on *theatrical* Shakespeare accounts for the ghost's distinctive appearance. Shakespeare's doublet, hose, and knee breeches recall nothing so much as the pseudo-Elizabethan costume invariably identified with stage Hamlets. The ghost's commanding stance and formal gesture are similarly theatrical.
[49] *Era* 23 April 1854.
[50] Qtd in T. Edgar Pemberton, *The Life and Writings of T. W. Robertson* (London: Richard Bentley, 1893), p. 90.
[51] The character impersonating Salvini snubs the character impersonating Irving by calling him a '[b]enighted slave of Tradition' (H. J. Byron, *The Rival Othellos* 1874 BL Add Mss 53,163 I, f. 8).
[52] *Illustrated London News* 7 December 1861.
[53] Not all nineteenth-century observers shared this view. One correspondent of the *Theatrical Times* protested that because of 'vile travestie' the 'magnificent specimens of human genius ... [are] pushed out of sight, and we cannot see them afterward without a sense of the ridiculous in connection with them' (2 December 1846).

from the burlesque's surprisingly wholesome influence in matters of Shakespearean 'taste'. While the burlesque ridicule of overweening tragedians certainly helps to explain the popularity of Fechter's informal manner, it bears remembering that such ridicule was equally directed at Fechter himself, as evidenced in *The Rival Othellos*. That the Shakespeare burlesque parodied the very acting style which it had helped to foster amply demonstrates just how suspicious the burlesque remained of all theatrical orthodoxies. Rather than 'solving' the problem of the legitimate, the burlesque operates as an ongoing *mode* of criticism which places itself in a consistently ambivalent relationship to the changing norms of theatrical legitimacy.

By no means limited to imitations of well-known performers, the burlesque criticism of legitimate Shakespeare extended equally to a satiric view of theatrical heritage. *Very Little Hamlet* provides a case in point. In October 1884, Wilson Barrett, the enterprising actor–manager of the Princess's Theatre, played Hamlet in a production which closely modelled itself after the one Charles Kean had staged at the same theatre nearly thirty years earlier. Less than a month after Barrett's production opened, the Gaiety premiered its own parodic version. The prologue to *Very Little Hamlet* mocked not only Barrett's ambition to play the Dane but also his quaint reverence for the late actor–manager of the Princess's. In an excruciatingly sentimental curtain speech on opening night, Barrett confessed that:

[f]ive-and-twenty years ago, outside this very theatre, stood a poor and friendless lad who had gone out after spending his last sixpence to go into the gallery . . . to see Mr [Charles] Kean. He swore to himself . . . [that] he would be the manager of the theatre and play 'Hamlet' in it himself. (Loud Cheers.) That boy kept his word. I am that boy – (loud cheers) – friendless no longer.[54]

Very Little Hamlet provided the Gaiety's audience with the *reductio ad absurdum* of Barrett's self-laudation. As reported in the weekly theatrical newspaper *Under the Clock*, the prologue to Yardley's play 'travesties' the young Wilson Barrett's 'adventures in the sixpenny gallery' (6 December 1884). The burlesque opens in Oxford Street, in front of the Princess's Theatre. The year is 1854. Nellie Farren played the twelve-year-old Barrett as a mere 'ragged street boy' who, to the strains of 'mysterious music', swears that he will one day act Hamlet in that very theatre (Hamilton, *Parodies*, II, p. 164). His boyhood companions – also played

---

[54] Unidentified newspaper clipping, bound in the *Theatre* n.s. 6 (July–December 1882), Folger Shakespeare Library, Washington, DC.

by burlesque soubrettes – lie in the gutter beside him. They exclaim 'Damn' when compelled to 'swear' by a 'ghostly actor'. The Shakespearean analogy is obvious. The prologue jestingly re-stages the famed moment in *Hamlet* when Horatio and Marcellus, assenting to the cries of 'Swear' which the ghost utters from beneath the stage, vow not to disclose what they have seen. By performing Barrett's juvenile oath as a *Hamlet* burlesque, Yardley's play effectively derides the adult actor–manager's desire to place his own performance as Hamlet within a self-promoting narrative of theatrical celebrity.

Apart from its mockery of actors and acting, the burlesque also engaged in a comic critique of the pictorial spectacles which increasingly dominated nineteenth-century productions of Shakespeare on both sides of the Atlantic. Pictorial staging entailed not only highly elaborate scenery, but also historically accurate costumes and properties, spectacular effects such as limelight, and the frequent use of *tableaux vivants*. The principal argument justifying such pictorial effects was that Shakespeare wanted them, but his theatre did not possess the resources required to achieve them. The 'machinist' and the 'scene-painter' were Shakespeare's rightful 'ministers and interpreters', the *Leader* decreed in 1858, because the poet himself 'would desire to be represented before a nineteenth-century audience with all the means and appliances which art, learning and science of the nineteenth century can furnish'.[55] This sort of argument is really about authenticity: that pictorialism is faithful to Shakespeare's true, but hitherto unrealized, intentions. And it is precisely the presumed authenticity of pictorial Shakespeare which made it particularly vulnerable to burlesque censure.

With its keen eye for exposing the absurd pomposities of dominant theatrical practice, the Shakespeare burlesque could hardly resist satirizing what Dallas termed the 'inane realism' of legitimate Shakespeare (*Blackwood's Magazine* 79, Feb. 1856, p. 219). In the weather vane from *King John (with the Benefit of the Act)*, we have already touched upon one example of how Shakespeare burlesques parodied the legitimate theatre's obsession with historical accuracy. For a para-performative instance of such ridicule, we can look at how the playbill essay for *Malone's Travestie of Macbeth* (Strand 1853), as shown in illustration 15, blatantly parodies the lengthy essay which Kean prepared for his antiquarian revival of *Macbeth*. Justifying the historical correctness of the scenery prepared specifically for his production, Kean explained that 'the architecture

[55] *Leader* 9 June 1858.

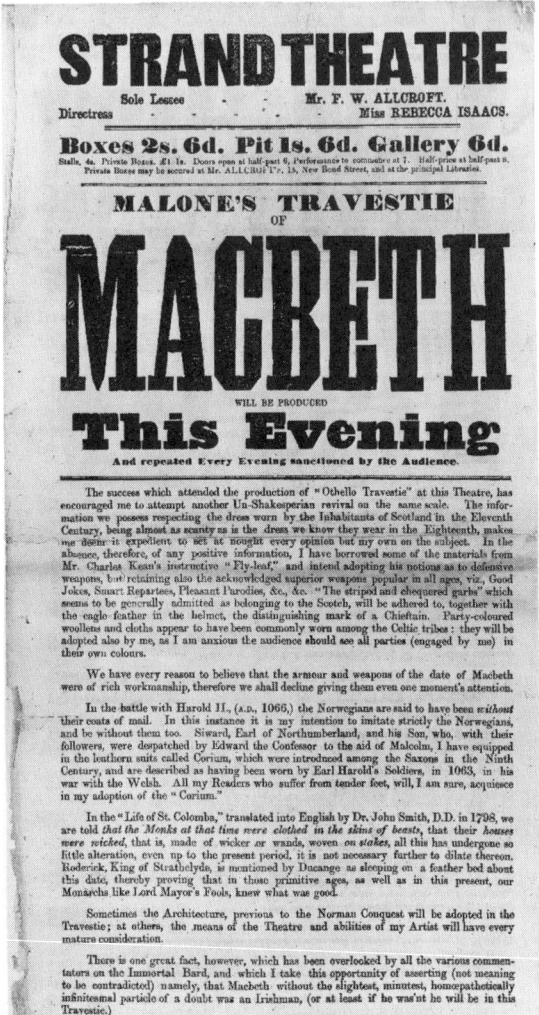

15. Playbill, *Malone's Travestie of Macbeth*, Strand Theatre, London, 1853. The essay by the Strand's manager F. W. Allcroft mocks the lengthy playbill essay Charles Kean wrote for his antiquarian revival of *Macbeth* (Princess's 1853). Compare the opening line of Kean's essay – '[t]he success which attended the production of *King John*, last season, at this theatre, has encouraged me to attempt another Shakespeare revival on the same scale' (Playbill, Princess's Theatre, London, 14 Feb. 1853) – with the opening line of Allcroft's mock version.

previous to the Norman Conquest has been adopted throughout the play. On this subject I have availed myself of the valuable knowledge of George Godwin, Esq., FRS, of the Royal Institute of Architects.'[56] The asserted historical accuracy of that scenery did not pass unnoticed at the Strand. 'Sometimes the Architecture previous to the Norman Conquest will be adopted in the Travestie', the manager F. W. Allcroft detailed in a telling paraphrase; 'at others, the means of the Theatre and abilities of my Artist will have every mature consideration'.[57] The Strand's manager not only ridicules Kean's pedantry but also – and more importantly – acknowledges a truth about theatrical production which high-minded actor–historians were inclined to forget: that the 'look' of a production was determined less by a commitment to abstract principles (such as historicism) than by a theatre's necessarily finite artistic and technical resources. Shakespeare at the Strand did not look like Shakespeare at the Princess's because those two theatres were different institutions – each with distinctive 'means' and 'abilities' – and not because the Strand was a categorically inferior theatrical venue.

The Olympic's production of *Shylock; or, the Merchant of Venice Preserved* provides an extreme example of burlesque Shakespeare revelling in the insufficiency of its own technical resources and, moreover, using that insufficiency to make a point about the ontology of performance. In a moment of nearly sublime simplicity, Launcelot Gobbo pulled across the stage a 'toy-spaniel on wheels'.[58] Dallas, for all his disparagement of burlesque frivolity, nonetheless acknowledged that the toy dog afforded the audience 'considerable satisfaction' because it successfully mocked the prevailing taste for 'pre-Raphaelite' – that is, detailed and realistic – mise-en-scène (*Blackwood's Magazine* 79, Feb. 1856, p. 219). At a time when the legitimate theatre realized with studied perfection every last image in Shakespeare's plays, the burlesque stage restored performance to its

---

[56] Playbill, *Macbeth*, Princess's Theatre, London, 14 February 1853 (Princess's Theatre production file, Theatre Museum, London).

[57] Playbill, *Malone's Travestie of Macbeth*, Strand Theatre, London, 18 April 1853 (Strand Theatre production file, Theatre Museum, London). The play was licensed by the Lord Chamberlain under the title *Macbeth According to an Act of Parliament* (British Library Add Mss 52, 939 I). The Strand's 'un-Shakespearean revival' starred the low comedian Hodson as Phelim O'Macbeth – Celtic to the power of two, as it were.

[58] Lacy's acting edition of *Shylock; or, the Merchant of Venice Preserved* makes no reference to Launcelot's dog, but the manuscript submitted to the Lord Chamberlain includes the stage direction 'Launcelot leading a Property Spaniel on Wheels' (BL Add Mss 52,941 I, f. 23). Since in Shakespeare's play Launcelot does not appear with a dog, it seems likely that Talfourd was thinking of the similarly named Launce – and his memorably unsympathetic dog Crab – from *The Two Gentlemen of Verona*. Additionally, burlesque Launcelot's inanimate canine wryly alludes to the spaniel named Portia which Edmund Kean had owned.

self-consciously illusionistic origins by displaying not an actual dog (it would not have been difficult) but an imitation one. Showing that theatrical presentments are not real – and need not be imagined as real – the burlesque echoes the opinion of *Blackwood's Magazine* that 'real things interfere essentially with the truthfulness of the scene. A great distinction should always be taken between mere representation and identity.'[59] Starveling, in *A Midsummer Night's Dream*, collapses the distinction between identity and representation when, as the emblematic character Moonshine, he presents his dog with a peremptory assertion of identity: 'this dog [is] my dog' (5.1.253). But Gobbo, in *Shylock; or, the Merchant of Venice Preserved*, knows better. He would never declare 'this toy-spaniel is my toy-spaniel' because he knows that the actuality of performance and the referentiality of performance are two different things.

The burlesque critique of legitimate Shakespeare was not lost upon nineteenth-century theatrical critics who, even if they displayed no particular affection for burlesque, nonetheless freely appropriated its critical lexicon to mount their own offensive against the legitimate. Exploiting the broad-based appeal of theatrical parody, these journalistic accounts exposed the underlying illegitimacy of ostensibly legitimate Shakespeare. G. H. Lewes, in his review of Kean's *Macbeth*, declared that its absurd solemnity made it seem the 'more genuine burlesque'.[60] Indeed, Lewes went so far in his acrimony as to assert that it would be 'impossible to realize a *Macbeth* more comic' than Kean's pompous archaeological spectacle. The Princess's manager 'has touched nothing that he has not burlesqued', Lewes complained, 'he has suggested the ludicrous side of all that is grand in art, and dignified in history . . . [and] leaves the field for those literary contortionists, the burlesque writers, so narrow and difficult'. At least for Lewes, writing pseudonymously as 'Vivian Latouche', legitimate Shakespeare was the true burlesque. Throughout the nineteenth century, 'burlesque' was the other name for legitimate Shakespeare gone bad. Less than a decade after Lewes derided Kean's *Macbeth* as more comic than its burlesque incarnations, the *Dublin University Magazine* indicted Charles Fechter's Othello as 'Shakespeare travestied in the most un-English guise'. Another reviewer similarly observed that Fechter's Hamlet, 'interesting though he may be, is decidedly "not Shakespeare"'.[61] Since the 'whole tragedy' had been converted

---

[59] *Blackwood's Magazine* 71 (April 1852), p. 471.   [60] *Leader* 30 July 1853.
[61] Unidentified review, Dramatic Records Scrapbook 4, f. 91, Folger Shakespeare Library, Washington, DC.

'into a pantomime', the journal argued, not even Robson could have added to its 'mirth'.[62] Neville Lynn, writing in 1887, argued that 'badly acted' productions of Shakespeare by provincial 'stock compan[ies]' encroached so much upon burlesque territory that they needed only a few 'mechanical burlesque changes' to rebrand themselves as out-and-out parodies.[63]

When burlesque playwrights were eclipsed by the ludicrous aspects of legitimate Shakespeare, then the work of these same 'literary contortionists', as Lewes described burlesque writers, became more contorted still. That is, if the legitimate became burlesque, then the burlesque itself must become legitimate. To argue for the piety and reverence of the Shakespeare burlesque was, on the face of it, simply irrational. What kind of veneration could there be in *Hamlet According to an Act of Parliament*, whose title-character, as described by the *Morning Chronicle*, 'meet[s] his father drunk' and 'fights Laertes in a ring with gloves'?[64] And yet such a claim did indeed have a nagging validity since the Victorian burlesque appeared a model of deference and circumspection when contrasted with the corruption of legitimate Shakespeare. Let us now expand the discussion by looking not only at how burlesques ridiculed the legitimate stage, but also how they rallied to Shakespeare's defence and, on occasion, corrected the flaws in his plays. In timely rebukes of their seemingly legitimate rivals, burlesques of *The Tempest* and *The Winter's Tale* attempted to be more legitimate than Shakespeare himself. *La! Tempest! Ah!*, an adaptation of Robert and William Brough's *The Enchanted Isle* (1848), opened at the Haymarket Theatre in the summer of 1850 as a satire upon Fromental Halévy and Eugène Scribe's opera *La Tempesta*, then enjoying a triumphant run at the nearby Her Majesty's Theatre.[65] The *Morning Chronicle* heralded the Brough brothers' revised comedy as the 'great event of the season', especially since London theatregoers had already 'heard and read much controversy upon the impropriety of founding an opera' based upon *The Tempest*.[66] In a parody of the ghost

---

[62] 'Shakespeare Travestied', *Dublin University Magazine* 59 (Feb. 1862), pp. 177, 171.
[63] Neville Lynn, 'The Shakespearian Réchauffé', in *The Thespian Papers* (London: Walter Scott, 1887), p. 87.
[64] *Morning Chronicle* 8 November 1853.
[65] No manuscript of the Haymarket production has survived except for the Prologue (BL Add Mss 43,028).
[66] *Morning Chronicle* 10 June 1850. The controversy betrays a stunning lack of historical perspective since *The Tempest* – in the Dryden–Davenant–Shadwell adaptation – was staged as a semi-opera from 1674 to 1838.

scene from *Hamlet* – with the ghost rewritten as that of Shakespeare himself – the poet denounces *La Tempesta* as 'murder most foul' (Pro. line 23). The spectre of Shakespeare thus haunts the boards of the Haymarket to decry his own murder at the hands of operatic meddlers who have reduced to 'Tom Thumb's level / The plot of [his] most seeming perfect play' (lines 4–5). In other words, Halévy and Scribe stand accused of having improperly burlesqued *The Tempest* in the guise of a romantic opera. Hamlet, upon hearing this woeful tale, resolves to avenge the death of father Shakespeare by performing yet another burlesque – that is, the Broughs' original comedy which will follow the prologue – thereby outsmarting the authors of *La Tempesta* 'on their own ground' (line 66). *La! Tempest! Ah!* thus ingeniously uses a deliberate travesty to malign an unwitting one.

Of course it would be wrong to presume that the self-laureation of Shakespeare burlesques went unchallenged. Some critics argued that *La! Tempest! Ah!* was doubly guilty of the very offence which it charged *La Tempesta* with having committed since it was itself an adaptation of an adaptation. The jokes directed against Scribe, the opera's librettist, were absurd, judged the *Morning Advertiser*, because the Brough brothers 'not only vulgarise Shakespeare, but render that which is itself "beautiful exceedingly", ridiculous and contemptible' (21 Oct. 1850). Such an argument cannot be sustained, however, because it confuses burlesques with adaptations. The opera *La Tempesta* certainly adapts *The Tempest*; but the same cannot be claimed for the Broughs' *La! Tempest! Ah!*

An even more strident example of Shakespearean defensiveness appears in *Perdita*, first performed at the Lyceum Theatre under Charles Dillon's brief management as a parody of Kean's revival of *The Winter's Tale*. In another of his elaborate playbill essays, Kean noted with some consternation the much-debated and (for the Victorians) lamentable historical errors in Shakespeare's play: the Delphic Oracle, Christian burial, and references to the Emperor of Russia and the painter Giulio Romano.[67] The burlesque took shrewd notice of the unseemly conflict between Shakespeare's shortcomings as a historian and Kean's passion for historical accuracy. How could a play replete with such errors, the burlesque openly wondered, be staged with the full antiquarian propriety expected of legitimate Shakespearean revivals? In a micro-manifesto on theatrical historicism, the burlesque Chorus deftly argues that *The Winter's Tale*

[67] Playbill, *The Winter's Tale*, Princess's Theatre, London, 28 April 1856 (Princess's Theatre production file, Theatre Museum, London).

> [A]s written by Shakespeare, won't do in our day.
> There's so strange an admixture of periods historical,
> An emp'ror of Russia, a pedlar, an oracle,
> That now in this critical age each man wonders
> The bard should have made such chronological blunders.
>
> (W. Brough, *Perdita*, p. 4)

As the Chorus frankly admits, the play 'as written by Shakespeare' cannot meet the rigorous and precise standards of historical research demanded in the 'critical age' of the mid nineteenth century.[68] Yet since Shakespeare wrote 'not for one age, but for all sorts of times' (as the Chorus neatly colloquializes Jonson's founding expression of Bardolatry), he must be continually revised to satisfy the expectations of subsequent ages.

From the perspective of the legitimate theatre, Kean was the ideal person to correct the embarrassing 'chronological blunders' in *The Winter's Tale* since his antiquarian dramaturgy transformed Shakespeare's fantastic romance into an animated picture of Periclean Athens. But as the burlesque Chorus further advises, the purportedly authentic 'Greek robes', 'Phrygian bonnets', and music of 'antiquity' (*Perdita*, p. 5) which figured in Kean's classicizing *mise-en-scène* did not so much purge *The Winter's Tale* of its errors as compound the play's incoherence because those artifacts, despite their presumed classical authenticity, could never find sanction within the text's own historicist imprecisions.[69] '[T]he bard says nothing', the Chorus pointedly reminds the audience, about whether the actors should wear Greek costumes. Although intended to liberate Shakespeare, Kean's antiquarian reforms resulted only in the 'worthy old dramatist's slaughter' by forcing his inexact play into a precise, yet arbitrary, historical framework. Kean's historicist version of *The Winter's Tale* failed to be either genuinely classical or genuinely Shakespearean. Equally false as both history and theatre, at least for its burlesque appraisers, the revival at the Princess's amounted to nothing more than a deadly retrospection of the picturesque.

Where, then, did all this criticism of *The Winter's Tale* leave a mid-Victorian audience? With the astonishing implication that the burlesque *Perdita* took full honours for both historical truth *and* Shakespearean

---

[68] The Chorus from *Perdita* recalls the Chorus from Planché's extravaganza *The Golden Fleece* (Haymarket 1845). As played by Charles Mathews, the Chorus interrupts the first line of the play to reassure the audience that he will 'rise to explain' the confusing moments in the performance when 'the author himself scarcely knows his own meaning' (J. R. Planché, *The Golden Fleece*, London: S. G. Fairbrother, n.d., Pro. lines 3, 8–9).

[69] Kean chose to have the *Hymn to Apollo*, 'which many consider genuine Greek', performed during the play (playbill, *The Winter's Tale*, Princess's Theatre, 28 April 1856).

fidelity. Safe and secure in the loving hands of burlesque artists, 'the poor old dramatist' was no longer condemned to 'slaughter' through overloaded antiquarian spectacle but could be successfully rehabilitated for performance in 'our day'. And yet the nature of the rehabilitation was altogether unforeseen. For *Perdita* claimed something startlingly new: not that the burlesque must be faithful to Shakespeare, but that Shakespeare must be faithful to the burlesque. The subtitle of Brough's comedy – *Being the Legend upon which Shakespeare is supposed to have founded his 'Winter's Tale'* – is unusually instructive. To allege that *Perdita*, rather than Greene's *Pandosto*, was Shakespeare's source text is obviously preposterous – and thus a source of delectation. But the allegation is no less serious for being amusing. The self-bestowed authority of the burlesque demands that Shakespeare's blundering play be corrected not by reference to some idealized authorial intent (that is, what the Victorians imagined Shakespeare would have written had he himself been a Victorian) but rather by alignment with its presumed (and newly recovered) source text. *Perdita* does not – indeed, cannot – rewrite Shakespeare precisely because Shakespeare had previously rewritten that very burlesque, itself now being revived for performance centuries later. *The Winter's Tale*, if we follow Brough's logic to its illogical conclusion, was thus always already an adaptation of a burlesque original. What is required in a contemporary performance, then, is a kind of unwriting – a *re*formance – which enables the burlesque to reassert its own normative a priori status over Shakespeare's play. Only with this ultimate reinstatement of the originary burlesque can the process of amendment and alteration which Shakespeare himself began come to an end. With the performance of *Perdita*, Shakespeare and his 'supposed' source are finally and conclusively reconciled. Reconciled, that is, to the burlesque's advantage. As the Chorus boasts, the burlesque has 'righted what Shakespeare left wrong' (W. Brough, *Perdita*, p. 4). So pronounced was the advantage that even Harley Granville-Barker, nearly eighty years after *Perdita*'s premiere, judged that in this instance Brough had 'a better sense of the fitness of things than had Shakespeare'.[70]

What emerges in *Perdita* is a two-faced Shakespeare: the sweet 'Swan of Avon' who, however illustrious, is estranged from nineteenth-century popular culture; and his burlesque alter ego, pedestrian to be sure, but who for that very reason can command appreciative audiences. The burlesque thus served the notable, yet ironic, function of repatriating

---

[70] Harley Granville-Barker, 'Exit Planché – Enter Gilbert', *London Mercury* 25.149/150 (March and April 1932), p. 565.

Shakespeare. The double feint of the burlesque was to proclaim its own historicity by mocking the 'peculiarities of the day'[71] and yet also to align itself with the ahistorical purity – 'for all sorts of times' (W. Brough, *Perdita*, p. 4) – attributed to Shakespeare once his plays were freed from the deformations wrought by intrusive actor–managers. Like the sempiternal national dramatist himself – 'radiant aloft . . . a thousand years hence', as Carlyle prophesied in 1840 (*On Heroes*, p. 114) – the Shakespeare burlesque equally purported to be outside of time precisely because it did *not* indulge in such passing fashions as antiquarian spectacle. Not held hostage to any historical moment, and least of all to its own, the burlesque descended to the level of contemporary *mise-en-scène* only to rescue the playwright from just those topical 'peculiarities'. Behind the undeniably pronounced localism of nineteenth-century Shakespeare burlesques, behind the bracing freshness of their slang and up-to-the-minute puns, there also lurked an equally pronounced universalism which secured their contorted authority and perverse canonicity, reminding us just how obligingly the Victorian stage acceded to Duffet's prescient injunction of 1673: 'Since with success great Bard's grow proud and resty, / To get good plays be kind to bad Travesty' ('Epilogue', *The Empress of Morocco*, p. 43).

The burlesque repatriation of Shakespeare was not solely a matter of *mise-en-scène*, but equally encompassed the actor's art. The career of Frederick Robson, the most acclaimed burlesque performer of the nineteenth century, offers a valuable case study not only of the recognition accorded to the most gifted burlesque performers as expositors of Shakespeare's genius, but also of how that seemingly laudatory recognition actually proved inimical to the burlesque itself. During his heyday at the Olympic in the 1850s, Robson, shown in illustration 16, appeared in Planché's extravaganzas *The Camp at the Olympic* (1853), *The Discreet Princess* (1855), and *The Yellow Dwarf* (1854), and Robert Brough's burlesques *Alfred the Great* (1859), *Masaniello* (1857), and *Medea* (1855). More to the point of this study, he also starred in *Macbeth Somewhat Removed from the Text of Shakespeare* and *Shylock; or, the Merchant of Venice Preserved*.[72] G. A. Sala recalled that Robson's Macbeth was a 'red-headed,

---

[71] Review of Francis Talfourd's *Macbeth Somewhat Removed from the Text of Shakespeare*, Olympic Theatre, London, *Bell's Life in London* 1 May 1853.

[72] Robson's signature song 'Villikins and his Dinah', although based upon a contemporary sensational murder, nonetheless recalls *Romeo and Juliet* since the heroine of the song takes poison to kill herself rather than forsake her beloved Villikins to marry the suitor named by her father. Indeed, Halliday's *Romeo and Juliet Travestie; or, the Cup of Cold Poison* deliberately invites comparison with John Parry's lyric describing 'poor Dinah stretched out on the ground / With a cup of cold poison poured down by her side'.

16. Portrait of Frederick Robson by Herbert Watkins, c.1855. Robson began his career in the 1840s singing in East London taverns. He made his debut at the Olympic in 1853 and remained associated with the theatre until his death in 1864. From 1857 to 1864 he was co-lessee of the theatre, along with W. S. Emden.

17. Robson as burlesque Shylock in Francis Talfourd's *Shylock; or, the Merchant of Venice Preserved*, Olympic Theatre, London, 1853. Dutton Cook described Robson's Shylock as a 'three-hatted Jew from Houndsditch, an old-clothes man with a snuffling guttural dialect, vehement of speech and eccentric of action' (*Gentleman's Magazine* 252, June 1882, p. 720). Note the strap holding Robson's false beard in place.

fire-eating, whiskey-drinking Scotchman' and his Shylock, depicted in illustration 17, a 'servile, fawning, obsequious, yet, when emergency arose, a passionate and vindictive Jew'.[73] Attestations of Robson's fidelity to Shakespeare were virtually a staple of mid-Victorian theatrical criticism. Most London critics praised the striking originality of Robson's acting in which he neither belittled the dignity of the role (that is, he did not mock Shakespeare) nor lowered himself to perform a mere slavish caricature of contemporary actors (that is, he did not mock eminent tragedians).[74] Because Robson was 'aware of the tragic foundation which lay at the bottom of the grotesque superstructure', claimed the *Observer*, his extravagant 'gestures and articulations' expressed an 'intrinsically serious feeling'.[75] For the *Era*, Robson's 'mock heroics' as Shylock illustrated his unquestionable 'appreciation' of Shakespeare's 'original' character.[76] The *Spectator* announced that only for the sake of the comedian's 'original conception' of Macbeth would it 'endure Lady Macbeth singing "tooral looral" in her sleep'.[77] Even though Robson 'broadly caricatured' Shakespearean heroes, Justin McCarthy remained confident that the poet's 'spirit' still ruled the actor's 'soul'.[78] Dallas, once having regarded burlesque acting as the 'most unnatural thing in the world', found himself astonished to discover 'perfect nature' in Robson's every look (*Blackwood's Magazine* 79, Feb. 1856, p. 214). And Dutton Cook, writing in the *Gentleman's Magazine* twenty-nine years after the fact, still remembered that in Robson's strangely compelling characterization

> Shylock might bring with him airs from Houndsditch, the actions and the accents of Petticoat Lane, his frenzy might culminate in an odd dance, his grief burst into comic singing; yet his original brightness was not wholly lost, his poetic and Venetian descent was still discernible; he was plainly a child of noble birth for all the gipsy stains upon his skin, the beggar's rags clothing him; the outlines of the Jew that Shakespear drew.[79]

The scene between Shylock and Tubal revealed Robson's uncanny ability – despite his East London dialect, shabby appearance, and

---

[73] G. A. Sala, *Robson: A Sketch* (London: John Camden Hotten, 1864), p. 47. The productions ran for a total of five consecutive months and were withdrawn only because William Farren's managerial lease of the Olympic had expired.
[74] See, for example, the *Illustrated London News* 30 April 1853 and *Lloyd's Weekly Newspaper* 8 May 1853.
[75] *Observer* 1 May 1853.   [76] *Era* 10 July 1853.   [77] *Spectator* 30 April 1853.
[78] Justin McCarthy, *Portraits of the Sixties* (London: T. Fisher Unwin, 1903), p. 404.
[79] Dutton Cook, 'Frederick Robson', *Gentleman's Magazine* 252 (June 1882), p. 721. Houndsditch was the centre of the garment district in the Jewish East End. Petticoat Lane, also in the East End, was famous for its open-air market in which dealers from rag shops, many of whom were Jewish, sold second-hand clothes.

bizarre mannerisms – to recreate 'the Jew that Shakespear drew'.[80] In *The Merchant of Venice*, Tubal brings the perversely cheering news of Antonio's misfortune to a Shylock devastated by Jessica's escape (3.1.75–122). Shylock's emotional reversals are especially powerful at the end of the scene, when Tubal's lines alternate between news from Genoa first of Antonio's ruin and then of Jessica's profligacy. '[T]hou torturest me', Shylock cries, unable to cope with the mixed reports (3.1.112). In the burlesque counterpart, a 'slightly intoxicated' Shylock fluctuates between the agony of realizing that Jessica has 'bolted' with his money and giddy excitement at the news that Antonio's 'fortunes [are] wrecked' (Talfourd, *Shylock*, BL Add Mss 52,941 I, fols. 33, 34, 36). His alternation between despair and exultation culminates in a version of Robson's own signature song 'Tippety Witchet', rewritten expressly for the comedian to sing as burlesque Shylock:

> From my first floor window handy
> Her impudence was such
> To the arms of that young dandy
> She took a drop too much.
>   But he shall see – a Jew may be
>   If he chance to cross my way,
>   As good as he – with my one – two-three
>   Ri – tol &c. (*pugilistic*)
>
> Of money she's bereft me
> And that's a serious thing,
> Besides that belle has left me
> A mourning for my ring.
>   In play or show – away she'd throw
>   My years expense per day,
>   And then no doubt my ring she'll spout[81]
>   Ri – tol &c. (*crying*)
>
> But since my own flesh rebelling
> Against me likes to fly,
> Its place within my dwelling (*with joy*)
> Antonio shall supply.
>   Tho' the tin[82] I've lost – and my Jewell's cost,
>   No time can e'er repay,
>   Yet the Christian's pound I'll dance around
>   Singing Ri – tol &c. (*laughing*)
>   (f. 37)

---

[80] As *The Times* observed, Robson spoke with a 'strong Jewish dialect, with the twang and lisp pushed to the last degree of exaggeration' (6 July 1853).
[81] *spout* – 'to pawn'.   [82] *tin* – 'money'.

The song re-articulates Shylock's conflicted emotions over Jessica's flight, his loss of money, and his impending revenge upon Antonio. The scene thus finishes with a compression – indeed, intensification – of feeling as each song verse conveys a distinct emotion. Shylock feistily imagines a boxing match against the 'young dandy' Lorenzo who stole his daughter, mourns his lost money and ring, and finally delights in his ingenious plot to exact a pound of flesh from Antonio. The relentless overturning of Shylock's jumbled sentiments throughout the entire scene, especially when repeated at hyper-speed within the virtuosic rendition of 'Tippety Witchet', exercised an overpowering effect upon the audience. It was precisely the frenzied acrobatics of Robson's Shylock – the flip-flops from the 'intensity of human passion' to the 'grotesque drollery of burlesque' and then back again – which made his performance unforgettable.[83] The experience was equally frenzied for the spectators since, as H. Barton Baker recalled, Robson first 'convuls[ed] them with laughter', then 'hush[ed] them into awe-struck silence', and finally held them 'midway between terror and laughter as he performed some weirdly grotesque dance' (*History of the London Stage*, p. 270). Another observer vividly recounted the 'undercurrent of passion' beneath Robson's 'apparently reckless drollery':

> Of a sudden, the actor would be in earnest; the eyes that had been winking with a knowing vulgarity, all at once looked you full in the face, mastered you at a glance; there was a passionate cry, a taunting shout, or a wail of utter heart-rending misery in the voice which had just been trolling a Cockney ditty; and then, ere your tears, so strangely surprised from you, were dry, the mime was again prancing or strutting, all the earnestness gone out of him, a mountebank, but one of bewildering and fantastic freaks, of swift and perplexing changes.[84]

Critical acclaim for Robson's 'swift and perplexing changes' ironically echoes the praise bestowed upon Edmund Kean after his debut as Shylock at Drury Lane in January 1814. As Hazlitt observed of that soon-to-be-legendary performance, Kean erased the memory of 'other actors' who had portrayed the Jew as a 'decrepid old man, bent with age and ugly with mental deformity, grinning with deadly malice'.[85] Overturning a stereotype which had held the stage for nearly eight decades, Kean displayed a 'conflict of passions' through the rapidity

---

[83] *Players* 9 January 1860.
[84] Unidentified obituary for Frederick Robson, qtd in Frederic Whyte, *Actors of the Century* (London: George Bell and Sons, 1898), p. 142.
[85] William Hazlitt, *Characters of Shakespear's Plays* (London: C. H. Reynell, 1817), p. 276.

of his 'transitions from one tone and feeling to another'.[86] The actor's breakthrough performance similarly inspired Coleridge's over-quoted simile that watching Kean act was like 'reading Shakespeare by flashes of lightning'.[87] The scene with Tubal, predictably, generated much comment. As John Doran recounted, audiences thrilled to Kean's 'alternations of rage, grief, and ecstasy'[88] – an emotional sequence which correlates precisely with the stage directions 'pugilistic', 'crying', and 'with joy' for Robson's concluding song. '[M]any of [Robson's] bursts are truly tragic', the *Illustrated London News* declared after witnessing his performances in burlesques of *Macbeth* and *The Merchant of Venice*, 'and might have done credit to Edmund Kean in his best days'.[89] In both burlesque and legitimate Shakespeare, audiences prized an actor's ability to portray the same emotions with equal intensity. But the burlesque tragedian's emotional range was prized not simply for its affective power, but also for how conclusively it defeated audience assumptions about the difference between burlesque and legitimate acting.

Robson's ability to reach both emotional depths and comic heights – and to move between them with lightning speed – brought about an unanticipated reversal of standards in Shakespearean acting which elevated the low comedian to the dignified and respectable status of a tragedian. Indeed, some Victorian theatrical observers called for Robson to turn 'legitimate' and thereby develop the full range of his talents in more creditable venues (and, presumably, before more creditable audiences). Confirming the unparalleled potential of Robson's histrionic genius, Henry Morley remarked that 'at a time when all serious acting is tending to the burlesque and unreal, a burlesque actor should start up with a real and very serious power in him. The only regret in observing [Robson's] execution of Mr. Talfourd's Shylock is that he had not made trial of Shakespeare's in preference.'[90] Morley's desire that Robson come face-to-face with Shakespeare – and so abolish the burlesque as a distinct theatrical form – betrays only too well the shocking realization that the poet could indeed be 'great in travestie' (*Bell's Weekly* 24 April 1853). So great, in fact, that consummate burlesque artists ought no longer to appear on the burlesque stage. As Morley's deceptive compliment implies,

---

[86] *Morning Chronicle* 27 January 1814; rpt in William Hazlitt, *A View of the English Stage* (London: Robert Stodart, 1818), p. 2.
[87] *Table Talk*, 2nd ed (1836), rpt in *The Romantics on Shakespeare*, ed. Jonathan Bate (London: Penguin Books, 1992), p. 160.
[88] John Doran, '*Their Majesties' servants'; Annals of the English Stage from Thomas Betterton to Edmund Kean*... 2 vols. (London: W. H. Allen & Co., 1864), II, p. 538.
[89] *Illustrated London News* 9 July 1853.   [90] *Examiner* 9 July 1853.

the burlesque – now perceived as a direct threat to the legitimate – had to be naturalized as an iteration of the legitimate; as the ever-flattering reflection of an unchanging and unchangeable Shakespeare. Yet the burlesque never aspired to naturalize itself as Shakespeare. Indeed, the burlesque's distinctive, though often unrecognized, virtue was that by performing 'not Shakespeare' it created an alternative space for thinking about just what performing Shakespeare means. To coerce the burlesque into merging with its own antecedent is to disable the very means through which the burlesque exercises its singular critique. In consequence, then, the repeated calls for Robson to turn legitimate do not recognize the burlesque's achievement but, in fact, return a calculated indictment against it. The apocryphal story that in his boyhood Robson appeared as a juvenile version of Richard III *à la Edmund Kean* in 'black wig and scarlet dress' at the Assembly Rooms in Mile End (*Gentleman's Magazine* 252, June 1882, p. 718) thus works against the interests of burlesque by establishing Robson's 'legitimate' pedigree in advance of his 'burlesque' pedigree.

Critics who eagerly affirmed Robson's histrionic genius declined to affirm the genius of burlesque itself. Indeed, they argued just the opposite: that burlesque was precisely what Robson needed to overcome if he were to fulfil his full Shakespearean potential. Journalistic accounts carefully distinguish between the performer's exceptional talents for Shakespeare and the inherently abject theatrical form through which he expressed those talents. Cook, one of Robson's most enthusiastic admirers, maintained that the comedian 'redeemed' the 'burlesque-writer's irreverence' (*Gentleman's Magazine* 252, June 1882, p. 721). Only by dint of his genius did the actor 'breath[e] poetic life' into the 'maimed and distorted figures . . . [which] he was required to embody'. Dallas similarly claimed that when Robson takes the stage 'glitter pass[es] for gold, the trash for truth' (*Blackwood's Magazine* 79, Feb. 1856, p. 211). The thrust of such arguments is clear enough: Robson's achievements owe nothing to the burlesque form. It was as if the burlesque were entirely incidental, a purely arbitrary theatrical medium which the actor could renounce at any moment without diminishing the overall effect of his performance.

But it is simply disingenuous to claim that the debased burlesque can transform itself into a more worthy substance only through the alchemy of exceptional performers. To claim that Shylock as a scripted character in Talfourd's play only burlesqued its Shakespearean original while Shylock as *characterized* by Robson in a performance of Talfourd's play incarnated that same Shakespearean original is to misunderstand the nature of burlesque. The extra-textual dimensions of a burlesque performance – songs, dances, winks, gags, ad libs, topicalities, exaggerated costumes, and outrageous properties – were not incidental to the burlesque. They cannot be summarily extracted from a spectator's perception of a successful performance and then dismissed outright as irrelevant to that success. Robson's Houndsditch persona, wild breakdown dances, and crooning of popular ballads did not comprise a dispensable, though amusing, overlay to an otherwise serious performance. Those comic acts constituted the burlesque's ambivalent disposition toward its Shakespearean origins. Likewise, the serious parts of Robson's performance – Shylock's 'utter heart-rending misery' – were not the rare moments of genius powerful enough to offset the play's essential triviality. Robson's admirers in Victorian higher journalism wrongly supposed that burlesque was a dramatic genre which could be contravened in the moment of its performance. His traditional audience, however, knew the score. When spectators at the Olympic laughed at Shylock's determined effort to sell cigars to the Venetian Senators in the trial scene,[91] they were laughing precisely at the contrast between a burlesque Shylock who treats a courtroom as if it were a market stall in Petticoat Lane and a legitimate Shylock who appears before the Doge '[t]o have the due and forfeit of [his] bond' with rather more circumspection (*The Merchant of Venice*, 4.1.37). And in that laughable contrast lay the burlesque's own ironic consciousness.

Throughout this chapter I have looked at the numerous ways in which Shakespeare burlesques claimed to be more Shakespearean than the objects of their ridicule. To that extent, I have taken the burlesques at their word. It is now time to turn the searchlight of burlesque criticism back onto itself. Yet as I hope to demonstrate, the burlesque was already doing just that. In thinking about the validity of burlesque criticism, we must acknowledge that the burlesque was the source of its own undoing. Since a parody 'belies the concept of a definitive or authoritative work altogether', as Michele Hannoosh has remarked, 'it cannot legitimately propose itself as the definitive [work]'.[92] Thus, the Shakespeare burlesque does not dismantle other performances so that it might assume their vacated canonical position. Rather, the burlesque abjures the entire notion of canonicity by removing the ground for all meaning, including

[91] *Daily News* 25 October 1884.
[92] Michele Hannoosh, 'The Reflexive Function of Parody', *Comparative Literature* 41.2 (Spring 1989), p. 114.

its own. Out of its necessary self-reflexivity, the burlesque comes into consciousness of its own susceptibility to critique. And it is precisely by being open to the possibility of self-ridicule that the burlesque can elude the charge of being gratuitously destructive.

These comic performances thus do not confirm pre-existing binaries (high/low, elite/popular, legitimate/illegitimate) by inverting them, but rather explode the hierarchies on which such accustomed meanings rely. Dispensing, then, with an outmoded 'true–false' propositional logic – *this* is Shakespeare, *that* is not – the burlesque proceeds according to the more deconstructive logic of performative free play. The result is not a new hierarchy but an aporia: the inability to choose. Phrased in more optimistic terms, the burlesque validates the continuing vitality of performances which, despite their necessarily non-authoritative status, still offer themselves for active interpretation by artists and audiences alike. To be sure, the burlesque frequently renounces the self-denying implications of its own rhetoric. But then it would, wouldn't it? As previously observed, burlesques frequently cited Shakespeare's own scenes of burlesque to appropriate his authority for their own parodic gain. That seemingly unassailable strategy nonetheless contradicts itself since if the burlesque is like Shakespeare inasmuch as he occasionally wrote burlesque, then it must also be like Shakespeare inasmuch as he is open to ridicule and parody. The burlesque cannot have it both ways. And, ultimately, it does not. All its bravado notwithstanding, the burlesque inevitably trumps its own claim to have redeemed Shakespeare by installing itself as his surrogate, to have 'righted what Shakespeare left wrong'.

How does this happen? Typically, a burlesque acknowledges that it possesses no singular privilege by enacting alternatives to itself. A burlesque actor's repertoire of 'knowing' winks, glances, and nudges allows the performance to realize momentarily something (often a sexual innuendo) which it immediately relinquishes. In this embedded counter-performance the burlesque teases its audience with a glimpse of a performance which they are destined never to see. When burlesques of *Hamlet, Macbeth*, and *Romeo and Juliet* resurrect dead characters in their finales, such performances at least suggest that burlesques do not remain committed to telling their story the same way every night. Characters recalled to life – that is, characters whose fates are not pre-ordained by the underlying Shakespearean narrative – endow the burlesque with an aura of unpredictability, as if tomorrow night Juliet might not be restored to life as an Ethiopian serenader but just might survive to marry Romeo.

Of course each burlesque enacts its own alternative in its own distinctive manner. *Hamlet* is a case in point. In February 1870 five productions of *Hamlet* were running at various New York theatres. Only two of the Hamlets – Booth and Fechter – were legitimate tragedians; the others – Fox, Tony Pastor, and Addison Ryman – were burlesque clowns. Performing at the Theatre Comique on lower Broadway, Ryman topically soliloquized,

> Another Hamlet!
> Who can it be?
> Is it Booth, Fechter,
> Or Fox, the sly one,
> Tony Pastor, or Addison Ryman?[93]

On the face of it, the observation is unremarkable. Different actors will be attracted to the same role, sometimes playing it simultaneously. But in Ryman's inventory of all the Hamlets available to New York theatregoers, we can also see how the performance alludes to its own alternatives, both burlesque and legitimate, to the point of doubting its own identity. 'Who can it be?', Ryman wonders on the audience's behalf. In *Rosencrantz and Guildenstern*, Ophelia raises a similar question when she complains that Hamlet is '[a]like for no two seasons at a time / Sometimes he's tall – sometimes he's very short – Now with black hair – now with a flaxen wig' (p. 79). Like Ryman, Ophelia refers to Hamlet's different incarnations through the performances of different actors. (The 'flaxen' bewigged Hamlet, for example, is Fechter.) Her speech creates a theatrical world of Hamlet possibilities in which no single possibility ever takes pride of place – or, indeed, even endures.

At other times, a burlesque unwittingly imitates an aspect of a production which it set out to criticize, thereby becoming the inadvertent object of its own ridicule. In its review of *Perdita*, the *Saturday Review* complained that Dillon's production displayed scenery 'as gorgeous as the original' when, for its satiric purposes, it should have used a 'heap of incongruities and absurdities' to depict a 'grotesque exaggeration' of the scenery used in Kean's revival.[94] *Perdita* thus defeated the power of its own critique by adopting the very conventions it should have repudiated. Dillon later staged *Perdita*'s ballet of 'Ladies personifying the Zodiac' as an afterpiece to *Belphegor* after he withdrew the burlesque from the Lyceum's repertoire. Once the astrological ballet became an attraction in its own right, it could no longer continue to function as a burlesque. This burlesque production kept reverting into the very type of performance which it was designed to criticize.

---

[93] Qtd in *Dramatic Mirror* 19 March 1901.   [94] *Saturday Review* 27 September 1856.

Moments when the burlesque performance reflects upon itself, redirects the course of its action, or forsakes itself are not moments of failure; rather, they signify the burlesque's openness to its own lack of authority and, consequently, its acceptance that matters might have proceeded differently – and yet still might. We cannot, however, rest content merely with exposing the inevitable contradictions of the burlesque's critique of Bardolatry. Because a burlesque makes demands on other forms of artistic expression, as the foregoing examples attest, we must look upon it as both a signifying act and a social phenomenon. That is, the burlesque's claims are worldly. In consequence, it would be impossible to account for its performance from a purely internal perspective. To be sure, all performances implicate themselves in their own historical moment. How could they not? But the worldliness of burlesque is especially pronounced in light of its aggressively topical allusions, citations, and comic misquotations. Accordingly, the next chapter investigates the social realities of the burlesque stage, emphasizing not only the representation of socially marked behaviour within the burlesque itself, but also the problematic relation between staged behaviour and the audience's own experiences and expectations.

CHAPTER 3

Shakespeare in Bohemia

The 'greatest puzzle among the theatres of London', a stymied Albert Smith noted in 1848, was how to describe the audience at the Adelphi Theatre, one of the principal metropolitan burlesque houses.[1] 'You cannot bring the frequenters under any category', the comic journalist conceded; '[i]t would trouble the keenest observer to tell to what class of society they belong'. Two years later, *Tallis's Dramatic Magazine* similarly remarked that the Adelphi was 'popular with a class, which it is difficult to define'.[2] If even these 'keenest observer[s]' could not accurately describe a contemporary burlesque audience, then how much more difficult that enterprise must be for the performance historian. Little scholarship exists on nineteenth-century burlesque audiences. Michael Booth's generalized claim that burlesques were 'almost entirely aimed at the relatively educated and middle classes' (*Prefaces*, p. 150) represents the extent of academic inquiry into the sociology of the Victorian burlesque. It also elides the distinction between audiences as demographically quantifiable communities and audiences as rhetorical constructions of theatrical performances. Both perspectives are valuable precisely because they are not identical. While the immediate task of this chapter is to begin to solve the puzzle of who attended nineteenth-century Shakespeare burlesques, its ultimate aim is to use knowledge about audience composition to frame – and assess – the social significance of burlesque performances.

On the face of it, Booth's assumption that burlesques appealed to the 'relatively educated and middle classes' appears sensible enough. Nineteenth-century theatres which attracted a strongly working-class audience – the Royal Effingham and the Britannia in the East End, the Surrey and the Victoria in south London – adopted a repertoire heavily weighted toward melodrama. 'Burlesques and extravaganzas have never

[1] Albert Smith, *Why Our Theatres Are Not Supported*... (London: n.p., 1848), pp. 12–13.
[2] *Tallis's Dramatic Magazine* November 1850.

been extremely popular on the south side of the river', one London newspaper explained in 1864, 'and the manager who would venture to place either of those innovations before a transpontine audience on Boxing Night would assuredly meet with the treatment that so daring an iconoclast would deserve'.[3] Mindful, as it were, of this journalistic proscription, the Surrey declined to produce Burnand's burlesque of *Black Eye'd Susan* on the grounds that its traditional audience would instead prefer to watch the 'genuine article' of Douglas Jerrold's original melodrama.[4] Nor were burlesques much performed at music halls, taverns, or penny gaffs. Their denunciations of burlesque notwithstanding, high-minded critics like Donne, Dallas, and Archer never employed the stereotypes reserved for 'ragamuffin' working-class audiences to describe the patrons of burlesque.[5] The audience for the Adelphi – and, for that matter, the Strand and the Olympic – may have been difficult to categorize, but it certainly did not include the dog-thieves, pick-pockets, and 'embryo and mature convicts' who, in T. W. Erle's comic inventory, comprised the loyal constituents of London's minor theatres (p. 101).

Some spectators' first exposure to burlesque occurred at school. Within elite educational settings, burlesques were not an illicit pleasure. Given that theatrical burlesque originated in seventeenth-century mock versions of epic poetry, the academic nurturing of burlesque playwriting and production only stands to reason. *Macbeth Somewhat Removed from the Text of Shakespeare* is a case in point. Written while its author was still at Eton, the play was first staged in 1847 at the Henley Regatta when Talfourd was a student at Christ Church, Oxford.[6] A year later, when the young Talfourd was disappointed with the low production values of the Strand Theatre, where his burlesque received its professional premiere, he dashed off a letter of protest to the *Theatrical Times* under the pseudonym 'Oxoniensis'.[7] Burnand's own experiences were similar. At Eton, W. G. Cookesley coached the future editor of *Punch* and his

---

[3] Unidentified newspaper clipping, December 1864, Theatrical Miscellany Scrapbook 10, Folger Shakespeare Library, Washington, DC.
[4] F. C. Burnand, *Records and Reminiscences* 2 vols. (London: Methuen and Co., 1904), II, p. 25. Burnand's play went on to run for two years at the Royalty Theatre, Soho.
[5] T. W. Erle, *Letters from a Theatrical Scene-Painter* (London: Marcus Ward & Co., 1880), pp. 81, 101.
[6] Talfourd played Lady Macbeth in what was by all accounts a high-spirited performance. One student was drunk, another insisted upon carrying a sword even though he played a 'Gentlewoman', and Macduff appeared wearing the 'straw hat and broad blue ribbon of the Oxford eight' (Alan Mackinnon, *The Oxford Amateurs*, London: Chapman and Hall, Ltd, 1910, pp. 22–3). The aspiring playwright reprised the role of Lady Macbeth in a private performance in his father's home later that year before an audience which included Henry Crabb Robinson (*The London Theatre 1811–1866: Selections from the Diary of Henry Crabb Robinson*, ed. Eluned Brown, London: The Society for Theatre Research, 1966, p. 247).
[7] *Theatrical Times* 6 May 1848.

contemporaries in playing the 'true serious vein' of 'old-fashioned, genuine burlesque' as they rehearsed William Rhodes' *Bombastes Furioso*.[8] Even as Cookesley shared with his charges the delights of burlesque, he also admired legitimate Shakespearean revivals, even corresponding with the old Etonian Charles Kean on the finer points of classical archaeology in *The Winter's Tale*.[9] It was not impossible, Burnand learned from his tutor, to enjoy burlesque *and* Shakespeare. When Burnand and the fellow members of the Amateur Dramatic Club (the 'A.D.C.') were not 'seeing Robson in his best days at the Olympic', they invited 'Little' Clarke from the Strand Theatre up to Cambridge to advise them on their own burlesque productions and to teach them the new 'dash-away, sparkling' dances (*The 'A.D.C.'*, pp. 22, 237). Of the young men who developed a taste for burlesque during their university career, many found ample means to satisfy that taste once they had settled in London. Indeed, Burnand attributed Edmund Yates' harsh review of his first burlesque, *Ixion* (St James's 1860), to the presence in the opening night audience of a 'strong contingent of A.D.C. men' who, out of a misplaced desire to encourage their friend, 'overdid the applause' (*Records and Reminiscences*, I, p. 375).

To be sure, more mature spectators were not insensible to the pleasures of burlesque, particularly at the Olympic in the 1850s and 1860s. In 1853, when Robson appeared as burlesque Macbeth and Shylock, the *Spectator* reported that the little theatre suddenly attracted 'throngs of persons who usually ignored its existence'.[10] '[N]oisome Wych-street', the magazine *Belgravia* noted, 'was crowded with West-end equipages' during Robson's 'brilliant' career.[11] Sala, in 1864, similarly noted that the Olympic 'has become one of the most favourite resorts of the British aristocracy. The Brahminical classes appear oblivious of the yellow streak of caste when they come hither.'[12] Among the Brahmins who crowded the Olympic were the pre-Raphaelites William Morris, Dante Gabriel Rossetti, and Edward Burne-Jones, all of whom lived nearby in Red Lion Square.[13] Charles Dickens had first seen Robson a decade before his success at the Olympic, when the aspiring actor was performing comic

---

[8] F. C. Burnand, *The 'A.D.C.' Being the Personal Reminiscences of the University Amateur Dramatic Club Cambridge*. 2nd edn (London: Chapman and Hall, 1880), p. 4.
[9] Revd W. G. Cookesley, letters to Charles Kean, April 1856, Folger Y.c. 606 (1, 3), Folger Shakespeare Library, Washington, DC.
[10] *Spectator* 9 July 1853.
[11] Walter Thornbury, 'London Theatres and London Actors. VI', *Belgravia* 9 (1869), p. 466.
[12] Sala, *Robson*, p. 32.
[13] J. W. Mackail, *Life of William Morris* (1922); qtd in Mollie Sands, *Robson of the Olympic* (London: The Society for Theatre Research, 1979), p. 89.

songs at north London taverns.[14] W. M. Thackeray, a man 'unused to the melting mood', found himself on the verge of tears during Robson's parody of *Othello* in *The Yellow Dwarf* (Planché, *Extravaganzas*, V, p. 37). More surprisingly still, the Shakespeare burlesque benefited from royal patronage when Victoria, in the summer of 1860, watched Robson in a revival of *Shylock; or the Merchant of Venice Preserved*.[15]

Anyone too respectable to set foot in a burlesque playhouse could still indulge in a range of vicarious experiences. Newspaper and periodical reviews written by such well-known critics as Dutton Cook, G. H. Lewes, Henry Morely, John Oxenford, and T. W. Robertson allowed readers to follow (if not necessarily to endorse) burlesque productions at a safe distance. Halliday and Burnand wrote essays on the history of burlesque for such eminent periodicals as the *Cornhill Magazine* and the *Universal Review*. Like other stage performers, burlesque artists were photographed for widely circulated *cartes de visite*. These popular photographs memorialized a performance which their owners may never have seen. The middle-class taste for private theatricals encompassed the burlesque no less than traditional poetic drama. Indeed, some burlesques were written specifically for private performance – most typically at Christmas – including *Hamlet! The Ravin' Prince of Denmark!!*, *Julius Caesar Travestie* (c. 1861), and the skit *O'Tello* (1833), written by a 21-year-old Charles Dickens. Acting editions of burlesque, although intended principally for use by provincial theatres in re-staging London productions, could also be read independently as dramatic literature. Among the more distinguished readers of burlesques was the Shakespearean scholar Edward Dowden, who owned an 1811 edition of *Hamlet Travestie*.[16] Some burlesques, such as *Coriolanus; a Burlesque*, were published as 'closet' dramas, with no intention that they would ever be performed, whether in a professional theatre or a private home.

The argument that burlesque spectators were drawn principally from the educated middle class seems equally persuasive from a theoretical perspective. That is, the very structure of the burlesque itself encodes a definition of competent – and incompetent – spectators. In *Perdita*, for example, the Chorus declares '[t]his is Bo – no, Bithynia to whose shores' the shipwrecked Antigonous and the infant Perdita have been carried (W. Brough, *Perdita*, p. 15). This declaration makes sense only if

[14] John Hollingshead, 'A Dramatic Meteor', *Entracte Annual* (London, 1898).
[15] Victoria was by no means ill-disposed toward Robson, for she invited him to perform in *Daddy Hardacre* and the farce *B.B.* at Windsor Castle in November 1860.
[16] See the copy in the Edward Dowden collection, Folger Shakespeare Library, Washington, DC.

spectators know that Kean changed the location of the corresponding scene in his revival of *The Winter's Tale* from the land-locked Bohemia to Bithynia, a place which did have a sea-coast. The Lyceum's playbill offers some assistance on the matter, describing the scene as taking place on a 'DESERT SPOT ON THE SHORES OF BOHEMIA, / Or BYTHINIA, or WHEREVER IT IS' (illustration 18).[17] Other allusions were more complex. Brough wrote the burlesque statue scene as a contemporized theatrical performance for Leontes and his royal entourage, who take their places in a make-shift 'Royal box' guarded by ersatz 'beef-eaters' (stage directions, p. 36). Paulina, as the stage-manager of this play-within-the-play, thanks her sovereign for 'the humble honour you bestow / By this state visit on my humble show / On this its opening night'. For the scene's allusive humour to work, the audience had to realize that it re-enacted Kean's welcome to Victoria and Albert on the opening night of *The Winter's Tale* five months earlier. Spectators not possessing the requisite foreknowledge still may have found *Perdita* amusing; but they would not have been able to situate their amusement within contemporary debates about the propriety of historicist *mise-en-scène* and the legitimate theatre's campaign for respectability by attracting royal patronage. From this example we can deduce a general proposition about the audience for nineteenth-century Shakespeare burlesques: that it knew enough about legitimate Shakespeare, by whatever means, to appreciate the burlesque's pointed topical satire. Just how much – or how little – it knew remains unquantifiable; but no theatrical form can survive if it attracts a predominantly incompetent audience. The *Era*'s observation that *Macbeth Somewhat Removed from the Text of Shakespeare* was more heartily enjoyed by those spectators 'who had seen the original at the Princess's' suggests that competence was the norm rather than the exception.[18] Godfrey Turner's indiscriminate theatregoing in the 1840s and 1850s – he recalled attending productions at 'Drury Lane, the Haymarket, the Lyceum, the old Olympic, and the old Adelphi' – gives us a sense of just how knowledgeable nineteenth-century theatre audiences could be.[19]

All these considerations – university background, social prestige, and thresholds of competence – seem only to confirm Booth's assessment that

---

[17] Playbill, *Perdita*, Lyceum Theatre, London, 15 September 1856 (Lyceum Theatre production file, Theatre Museum, London).

[18] *Era* 1 May 1853.

[19] One of the productions he saw at the Lyceum was *Perdita* (Godfrey Turner, 'First Nights of My Young Days', *Theatre* 1 September 1887, pp. 115–16).

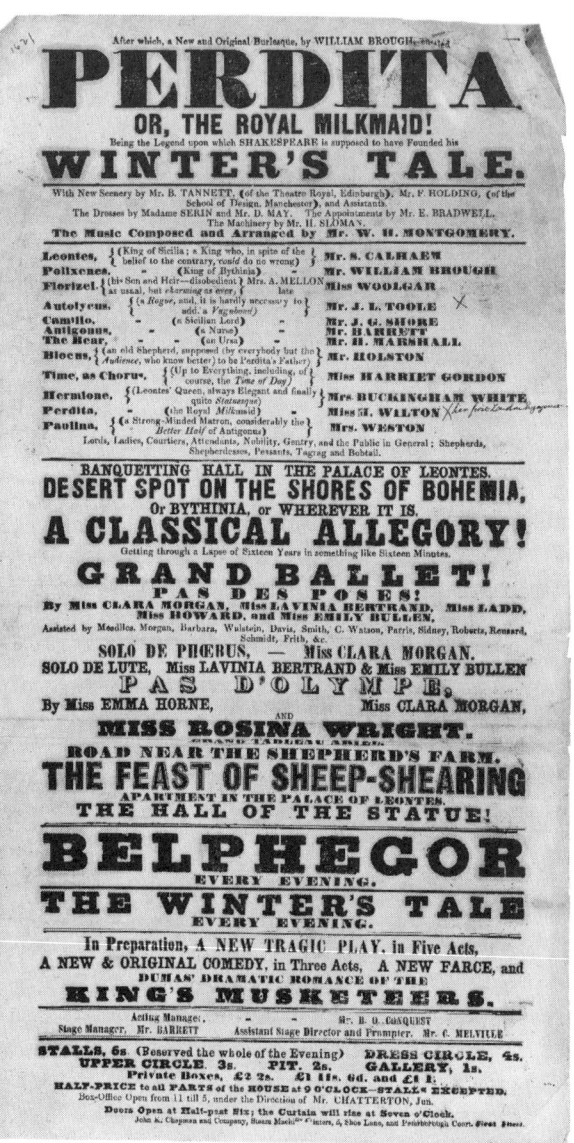

18. Playbill, William Brough's *Perdita; or, the Royal Milkmaid*, Lyceum Theatre, London, 1856. Like Kean's production of *The Winter's Tale*, the burlesque consists largely of *tableaux vivants*, songs, and dances, including 'A Classical Allegory', a *Pas des Poses*, the '*Solo de Phoebus*', and the 'Feast of the Sheep-Shearing'.

burlesques appealed most of all to the educated, middle class. Yet that assessment obscures more than it reveals, primarily because the Victorian middle class was never a singular social category. What historians long presumed was a stable, coherent entity actually comprised 'diverse social groupings', Patrick Joyce has explained, 'split among economic, social, political, and religious lines'.[20] Most of the urban middle classes in the nineteenth century did not have an education, write letters to newspapers, read literary and scientific journals (let alone contribute to them), own property, or belong to learned societies. They were, in F. M. L. Thompson's description, the 'small shopkeepers, traders, and dealers' who lived in Clerkenwell and Islington; they were of lower professional standing than the lawyers and bankers who controlled most middle-class political and reform activity.[21] Who belonged to the middle class was, moreover, a question not simply of demographics, but of ethics. Dror Wahrman has argued that the Victorian middle class, as a moral force, was principally an 'imagined constituency': a mythologized vision of how *all* members of society should conduct their private lives.[22] To think of the middle class as having a precise social referent would thus be to diminish the pervasive influence of its moral precepts. The variety of experiences, actual or imagined, which might all be termed 'middle-class' suggests that we cannot expect *any* class-based reception of theatrical productions to have been either uniform or predictable.

A further objection to an easy identification of the burlesque with London's educated middle class – to the extent that we can even speak of the 'middle class' – lies in the incongruity of their moral values. While audiences had to comprehend the aesthetic and social values of legitimate Shakespeare in order to understand its burlesque critique, it does not follow that they accepted those values unreservedly. Indeed, anyone sympathetic to burlesque would be more inclined to question – not affirm – the values associated with legitimate culture. Otherwise, there would be no need for a burlesque in the first place. Perhaps the most cherished middle-class value was respectability, a value which the legitimate nineteenth-century theatre wholeheartedly embraced for itself as a cultural institution, for the acting profession, and even for the social standing of its audiences. No nineteenth-century comic genre – burlesque,

---

[20] Patrick Joyce, *Democratic Subjects* (Cambridge: Cambridge University Press, 1994), p. 164.
[21] F. M. L. Thompson, *The Rise of Respectable Society* (Cambridge, MA: Harvard University Press, 1988), p. 19.
[22] Dror Wahrman, *Imagining the Middle Class* (Cambridge: Cambridge University Press, 1995), p. 263.

pantomime, extravaganza, or farce – ever respected the decorum and etiquette of legitimate Shakespeare. In Planché's extravaganza *The Camp at the Olympic* (1853), the energetic spirit of Burlesque, played by Robson, merrily taunted the spirit of Tragedy by singing that 'Burlesque is up! up! up! / And Tragedy down! down! down!'[23] Let us investigate more closely how Shakespeare burlesques repudiated core middle-class values.

In 1852, *Blackwood's Magazine* explained that the two million residents of 'this united Rome-Babylon-and-Nineveh which rejoices in the name of London' should be amused '[r]espectably, of course; improvingly by all means; intellectually if possible' (71, April 1852, p. 461). Just as 'mechanics' benefited from 'literary and scientific institutes' and the 'humble classes' from 'lectures on temperance', so, too, Londoners benefited from a respectable, improving, and intellectual theatre. Indeed, London's leading tragedians were among the first members of the theatrical profession to renew their commitment to legitimate drama and thereby reinvent themselves as gentleman proprietors of respectable public establishments. During his brief managerial career at Covent Garden (1837–9) and Drury Lane (1841–3), Macready was renowned for a noble, if failed, effort to establish a respectable theatre where the national drama would be produced with appropriate reverence. Achieving that worthy distinction entailed not only restoring the integrity of Shakespeare's texts, but also attracting royal patronage, and expelling prostitutes from the theatre. Kean, the recipient of even greater royal favour, managed the Princess's with 'the greatest possible decorum' and, as Arthur William à Beckett recalled, remained 'a thorough gentleman' during his forty-year career.[24] Phelps, the longtime manager of Sadler's Wells, was lauded for taking Shakespeare into the hinterlands of suburban north London. The knighthood bestowed upon Henry Irving in 1895 represents not a sudden leap in the respectability of the legitimate theatre but rather the culmination of a century-long process.

Unlike the productions which they satirized, nineteenth-century Shakespeare burlesques never formed part of middle-class attempts to educate mass audiences through popular culture. As its detractors asserted, burlesque contributed nothing to the education or morals of its audience. When Donne, the Examiner of Plays, urged the government to provide 'recreations which may divert the masses from sensual indulgence and specious temptations', he viewed burlesque not as

[23] J. R. Planché, *The Camp at the Olympic* (1853; *Plays*, p. 176).
[24] Arthur William à Beckett, *Green-Room Recollections* (London: Simpkin, Marshall, Ltd, 1896), p. 63.

the wholesome cure, but as the pernicious affliction.[25] These 'foul excrescences' of the stage, he insisted, jeopardized the theatre's mission to provide 'rational entertainment'.[26] He predicted, moreover, that if the theatre failed to accommodate 'the more cultivated and critical portion of the public' it would soon be overrun by 'those who are content with rant, buffoonery, spectacle, and burlesque'.[27] Donne's apocalyptic verdict was hardly idiosyncratic. As *Blackwood's Magazine* had advised two years earlier, '[n]othing has so depreciated the drama' as the 'contemptible' burlesque (71, April 1852, p. 468). Surely no one, the magazine presumed, would prefer 'miserable jargon' and the 'oratory of the cabstand' over the loftiness of dramatic poetry. And, almost a decade earlier, an outraged reader of the *Theatrical Times* had issued a call to 'shame the public' out of the 'indecency' of burlesque.[28] The writer specifically contrasted the success of Shakespeare at Sadler's Wells with the success of burlesque at 'the Adelphi and Lyceum'. The informality, ridicule, and nonsense of burlesque could only ever be at cross purposes with the legitimate theatre's stalwart efforts to be recognized as respectable. Sala welcomed Victoria's occasional visits to the Olympic, yet remained conscious that burlesque could never eliminate its 'yellow streak of caste' (*Robson*, p. 32). And John Coleman observed that even as the Olympic's audience grew increasingly fashionable at mid-century, the theatre never expunged the 'ancient and fishlike smell which permeated every corner of the building'.[29]

But why should the Olympic have expunged its 'ancient and fishlike smell'? If there was anything the burlesque sought to dispel, it was the air of good breeding. A particularly memorable instance of the burlesque renunciation of respectability occurs in the final moments of *Perdita*, when Antigonous unexpectedly reappears accompanied by the bear which presumably had devoured him much earlier in the play. Yet as Antigonous relates, he 'tamed' his man-eating captor, taught him to dance, and 'advanc[ed]' his 'tastes' (W. Brough, *Perdita*, p. 38). The 'respectably dressed' bear not only bows to the assembled company but also gently kisses Perdita's fair hand. The astonished milkmaid-turned-princess (she, too,

---

[25] W. B. Donne, 'Popular Amusements' (*Westminster Review* July 1856), rpt in *Essays on the Drama* (London: John W. Parker and Son, 1858), p. 256.
[26] W. B. Donne, 'Plays and Their Providers' (*Fraser's Magazine* September 1853), rpt in *Essays on the Drama*, p. 83.
[27] W. B. Donne, 'Charles Kemble' (*Fraser's Magazine* December 1854), rpt in *Essays on the Drama*, p. 158.
[28] *Theatrical Times* 2 December 1846.
[29] John Coleman, *Fifty Years an Actor's Life*; qtd in Sands, *Robson of the Olympic*, p. 89.

has risen in social status) praises the bear's 'extreme civility'. Antigonous then invites the audience to provide music for the dancing bear through its applause. Here is the exchange in full:

Enter Antigonous, followed by the Bear, respectably dressed, L.
PAULINA: 'Tis he! (*runs to embrace him*)
FLORIZEL: It may be, but who's this?
A bear?
(*Bear bows to the Company, and kisses Perdita's hand.*)
PERDITA: Good gracious! what extreme civility.
FLORIZEL: You wouldn't think it a *bare* possibility.
ANTIGONOUS: He took me home to dinner years ago,
I couldn't get away he pressed me so.
I tamed him – by degrees, his tastes advancing,
And finally instructed him in dancing.
Say, would you like to see him dance?
FLORIZEL: I should[.]
[ANTIGONOUS]: If you, kind friends, (*to Audience*) would only be so good
As [to] furnish music. (*indicates clapping*) Poor the best of bands
To the sweet sound of your applauding hands.
(pp. 38–9)

In this ludicrous image of manufactured manners, *Perdita* clearly mocks the canons of respectability. It bears remembering that a moral precept so deeply cherished as respectability migrated both up and down social hierarchies. Industrialists adapting to the social prominence which their newly obtained wealth afforded them and the so-called 'aristocracy of labour' both eagerly adopted the codes of respectability in order to distinguish themselves from uncultured captains of industry no less than from the proverbial 'great unwashed'. It is impossible, then, to say whether *Perdita*'s rehabilitated bear evokes brutish entrepreneurs (bearish, one might say) who aspired to gentlemanly status or a lower middle class anxious to separate itself from the perceived vulgarities of labourers (the kinds of people who might crowd around to watch a dancing bear). The comic image sustains both readings. Of course we need not attach a precise social standing to the 'respectably dressed', hand-kissing bear since what matters most of all is that the performance sardonically disavows the virtue of respectability. When Antigonous invites the 'sweet sound' of the audience's 'applauding hands' to keep time for the dancing bear, the burlesque articulates just how fraudulent respectability can be. The closing image of the respectable bear forced to dance by its master certainly tells us that respectability, at least from the burlesque's point of view, amounts to nothing more than a diligently learned trick. The image tells us, moreover, that respectability entails coercion. Behind every bear which displays good manners stands an Antigonous who compels those manners to be displayed; behind every person who would acquire respectability stands an authority empowered to dictate its controlling terms. For all its immaculate grooming, all its *politesse*, the bear is still a bear. It must still dance in public when its owner commands. Indeed, being respectable means being forced to dance someone else's steps, as the 'royal milkmaid' Perdita, lost no more, may well discover.

One of the key terms for understanding the burlesque's refusal to endorse respectability was 'fast' – Victorian slang shorthand for a flamboyant disregard of the conventional, the expected, the wearyingly slow. For those who sought to safeguard their own respectability, the epithet 'fast' implied more than a hint of moral censure. Here is ample testimony, published in 1848, from an incensed reader of the *Theatrical Times*:

> Great attempts have been made in this our day, and indeed are yet being made, to drive the legitimate drama off the stage, and to substitute for it, a drama without thought, or feeling, or imagination, above all, without poetry and moral purpose. This latter drama is the offspring of certain people who call themselves 'Fast men', and whose heroes are gents, coxcombs, snobs, &c., whose heroines are ballet-girls, flirts, coquettes – It consists chiefly of pert flippant dialogues, without plot or story, incidents at once absurd and improbable, scenes which all who laugh at them feel angry with them[selves] for doing so, for a rightly constituted mind would rather hiss than applaud them, and characters that are all outrageous and indecent caricatures.[30]

As such impassioned invective confirms, 'fastness' was a toxin which quickly spread throughout the entire theatrical establishment, contaminating not only playwrights, but also actors and audiences. In *Shylock; or, the Merchant of Venice Preserved*, the flunkey Gratiano refers to his master Bassanio as a 'Fast young man' (BL Add Mss 52,941 I, f. 27). In its review of *Macbeth According to an Act of Parliament*, the *Spectator* confessed its 'weariness at hearing every tragical or fanciful subject discussed in the language of those very limited beings the "men about town"'.[31] In *Perdita*, the Chorus – in the role of Chronos – punningly described itself 'not [as] the Old Time', but as 'the modern, the go-a-head fast Time' (p. 4). Harriet Gordon's impersonation of 'fast Time' in *Perdita* was singled out, appropriately enough, for its 'vulgarities', 'impertinences', and 'bad taste'.[32] The *Era* took particular offence at the actress's 'familiarity

---

[30] *Theatrical Times* 28 October 1848.   [31] *Spectator* 30 April 1853.   [32] *Era* 21 September 1856.

with the audience' and counselled her to 'check this display' if she wished 'to maintain a creditable position in the profession'.

Capturing the hustle and bustle of theatre, journalism, and the arts in London's West End, Robert Brough referred to his own time as the 'age of railway literature'.[33] Indeed, successful burlesque performances were deemed to possess 'go', a kind of vivacious, unstoppable locomotion. Since the *Theatrical Times* was a principal site of debate around questions of theatrical legitimacy, we ought not to be surprised that some correspondents championed 'fast' drama. The track record, if you will, of a self-professed 'Railroad Man' offers a high-spirited survey of 'fast' theatrical tastes:

> I dislike Shakespeare, I contemn Macready; Helen Faucit is a bore; and as for all our present dramatists, acted and unacted, I wouldn't give twopence for them... I like pretty girls – I love to see, and to be seen!... What's the use of the 'legitimate'? I vote that we do away with such humbug... We want some lovely actresses... and then fast men would go to the play fast enough... What the deuce is the fun of going to see Macready, Phelps, Miss Faucit, &c. &c.; They don't excite you.... I'm sure I've spent two hundred pounds in the saloons of Drury Lane and Covent Garden – ruined myself to support the legitimate! I now declare for the *il*legitimate... Let us have novelty – no more Shakespeare.[34]

The tone is facetious, but only just. Indeed, the manifesto for 'no more Shakespeare' reminds us that the Shakespeare burlesque functioned as a site of particularly intense focus on matters of theatrical propriety, and so cannot be dismissed as a harmless *jeu d'esprit* for a polite middle-class audience pleased with its ability to 'get' burlesque jokes.

Let us continue, however, to resist rigidly class-based explanations of the social forces at work in burlesques. While burlesques satirized the cult of respectability which rendered the middle class ever more protective of legitimate Shakespearean culture, they did not do so on behalf of a working class sceptical of respectability and less nervous about the pursuit of pleasure for pleasure's sake. Working-class theatres rarely performed burlesques, and their core audience seldom migrated to the minor theatres along the Strand. Robson played Shylock in the guise of an East End rag merchant – an image familiar enough to any Londoner who visited Whitechapel or Mile End – but almost certainly no one in the audience actually was an East End rag merchant. Nor did Shakespeare burlesques 'speak' from a labouring-class perspective even though they comically

---

33 Robert Brough, Introduction, *Béranger's Songs of the Empire, the Peace, and the Restoration* (London: Addey and Co., 1856), p. x.
34 *Theatrical Times* 23 October 1847.

represented the clichéd behaviour and leisure pursuits of urban workers. Burlesque characters rarely articulate class-based antagonism. For all their topicalities and domestications, Shakespeare burlesques did not construct their audiences as working-class subjects. Such plays routinely demote Shakespeare's tragic heroes and noble characters to the level of ordinary Londoners, but the reverse was almost never true. Ordinary characters – clowns, servants, and rustics – never benefited from upward mobility. In many instances such roles were simply eliminated.

The Apothecary in *Romeo and Juliet Travestie* cannily demonstrates how the Shakespeare burlesque satirizes respectability – or, more precisely, certain people's attempts to acquire respectability – while simultaneously resisting an easy alliance with populist rhetoric.[35] In Shakespeare's *Romeo and Juliet*, the Apothecary is a minor, but dramaturgically central, character. He appears briefly in the fifth act to sell poison to Romeo, an action without which the play could not proceed. As a figure of mortality and death, the Apothecary brings the various forces of the play together and so enables its conclusion. M. M. Mahood has helpfully observed that such minor, yet essential, Shakespearean characters typically appear only in the second half of a play, since appearing any earlier would only defeat their function.[36] In Halliday's burlesque, however, the Apothecary amusingly rebels against his secondary status and insists upon greater visibility in the play. He thus intrudes upon the *first* scene, finding himself sharing the stage with Mercutio, a character to whom he never speaks in the original tragedy. In this opening exchange, the Apothecary pleads for emancipation not just as a Shakespearean character, but also as a member of the electorate and as a credentialed professional. Here is the first part of their dialogue:

MERCUTIO: Who are you?
APOTHECARY: The Apothecary.
MERCUTIO: Pooh!
Romeo and Juliet, I know all through.
And the Apothecary don't arrive
Upon the scene, you know, 'till act five.
APOTHECARY: Look here, old chap, the times and seasons varies –
There's several new acts for apothecaries.
I'm daily [duly?] qualified; one of those who will

---

[35] The satiric treatment of the Apothecary in *Romeo and Juliet Travestie* recalls Rafe, the eponymous 'Knight of the Burning Pestle' in Beaumont and Fletcher's comedy. It also hints at the contributors to *Punch*, including Albert Smith, who were failed apothecaries and medical students.
[36] M. M. Mahood, *Bit Parts in Shakespeare's Plays* (Cambridge: Cambridge University Press, 1992), pp. 85–6.

	Be made a voter by the new Reform Bill.
	I'll brook no longer to be stowed away
	In the fifth act, of even Shakespeare's play.
MERCUTIO:	This comes of giving franchise to the masses,
	Apothecaries, and the lower classes.
	(Halliday, *Romeo and Juliet Travestie*, p. 6)[37]

From the Apothecary's perspective, the right to enhanced status in Shakespeare's play, the right to vote, and the right to practise his profession are all bound together in his hope for what the new 'times and seasons' will make possible. By eroding the distinction between major and minor characters, *Romeo and Juliet Travestie* appears to enter a plea for broadly based equal rights. But Mercutio, confident in his own Shakespearean knowledge, blocks the Apothecary's advancement. '[T]he Apothecary don't arrive / Upon the scene', he explains, "till act five'. In reply, the Apothecary informs Mercutio that 'the times and seasons' effectively trump Shakespeare, allowing even minor figures like himself to be dramaturgically promoted – moving up, as it were, from the final act to the first scene. In other words, the enhanced social position of real-life apothecaries calls for a corresponding enhancement of the theatrical representation of apothecaries. Faced with a turn of events not to his liking, Mercutio can only complain that '[t]his comes of giving franchise to the masses, / Apothecaries, and the lower classes'.

While the Apothecary proudly asserts his new credentials, the play itself does not recognize those assertions. Indeed, the play overturns each of the new rights which the Apothecary claims. The burlesque allows him to play an expanded role, yes; but it prevents him from ever playing a significant role. Whether in *Romeo and Juliet* or *Romeo and Juliet Travestie*, the Apothecary remains a disreputable character. The only difference is that the burlesque offers more direct evidence of his disrepute. Inheriting some of the actions performed by the servant Peter in Shakespeare's original tragedy, the Apothecary discovers a 'blank invite / To sup at the rich Capulet's' (Halliday, *Romeo and Juliet Travestie*, p. 9). Being illiterate, however, the Apothecary does not know what he has found and so asks Romeo to decipher the handwriting. The Apothecary's illiteracy

---

[37] The Apothecary's topical boast that he would '[b]e made a voter by the new Reform Bill' was optimistic. For although Parliament debated electoral reform throughout the 1850s, it never ventured beyond the Reform Bill of 1832 which enfranchised the urban middle class. Indeed, the Tory reform bill to which the Apothecary alludes was defeated in 1859, the year in which Halliday's play premiered.

hardly surprises Romeo, who disdainfully observes that '[l]earning we don't expect from such as you'. Mercutio and Romeo then rebuff the Apothecary's ill-judged attempt to sell them a comb, a toothbrush, and a bar of soap. At Capulet's ball that evening, the Apothecary gorges on cherry pie, gets drunk on Tokay, and passes out underneath Juliet's balcony. After Romeo and Juliet profess their love in a burlesque version of the balcony scene, the Apothecary awakes and, in what amounts to a parody of a parody, professes his love for the Nurse. His drunken serenade comes to an abrupt end when the indignant Nurse hurls a flower pot at him and, brandishing an umbrella, chases him offstage. In scene five, the Apothecary duly fulfils his required dramaturgical function and sells poison to Romeo. Yet even this necessary action includes a joke since the poison turns out to be South African port. In the final scene, once the menacing figure of Shakespeare appears onstage, the Apothecary loses his former resolve. At the precise moment when the performance permits him to confront the tyrannical playwright who had kept him 'stowed away / [i]n the fifth act', the would-be protagonist reveals his true cowardice. '[Y]ou / [a]re the hero here', the sheepish Apothecary informs Romeo, urging him to 'face it out' with Shakespeare (p. 38). Despite wanting to advance himself within the play, the Apothecary ultimately realizes that Mercutio was right all along: he should appear only in the single scene which Shakespeare had written for him. Otherwise, the results are embarrassing. The disgraced Apothecary fails to behave at parties, peddle his wares, hold his liquor, serenade his beloved, or challenge the authority of his dramatic oppressor.

The Apothecary's ineptitude as a dramatic character really functions as social criticism, for his obsession with being 'qualified' provides *Romeo and Juliet Travestie* with the means to satirize the contemporary obsession with professional respectability, particularly among petty tradesmen who sought to transform themselves into gentlemen. In Shakespeare's original play the Apothecary was an impoverished criminal, someone so 'bare and full of wretchedness' that he would sell drugs not to heal the sick, but to kill the healthy (*Romeo and Juliet*, 5.1.68). The Apothecary's necessary corruption (were he honest, there would be no play) makes him an effective vehicle for satirizing the medical profession's ongoing attempts to make the long-maligned apothecary trade at last respectable. To understand why the audience for *Romeo and Juliet Travestie* would have been pre-disposed to view the Apothecary as a potential object of ridicule, we need first to establish the changing social status of medical practitioners in the nineteenth century. Like physicians and surgeons, the members of the Worshipful Society of Apothecaries of London were subjected to continuing external pressure to adopt rigorous professional standards. The Apothecaries Act of 1815 created a new class of educated and trained professionals by stipulating that apothecaries undergo a five-year apprenticeship, pass an examination, and be licensed by the Society of Apothecaries. The statutory imposition of these requirements stemmed the tide of unqualified practitioners – as typified by the burlesque Apothecary – who catered to the rapidly expanding working classes in Britain's major cities and towns. By the 1830s, a properly licensed apothecary was regarded not only as a 'qualified general practitioner', Penelope Hunting has observed, but also as a 'well-educated gentleman'.[38] The Medical Act of 1858 (what the burlesque Apothecary calls one of the 'new acts') established the General Council of Medical Education and Registration to oversee the licensing of medical practitioners. Qualified apothecaries welcomed these regulatory statutes because they were eager to distinguish themselves in the public's mind from the unqualified, rogue druggists who still dispensed medicine to unsuspecting patients. One of the principal methods for the apothecaries to establish themselves as respected professionals was to host scientific *conversazione* in Apothecaries' Hall (Hunting, *Society of Apothecaries*, p. 211), thereby participating in the Victorian cult of rational amusement. '[T]he parish Hippocrates has been transformed from a rough, boorish half-educated bi-ped into a thoroughly presentable gentleman', the *City Press* approvingly observed in 1864; 'the absurdity of the apothecary has died out and the licentiate of the [Apothecaries'] Hall may now take his place among gentlemen'.[39]

But respectability was an exclusive virtue, acquired only by apothecaries at the top of their profession. Indeed, the social distinction obtained by the professional elite only widened the gulf between qualified apothecary / practitioners and unqualified druggists. Even after the Medical Act of 1858, 'disreputable, unqualified chemists' – outside the reach of regulatory authority – presented a continuing danger to the public (Hunting, *Society of Apothecaries*, p. 217). As the Strand audience would have immediately recognized, the burlesque Apothecary represented not

---

[38] Penelope Hunting, *A History of the Society of Apothecaries* (London: The Society of Apothecaries, 1998), p. 193.
[39] *City Press* 4 June 1864; qtd in Hunting, *Society of Apothecaries*, p. 211.

the earnest gentleman of the scientific *conversazione* but rather the scurrilous dispenser of illegal drugs. Nowhere in *Romeo and Juliet Travestie* does the Apothecary produce evidence of his boasted qualifications: he does not possess a certificate from the Society of Apothecaries, recite the Latin names for various drugs (a requirement for licensing), consult a medical text, allude to a *conversazione*, or even appear to possess a microscope, a beaker, or any instrument of calibration. The burlesque Apothecary, in short, is a quack. An illiterate drunk – an '(in)toxicologist' in the playbill's punning description – the Apothecary cannot claim even the slightest contact with the medical profession.[40] Nothing more than a purveyor of herb, spices, exotic imports, and illegal substances, the Apothecary tries to sell 'Sarsasparilla' cough drops to Mercutio, who understandably protests 'you're not an M.D. / Don't think to sell your rubbish to me' (Halliday, *Romeo and Juliet Travestie*, p. 7).[41]

The Apothecary's expanded role in *Romeo and Juliet Travestie* might suggest that the play will advocate the cultural, social, and even political emancipation of the urban lower middle class. In other words, the burlesque appears capable of using its 'popular' characters, minor though they are, to conduct an emancipatory project. But none of this happens. Although the Apothecary declares himself emancipated, he remains subjected throughout the play to forces which he cannot control. He has greater scope for action; but all his actions are in vain. He fancies himself an ersatz Romeo; but in the play's moment of crisis he begs Romeo to act like a hero. Unlike the Nurse who successfully challenges Shakespeare's authority, the Apothecary retreats from the burlesque's own bravado. The burlesque does indeed reconcile Shakespeare to its comic deformations, but the Apothecary plays no part in that reconciliation. While the other characters achieve a measure of theatrical emancipation, the timid Apothecary lags behind: not emancipated, but subjugated still. The Apothecary's compromised position throughout all of *Romeo and Juliet Travestie* prevents us from reading any populist rhetoric into the performance itself. This is not to

---

[40] Playbill, *Romeo and Juliet Travestie*, Strand Theatre, London, 3 November 1859 (Strand Theatre production file, Theatre Museum, London).
[41] In a similarly satiric view of morally dubious apothecaries, burlesque Autolycus sings of the '[c]heap druggists [who] somehow fill their tills / As they go robbing around' (W. Brough, *Perdita* BL Add Mss 52,961 K, f. 31). Since apothecaries could not charge fees for medical advice, their income depended entirely upon the volume of drugs which they dispensed. Disreputable apothecaries supplemented their income by selling patients more drugs than they actually needed.

say that populist concerns formed no part of the audience's horizon of expectation, but only to say that the performance neither articulated nor encouraged such concerns.[42]

We might suppose that burlesque topicalities, which routinely referred to clichéd patterns of working-class behaviour, encode a socially progressive outlook. But close readings of the performances only demonstrate that such topicalities do not sanction what they represent. Because the mock prizefights, odes to beer, and street slang which appear throughout nineteenth-century Shakespeare burlesques do not affirm working-class culture, such dramatized behaviour does not 'prompt' the audience to validate the social realities of the urban working class. References to boxing, whether through slang, allusions to champions of the ring, or even comic fights, occur most frequently in burlesques of plays which feature scenes of combat and fighting, such as *Hamlet*, *Macbeth*, *Richard III*, and *Romeo and Juliet*. In *Kynge Richard ye Third*, for example, Richard contemptuously calls Henry VI a 'Pedestrian' and a 'walker' (BL Add Mss 42,973, f. 395) – nineteenth-century slang for a labourer who travelled on foot during the night to boxing matches outside London because he could not afford a seat on a specially chartered train or steamer. In *Hamlet According to an Act of Parliament*, Hamlet calls on the champion fighter Thomas Bendigo to 'defend' him as he catches sight of his father's ghost (BL Add Mss 52,943 M, f. 15). Mock prizefights were incorporated into Shakespeare burlesques as comically 'low' versions of swordfights, thus continuing the tradition begun with Poole's *Hamlet Travestie* of substituting a 'pugilistic trial of skill' for 'the more elegant exercise of the rapier' (Preface, p. xi). Both *Romeo and Juliet Travesty* (1812) and *Romeo and Juliet as the Law Directs* feature bare-knuckle boxing matches. In the former, Mercutio bawls 'O what a thump he's tipped me on the chops' (*Romeo and Juliet Travesty*, p. 33). *Macbeth Modernised* features two boxing matches: in one, Banquo and Fleance knock out their would-be assassins; in the other, Macduff challenges Macbeth (pp. 23, 32). Hamlet and Laertes box each other in *Hamlet the Dane* (1847) and *Hamlet! The Ravin' Prince of Denmark!!* In the latter play, Hamlet adopts the

---

[42] *Perdita* offers a further example of how the Shakespeare burlesque cites, but does not affirm, the conventions of working-class life by depicting Autolycus as a trafficker in stolen goods. He encourages chambermaids and other domestic servants to steal from their masters. '[M]elting pots – always hot', he informs his potential accomplices; '[m]arks effaced – can't be traced' (W. Brough, *Perdita* BL Add Mss 52,961 K, f. 23).

swaggering bravado – and colourful nicknames – of prizefighters, defiantly declaring

> Here I stand, the Danish Chicken
> Ever fit to face the foe,
> Won't he get a fearful lickin'?
> Does I tremble at him? Oh dear no!
> (Wells, *Nineteenth-Century Shakespeare Burlesques*, IV, p. 133)

The boxing matches in *Hamlet According to an Act of Parliament* and Halliday's *Romeo and Juliet Travestie*, both performed at the Strand, strikingly recreate the liveliness of the actual sporting event, for the spectators no less than for the fighters themselves. The final scene of the *Hamlet* burlesque takes place around a 'rope ring' at centre stage. Hamlet and Laertes spar inside the ring, each wearing a pair of gloves blackened with soot (BL Add Mss 52,943 M, f. 48, stage direction). The assembled courtiers, who have placed wagers on the match, urge on their favoured combatant. Thus, Claudius tells Bernardo that he will bet on the 'Rabbit' – Laertes, throwing 'rabbit' punches – whose odds are 3:1. Horatio, supporting Hamlet, cries out 'Bravo Bantam' when his man lands a punch on Laertes for the third time. *Romeo and Juliet Travestie* offers an even more ludicrous example of burlesque boxing. As in Shakespeare's tragedy, the Nurse tells Juliet that Romeo killed Tybalt to avenge Mercutio's death. But as the burlesque Nurse narrates these events, the swordfight becomes a boxing match as reported in the sporting magazine *Bell's Life in London*. Rather than read out the 'particulars of the strife', the Nurse re-enacts the entire fight herself, playing the referee, Mercutio, Tybalt, and Romeo (Halliday, *Romeo and Juliet Travestie*, p. 26). The result, as performed by John Clarke, was a comic tour de force. Singing to the tune of 'King of the Cannibal Islands', the Nurse acts out Tybalt knocking Mercutio's 'box of dominoes' (i.e., his teeth) down his throat, Mercutio 'bit[ing] the dust', Romeo hitting Tybalt 'with such an awful whack, / That down he goes upon his back', and, finally, Romeo winning the champion's 'belt' (pp. 26, 27). In between 'rounds', the Nurse retreats to her corner, where she drinks from a 'flask' and has Juliet wipe her perspiring face with a sponge (p. 26). No doubt the sponge was welcome since 'Little' Clarke must have worked up a sweat playing four characters at once.

As these examples suggest, audiences for Shakespeare burlesques were only too familiar with the culture of the 'ring'. Of course that familiarity did not necessarily entail firsthand experience of prizefighting. Such knowledge could have been acquired through reading (*Bell's Life in London, Sporting Life*, or even Vincent Dowling's *Fistiana* (1841)), looking at prints or photographs of championship fighters, striking up a conversation in a pub (many of which were run by retired pugilists), or even attending an exhibition match mounted in a rented hall or theatre. That boxing matches were parodied on the stage by the middle of the nineteenth century tells us that the sport had seen better days. Indeed, the Nurse's ludicrous prizefight *à seul* in *Romeo and Juliet Travestie* mocks the prize ring for its faded glory. And the use of boxing gloves in *Hamlet According to an Act of Parliament* reveals more than we might presume. Although their use was not stipulated until 1866 in the Marquess of Queensberry Rules, boxing gloves always indicated that the fighters were gentlemen amateurs. By contrast, working-class prizefighters, particularly from London's East End, traditionally fought bare-knuckled. The excitement of such matches was precisely their brutality. Bare-knuckle boxers also fought however many rounds were necessary until one man was knocked out, while amateurs generally fought a predetermined number of rounds.

    The gentlemanly aspects of burlesque boxing matches, coupled with their broad physical humour, suggest that the burlesque was only too aware that the ferocious blood sport once patronized by Regency 'Corinthians' was becoming tamed and domesticated. The aristocrats whose patronage effectively protected boxing and other illegal blood sports during the Regency gradually deserted the sport, so that by the 1840s, as Dennis Brailsford explains, 'a miscellaneous band of publicans, ex-pugs, and minor financiers' controlled the ring.[43] The sport's prestige declined as more fights became fixed and unruly crowds surged upon the ring itself. In satirizing the sport's decline, the burlesque distanced itself from the working-class, frequently immigrant, backgrounds of most prizefighters. Moreover, the principal spectators for boxing matches never came from the labouring and artisanal classes. Indeed, organizers of prizefights considered manual workers to be the least valued spectators not only because they could not afford to buy tickets, but also because their unruly behaviour threatened to disrupt fights.

    Just as boxing matches replaced duels and swordfights in Shakespeare burlesques, so did beer substitute for wine in banquet scenes. The Shakespeare burlesque readily took advantage of opportunities for its characters to sing drinking songs, get drunk, and allude to West End taverns. In Craig's *Hamlet; or, Wearing of the Black*, Gertrude drinks not

---

[43] Dennis Brailsford, *Sport, Time and Society: The British at Play* (London: Routledge, 1991), p. 57.

from a goblet of poisoned wine but from a mug of beer into which Claudius has dropped an onion (Fol. D.a. 68, f. 35). The banqueteers in *Macbeth Bottled into a Burletta* (1842) – a play whose very title evokes distillation – quaff '[l]ashings of beer and plenty of grog'.[44] Shakespeare burlesques also interpolated drinking songs into scenes which, in their original versions, had nothing to do with either drinking or feasting. Thus, in Coyne's burlesque of *Richard III*, the inebriated monarch trills the song 'We won't go home 'till morning' with the 'two fat priests' who have been his drinking companions (BL Add Mss 42,973, f. 9b). And in *Macbeth Modernised*, a drunken Rosse stumbles upon Macbeth and Banquo just after the witches have vanished. To the tune of 'Vive le Roi', he swears allegiance not to his sovereign, but to beer:

> All but beer shall be forgot;
> 'Tis for thee alone I care.
> Heaven defend the pewter pot!
> Vive la bierre! Vive la bierre!'
> (p. 8)

Admittedly, turning Shakespeare's noble personages into sloppy drunks requires little ingenuity. But ingenuity is not the point. The burlesque's preoccupation with alcohol enables us to locate it within a precise network of urban leisure pursuits. How drunken burlesque characters relate to other characters tells us a good deal about the burlesque's sense of its own – and its audience's – social standing. The opening scene of *The Merchant of Venice (very far indeed) from the Text of Shakespeare* provides a case in point. Blanchard's play begins at daybreak on an empty market square, perhaps intended to remind the Strand's spectators of the nearby Covent Garden piazza. To the strains of a tarantella from Daniel François Auber's opera *La Muette de Portici* (1828), a chorus of chimney sweeps, costermongers, and flower girls assembles onstage. They begin to ply their wares, merrily singing '[f]lowers I've here of every hue' and '[c]resses quite fresh with the morning dew' (Blanchard, *Merchant of Venice* BL Add Mss 42,968, f. 688b). Here is the London burlesque version of picturesque operatic peasants who lighten their labours with song. Moreover, this *faux pastorale* also mocks the London street folk whose travails Henry Mayhew would faithfully document in his monumental *London Labour and the London Poor* (1861). In her daintiness, the burlesque's Flower Girl suggests nothing of the penury and prostitution which marked the

---

[44] Anon., *Macbeth Bottled into a Burletta* 1842 British Library Add Mss 42, 962, f. 440.

lives of girls sent into the street to earn their living. As Mayhew melodramatically observed, the 'beauty and fragrance' of the flowers sharply contrasts with the 'stench and squalor' of the lodgings even for the 'better class' of flower girls.[45]

The young bucks Antonio, Salarino, and Salanio, stumbling home at dawn after a night of heavy drinking, boisterously intrude upon this parodic *rus in urbe*. Admitting the hypocrisy of their self-professed 'moral propriety', the revellers confess that they have just returned from the 'well known Cider Cellars / Where song and stout to one vast ocean flows [*sic*]' (Blanchard, *Merchant of Venice* BL Add Mss 42,968, fols. 688b, 689). The street sellers, whose work ethic cannot be doubted, quickly leave the stage, and the scene shifts from propriety to irresponsibility, pedlars to 'fast' young men, and lyricism to slang. To be sure, the drunken louts are stereotyped just as much as the sprightly chimney sweep who chirps 'Sweep! soot ho!' (f. 688b). But underneath the stereotype lies an indisputable social reality. By the 1840s, 'fast' young men about town, notorious for their prodigality and intemperance, had emerged as a recognizable constituency within London's West End. They were the kind of men who actually did seek out pawnbrokers – like burlesque Shylock – to underwrite their drunken escapades. For all their broad humour, Antonio, Salarino, and Salanio define with considerable precision the behavioural patterns of a well-documented urban sub-culture.

The drinking establishments regularly cited in Shakespeare burlesques, such as the Evans's Supper Rooms, the Coal Hole, and the Cider Cellars, were neither gentleman's clubs along Pall Mall nor local gin palaces in ordinary neighbourhoods. These West End establishments were patronized chiefly by 'swells' and 'fast' young men. For all its seeming earthiness, the burlesque does not invoke the centrality in working-class life of the local pub, a place where families gathered, friends conversed, and business was conducted. Since the burlesque vigorously resisted the cult of respectability, it offered scant encouragement to the temperance movement. Nor, for that matter, did 'legitimate' West End theatres advocate temperance. Middle-class social reformers presumed that theatregoing and drinking were equally deviant, and thus hardly looked to the stage for morally uplifting amusement. Anyone who attended a West End theatre, particularly a burlesque house, was unlikely to have taken the teetotaller's 'pledge'. The rakish spectators at the Adelphi and the Strand more likely appreciated Alfred Crowquill's

---

[45] Henry Mayhew, 'The London Flower Girls', in *London Labour and the London Poor* 3 vols. (London: C. Griffin and Co., 1861), I, p. 135.

comic essay 'The Philosophy of Drinking' (1842) which gleefully catalogued contemporary slang expressions for alcohol consumption: 'Boozing, Bibbing, Fuddling, Swilling, Guzzling, Tippling, Toping, Lushing, Cracking a bottle, Sucking the money, [and] Sluicing the ivories'.[46] It hardly needs to be added that these were the same sort of words spoken by burlesque characters.

Crowquill's overdose, we might say, on slang terminology for drinking should remind us once again of how the cultural practices dramatized within burlesques formed a set of common experiences. People who read *Bell's Life in London* also drank beer, used slang, and attended burlesques. One of the obvious ways burlesques reformulated the language of their antecedent texts was to translate the original dialogue into modern-day slang. Yet when compared with W. T. Montcrieff's play *Tom and Jerry* (1821), Mayhew's *London Labour and the London Poor*, or Thackeray's *The Yellowplush Papers* (1837–8), nineteenth-century Shakespeare burlesques are comparatively restrained in their use of slang. Unlike these other texts, the Shakespeare burlesque could use slang only as a parodic response to an antecedent text; it could not be entirely 'free and easy' with its own speech. In Blanchard's burlesque, Shylock reminds Antonio that 'the other day / You threw your oyster shells across the way' (*Merchant of Venice* BL Add 42,968, f. 690b). To 'throw one's oyster' was to spit on someone, 'oyster' being a nineteenth-century slang term for phlegm. The burlesque line thus stands in for Shylock's original, though less picturesque, declaration that Antonio 'spet upon [his] Jewish gaberdine' (*The Merchant of Venice*, 1.3.110). The line also makes sense dramatically, given that burlesque Antonio was a fishmonger. Later in the play, Portia's suitors choose from barrels of gin, rum, and brandy. When examining the barrels, Bassanio uses slang terms for the three different spirits. Gin, for example, was colloquially known as 'cream of the valley', thus leading Bassanio to sing

> The Cream of the Valley hath fled
> Not a drop now remains in the bottle
> To send one quite muggy [i.e., drunk] to bed
> Or even to moisten one's throttle.
> (BL Add 42,968, f. 694)

In itemizing the various usages of burlesque slang, we must remain aware that slang is a social practice. As socio-linguists have long noted,

---

[46] Alfred Crowquill (pseud. Alfred Henry Forrester), 'The Philosophy of Drinking', *Bentley's Miscellany* 11 (1842), p. 150.

concepts of standard language (e.g., learned from elocutionary manuals) and non-standard language (e.g., picked up in the streets) possess no meaning apart from the people who actually use those languages. '[I]mportant social and historical processes', Raymond Williams observed in his classic text *Keywords*, 'occur *within* language'.[47] Branding a form of speech as 'improper' – such as slang references to petty crimes, pawnshops, blood sports, and gin palaces – impugns not just a list of words, but also the people who use those words and, moreover, the cultural experiences which those words signify. As Lynda Mugglestone has observed, slang was one of the 'style' markers upon which nineteenth-century 'social affinities' were based.[48] Such markers, she maintains, were more significant in determining 'notions of social cohesion or division' than parities (or disparities) in financial status (p. 78). In looking, then, at the burlesque's relentless use of slang, we are looking not at a gratuitous recitation of vulgarities but rather at the public performance of a socio-cultural identity through a particular mode of speech.

But just whose identity does burlesque speech perform? The 'dialogue' of burlesque, Dallas disapprovingly noted in *Blackwood's Magazine*, echoes 'the vernacular of the London taverns and caves of harmony' (79, February 1856, p. 229). *Lloyd's Weekly London Newspaper* similarly complained that phrases 'dragged out of their tap-room obscurity' could be heard upon the stage of a 'respectable theatre'.[49] When *Blackwood's*, in an 1852 article on life in London, cited the slang expression 'cut their sticks' (a locution, endlessly repeated in burlesques, meaning 'to run away'), the respectable journal quickly distanced itself from such uncharacteristically low speech by referring to it as the 'figurative language of the Coal-hole'.[50] Such remarks confirm what a close study of burlesque texts will reveal: that popular slang does not reproduce 'cant' (the secret street-language of criminals) but rather what the Victorian etymologist J. C. Hotten termed 'the vulgar language of fast life'.[51] Whether in Thackeray's novels, *Punch*, the *Comic Almanack*, Evans's Supper Rooms, or the burlesque stage, popular slang was the everyday language of young, unmarried men about town. '[T]he writing of a burlesque should rank higher in literary merit', *Lloyd's Weekly* asserted in its review of *Macbeth*

---

[47] Raymond Williams, *Keywords: A Vocabulary of Culture and Society* (New York: Oxford University Press, 1985), p. 22.
[48] Lynda Mugglestone, *'Talking Proper': The Rise of Accent as Social Symbol* (Oxford: Clarendon Press, 1995), p. 78.
[49] *Lloyd's Weekly London Newspaper* 8 May 1853.
[50] 'Our London Commissioner', *Blackwood's Magazine* 71 (April 1852), p. 460.
[51] J. C. Hotten, *The Slang Dictionary* (1859; rpt London: Chatto & Windus, 1891), p. 34.

Somewhat Removed from the Text of Shakespeare, 'than the report of a prize fight from a sporting newspaper' (8 May 1853). But nobody who enjoyed Shakespeare burlesques shared that belief. As we have seen, part of the burlesque's appeal was that it unashamedly borrowed the *patois* of the newsroom and the boxing ring, to say nothing of the bar, the tavern, and the supper club.

In identifying the boundaries of London 'fast life' which nineteenth-century slang demarcated, we must be careful not to assume that the experiences described through burlesque slang simply reflected the experiences of burlesque audiences. Although burlesque slang clearly defined – and privileged – the 'fast' spectator, it did not define the totality of all spectators' social experiences. Like all non-standard forms of speech, slang was understood by more people than those who actually used it. Yet to understand slang was not to sanction its usage. And thus *The Times* complained that Talfourd, in *Shylock; or, the Merchant of Venice Preserved*, 'addresse[d] himself rather too exclusively to that interesting class of our fellow citizens who are known as "men about town"'.[52] While the 'vulgar' speech and 'double-entendre' of Edward Wright's comic performances at the Adelphi would be acceptable to the louche patrons of the 'coal-hole', the *Theatrical Times* claimed that such speech was 'not quite the thing' for the 'modest ladies of the galleries and the pit'.[53] As these cautious remarks confirm, spectators who understood but did not use slang felt excluded (or were perceived as feeling excluded) from burlesque performances. Given the diversity of nineteenth-century theatre audiences, we can hardly expect that burlesque audiences would conform to a consistent demographic profile, let alone that their response to a performance would be uniform. We can more reliably conclude that through 'improper' language the burlesque grounded itself in a precise social actuality and, moreover, attempted to constitute its audience as participants in that same actuality. In other words, the burlesque constructed its audience as a collective of 'fast' young men.

But what did it mean to live a 'fast' life? As Burnand recalled, beer drinking, slang, and prizefighting – the very kinds of practices represented within the burlesque – featured prominently in the daily life of London's 'fast' young men in the 1850s and 1860s.[54] But, then, so did attending burlesque performances at the Adelphi, the Strand, and the Olympic. The *experience* of watching a burlesque needs to be set alongside other more or less disreputable practices, including late-night carousing,

---

[52] *The Times* 6 July 1853. [53] *Theatrical Times* 25 November 1848.
[54] Burnand, *Records and Reminiscences*, I, pp. 130–1.

attending illegal prizefights at secret locations outside London, smoking clay pipes in the streets, playing billiards, and reading the gossip columns in *Bell's Life in London*. For an example of how inter-connected these leisure pursuits were, we need look no further than Clement Scott's memoirs. After putting in a full day at the War Office, the aspiring drama critic often spent the evening at Evans's Supper Rooms, where Sam Cowell sang comic narrative-ballads of *Hamlet* and *Macbeth*. 'The first verse of Cowell's *Hamlet* I shall never forget', Scott vowed, 'for it recalls not only Sam Cowell, but my dear old friend Frank Dowling, the editor of *Bell's Life*, with whom I went, not only to Evans's, but to many a merry "mill", or prize fight, down the river by Purfleet, in the days of the "pugs"' (*Drama of Yesterday and Today*, I, p. 350).[55]

Scott witnessed Cowell perform Hugo Vamp's 'Comic Dramatic Shakesperean Scenas' (illustration 19), which included parodies of *Hamlet, King Lear, Macbeth, The Merchant of Venice*, and *Richard III* set to the tune of contemporary popular songs. Even the iconography of Vamp's musical reveries was in the spirit of burlesque, since the cover page for 'Hamlet: The Black Prince of Denmark' features caricatures of famous moments from various Shakespearean plays, including Richard III confronted by King Henry's ghost in the form of a carved pumpkin head atop a white bed sheet. While Cowell's solo act did not match the scale of fully staged burlesques at the nearby theatres on the Strand, they nonetheless traded on the same comic sensibility, theatrical 'knowingness', and topicality of the Shakespeare burlesques written by Blanchard, Dowling, Talfourd, and the Broughs. The recitative prelude to 'Kynge Rycharde Ye Thyrde' historicizes the reign of Henry VI as a time '[e]re railways or telegraphs were known, / Ere theatres were brought about, / Or Jenny Lind was thought about'.[56] And one of the punning lyrics was accompanied by the direction, 'spoken à la [Charles] Kean'. Scott's recollection demonstrates the degree to which burlesques implicated themselves in a network of mutually reinforcing cultural practices. Shakespearean parodies were performed not only in theatres, but also in drinking clubs whose patrons attended illegal boxing matches, spoke the *argot* of the

---

[55] The opening verse was 'A hero's life I sing, his story shall my pen mark; / He was not the King, but Hamlet, Prince of Denmark; / His mama was young, the crown she had her eyes on; / Her husband stopp'd her tongue: – she stopped his ears with poison. / Tooral, looral, lay, ti, rol, rumpti, edy, / Tweedle, deedle eh! ri, fol, rumpti, doodle eh!' (Anon., *Hamlet, A Comic Song*, London, *c*. 1853).

[56] Hugo Vamp (pseud. John Robert O'Neill), 'Kynge Rycharde Ye Thyrde – Hys Historie, as Literally Per-verted from the Text of Shakespeare' (London: Davidson's Musical Treasury, n.d.).

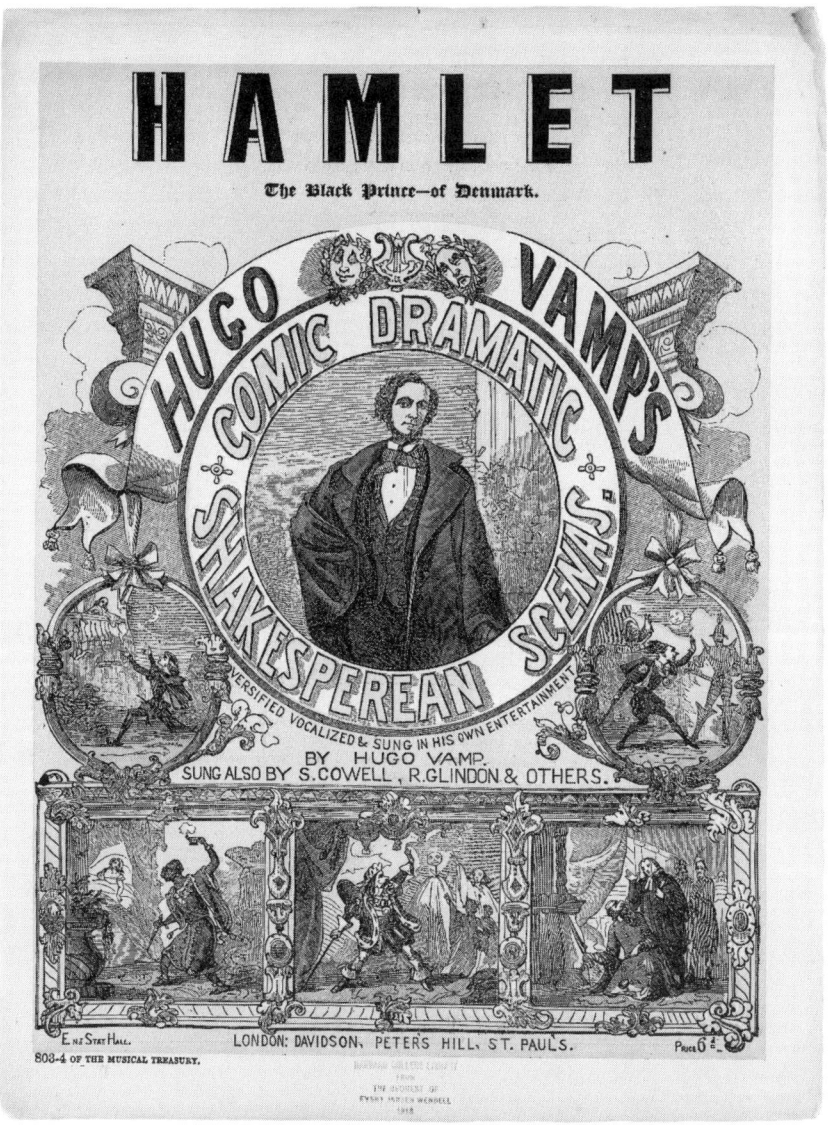

19. Hugo Vamp's 'Comic Dramatic Shakesperean Scenas', *c*. 1850s, The Harvard Theatre Collection, The Houghton Library. Compare the ghost of Henry VI in the cartoon of the tent scene from *Richard III* with the ghost of Old Hamlet in illustration 4. Compare the smiling crescent moon in the cartoon of the balcony scene from *Romeo and Juliet* with the smiling mask in illustration 1.

ring, and even performed comic versions of Shakespeare for their private amusement.

Unlike the respectable middle class, the 'swells', 'sparks', and 'men about town' who comprised the burlesque's target audience were by no means an imaginary constituency. Demographic changes in the mid nineteenth century consolidated London's bachelor sub-culture. With a suburban railway network fully in place by the 1850s, middle-class families relocated from the West End and the City of London to the suburban regions of Islington, Highgate, Clapham, and even Richmond. As these families moved out, single young men moved in. In many instances, these educated young men were the sons who stayed behind as the rest of their families decamped to the suburbs. In consequence of these population changes, the West End and its environs housed a growing number of 'men about town' who had professional careers, disposable income, leisure time, and no domestic responsibilities.[57] The *Era* described them as 'young gentlemen who float about town after nine o'clock cogitating where they shall invest their odd shilling in exchange for a little fun'.[58] Since many of these men lived in 'chambers and lodgings', as Sir Walter Besant observed in his monumental survey of London, they had neither the means nor the desire to entertain at home.[59] Their leisure pursuits were predominantly public, whether in clubs, theatres, or song-and-supper rooms, where they were joined by travelling businessmen and tourists. One visitor from Edinburgh who came to London to testify before a House of Commons committee on railways reported that some of the 'engineers, surveyors, solicitors, [and] agents' also presenting evidence had visited the Coal Hole the night before.[60] '[T]here are no poor people here', J. Ewing Ritchie noted of the audience at Evans's Supper Rooms.[61] The 'majority in the room are clerks, and commercial gents, and fellows in Government situations', he observed; yet the entertainments also attracted 'wealthy swells, moustached, and with white kid gloves'.

[57] As Burnand recorded, a corner table at Evans's was always reserved for Mark Lemon, Shirley Brooks, Thackeray and, on occasion, Albert Smith, the Brough brothers, and J. B. Buckstone. These 'notables, literary and dramatic' spent 'four evenings out of six' at Evans's, where they were welcomed 'by the amiable snuff-taking Paddy [Green]', who referred to the young men as his '"Dear Boys, Dear Boys"' (Burnand, *Records and Reminiscences*, I, p. 246).
[58] *Era* 12 March 1854.
[59] Walter Besant, *London in the Nineteenth Century* (London: A&C Black, 1909), p. 262.
[60] 'Letter from a Railway Witness in London', *Blackwood's Magazine* 62 (July 1847), p. 73. The Coal Hole's move to the Strand in 1851 was calculated to attract tourists who had spent the day visiting the Great Exhibition in Hyde Park.
[61] Qtd in Harold Scott, *The Early Doors: Origins of the Music Hall* (London: Nicholson & Watson, 1946), p. 42.

The 'fast' young man's relentless pursuit of nocturnal pleasures is confirmed, at least as a cultural stereotype, in *The Comic Almanack*. The satiric magazine purported to offer 'conclusive facts' proving that the 1851 census was flawed because it failed to count those people who had not spent the 'census' night under their own roofs (*The Comic Almanack* 2nd ser. 1844–53, p. 334). Here is the testimony, reported in the *Almanack*, from Mark Lane, a bachelor working in the Corn Exchange:

> I never slept anywhere on the night in question. I went to dine at the Divan, and then I went to the play, and then I went to the Albion, and then I went to the Cyder Cellars, and then I went about, and then I went to a coffee-house, and then I went to Westminster Bridge to see the sun rise, and then I went to my office, and then I went to bed on the counting-house table, and upset the inkstand into the wafers; and then I went to sleep until the clerk came. (p. 334)

Despite its obvious exaggeration, the fanciful account of Mark Lane's night on the town gives us a strong sense of the kinds of people who lived their social lives in public and the kinds of places where they found amusement at any hour of the day or night. Sala's 'Twice Round the Clock; or, the Hours of the Day and Night in London', serialized in the *Welcome Guest* (1858), publicized even more widely London's transformation into a twenty-four-hour center of entertainment. The 'fast' young man's insatiable desire for pleasure contrasts, of course, with the sober diligence of his more earnest elders. But like the fictive Mr Lane, who preferred to sleep in his office, the 'man about town' took a more relaxed view of professional responsibilities. It was by virtue of their own profligacy (though not immorality) that the burlesque's core audience understood itself to be a dissenting audience. And burlesque was a favoured means for articulating dissent from dominant cultural and social hierarchies. Ultimately, what was most distinctive about the burlesque audience was not its socio-economic profile, but the disposition of its values. The more familiar name for the burlesque's irreverent disposition was Bohemian.

Like Shakespeare, who, in *The Winter's Tale*, referred to Bohemia's non-existent seacoast, the Victorians understood Bohemia not as a precise geographic place but as a symbolic space. For *Blackwood's Magazine*, Bohemia was a 'space without borders'; for the *Saturday Review*, an 'imaginary country'.[62] This zone of impropriety, the Bohemia not to be found on any map, encompassed literary and artistic clubs, newspaper

[62] *Blackwood's Magazine* January 1883; *Saturday Review* 3 March 1877.

and magazine offices, artists' studios, song-and-supper rooms, and, above all, the minor West End theatres in and around the Strand. This virtual Bohemia consisted not merely of renegade artists, writers, and performers, but also of the 'jaunty young clerks' and 'incipient men about town' who aspired to a similar status.[63] Yates, looking back upon his first years in London, recalled that the denizens of '[o]ur British Bohemia' were 'young, gifted, and reckless; that they worked only by fits and starts, and never except under the pressure of necessity; that they were sometimes at the height of happiness, sometimes in the depths of despair'.[64] They unfailingly harboured a 'thorough contempt', Yates elaborated, 'for the dress, usages, and manners of ordinary middle-class civilisation' (p. 300). The *Cornhill Magazine* similarly observed that the Bohemian experience constituted 'alienat[ion] from society in its established, conventional, and certainly very convenient sense'.[65]

Most burlesque playwrights were confirmed Bohemians. Talfourd was the 'most irregular of irregular livers, and the most careless', Burnand recalled (*Records and Reminiscences*, I, p. 387). The dashing young playwright, shown in illustration 20, 'would dine when others breakfasted, and breakfast when other men dined'. Robert Brough led an even more erratic life, having been born with a 'slop-work constitution' (Hollingshead, *My Lifetime*, I, p. 84). In Hollingshead's poignant character sketch, Brough appears 'as a lost soul, an awful example, a misguided being – a man with his eyes open who had gone down the wrong turning'. Brough himself complained of constant 'bad health' which prevented him from writing at all. 'The very shaky old head on my young shoulders', he wrote to one of his editors after missing yet another deadline, 'has been playing me such tricks lately – I have not been able to write a line since I saw you'.[66]

One of the most important social affiliations which embodied the Bohemian antipathy toward established cultural orthodoxies was the club. The Savage Club, founded in 1857, was the first and most well-known Bohemian club in Victorian London. While the origins of the

---

[63] G. A. Sala, 'Twice Round the Clock; or, the Hours of the Day and Night in London', *Welcome Guest* 17 (21 August 1858), p. 279.

[64] Edmund Yates, *Edmund Yates: His Recollections and Experiences* 3rd edn 2 vols. (London: Richard Bentley and Son, 1884), I, pp. 299–300.

[65] *Cornhill Magazine* 11 (February 1865), p. 214.

[66] Robert Brough, a letter, n.d., Harry Ransom Humanities Research Center, The University of Texas at Austin, Austin, Texas.

20. Portrait of Francis Talfourd by Herbert Watkins, *c*. 1850s. Burnand remembered him as 'tall, handsome, [and] easy-going. Not of a strong constitution, he loved Bohemia and was an utter Bohemian' (*Records and Reminiscences*, I. p. 387).

club's name remain disputed, Halliday recalled in *The Savage-Club Papers* that Robert Brough had proposed the name 'Savage' as a testament to the members' lack of pretence.[67] 'If we must have a name', Brough argued, 'let it be a modest one – one that signifies as little as possible' (qtd in Halliday, *Savage-Club Papers*, p. x). Brough's desire that the club signify 'as little as possible' is manifestly disingenuous. The 'tap-room character' of the Savage Club, as characterized by John Hollingshead (*My Lifetime*, I, p. 151), ought not to obscure the considerable talents and accomplishments of its members – men like à Beckett, Blanchard, Byron, Gilbert, Halliday, Planché, Robertson, and Sala. The feigned insignificance of Bohemian culture, as encoded in the name of the Savage Club, reminds us that while the burlesque appeared to signify 'as little as possible' – appeared to be nonsensical – it actually mounted a concerted resistance to all forms of cultural 'humbug'. Indeed, the burlesque is the genre *par excellence* of Bohemianism: slap-dash, 'fast', highly ephemeral, scarcely remunerative, and with no pretence to lasting effect. 'Bohemians had raised to a positive profession', Justin McCarthy noted, 'the production of the theatrical burlesque' (*Westminster Review* 79, January 1863, p. 51). In the summer of 1845, *Blackwood's Magazine* published a 'Letter from London' which attested to the prominence of burlesque – and, more particularly, Shakespearean satire – within Bohemian culture:

> The literary youth of London are all in the facetious line. They have regular clubs, at which they meet to collate the gathered slang and pilfered witticism of the week; periodical compotations to work these materials into something like a readable shape; and hebdomadal journals, by means of which their choice productions are issued to a wondering world... [I]n London, you are surrounded with these philosophers of the Cider-cellar. Their works stare you every where in the face; the magazines abound with their wit; their songs, consisting for the most part of prurient parodies, are resonant throughout the purlieus of Covent Garden. What is worse than all, they have wriggled themselves into a sort of monopoly of the theatres, persuaded the public to cashier Shakespeare, who is now utterly out of date... The form of dramatic composition now most in vogue is the burlesque.[68]

We can align Shakespeare burlesques even more closely with Bohemian culture by looking at examples of how Shakespeare burlesques and the 'philosophers of the Cider-cellar' quoted each other. One of

[67] Andrew Halliday, Preface, *The Savage-Club Papers* (London: Tinsley Bros., 1867), p. x.
[68] 'A Letter from London', *Blackwood's Magazine* 58 (August 1845), pp. 177–8.

the most sustained references to Bohemian culture occurs in *Shylock; or, the Merchant of Venice Preserved*.[69] The manuscript licensed by the Lord Chamberlain's Office in July 1853 indicates that during the trial scene the 'Judge and Jury Society of Venice' appears on stage, with the 'Duke in the Chair' (BL Add Mss 52,941 I, f. 38).[70] When Robson first performed burlesque Shylock, the 'Judge and Jury Society' – a late-night revue which staged mock versions of the most sensational trials of the day – had been running for over ten years. 'Baron' Renton Nicholson, a former pawnbroker, imprisoned debtor, and editor of the scurrilous newspaper the *Town*, first conducted his mock court at the Garrick's Head Hotel, Bow Street, in 1841. A decade later the proceedings moved to the Coal Hole and, in 1858, finally relocated to the Cider Cellars, Maiden Lane, next to the Adelphi Theatre's stage door.[71] All three song-and-supper rooms catered for an almost exclusively male clientele, who ate steaks and chops, drank beer or brandy, and smoked cigars while being entertained with performances of varying degrees of lewdness. The Coal Hole took its name both from the coal heavers who numbered among its original patrons and from the establishment's low ceiling and dimly lit interior.[72] Perhaps because of its impropriety – and its sheltering darkness – the Coal Hole was exceedingly popular.

The 'Judge and Jury Society' consisted of Nicholson, in full judicial regalia, imitating the Lord Chief Justice; actors playing sham lawyers; Nicholson's side-kick H. G. Brooks impersonating witnesses of both sexes (a feat which earned him the sobriquet 'the Protean Witness'); and twelve customers empanelled to form the jury. The burlesque court of law being fully assembled, the participants proceeded with that evening's mock

---

[69] Burlesques of *Richard III* are also instructive. In *Kynge Richard ye Third*, Lady Anne complains of her new husband's irresponsible behaviour. 'Instead of coming home to sup and sleep', she distressingly reports, '[a]ll night in [Cider] Cellars and Coal holes he'll creep – / Smoking and singing Barcarolles' (BL Add Mss 42,973, f. 402). Similarly, Malone's burlesque *Richard III* refers to the '[g]ridiron' in the 'Coal Hole Kitchen' (Malone, *Richard the Third. A Burlesque Operatic Edition of Master Shakespeare's Celebrated Tragedy with Additional Notes* 1854 British Library Add Mss 52,947 B, f. 3).

[70] '[The Duke] and the Senate generally accommodated with pipes, cigars, etc. Antonio, Bassanio, Gratiano, Lorenzo &c discovered L. Clerks of the Court, Spectators, Witnesses, Jurymen, &c. R' (Talfourd, *Shylock* BL Add Mss 52,941 I, f. 38). The same stage directions appear in the anonymously published version of Talfourd's play. See *The Merchant of Venice Travestie. A Burlesque in One Act* (Oxford: E.T. Spiers, 1849), p. 24.

[71] The Coal Hole furnished Thackeray with the prototype for 'The Cave of Harmony' in the opening chapter of *The Newcombes*, and the Cider Cellars became the model for the 'Back Kitchen' in *Pendennis*.

[72] Leopold Wagner, *London Inns and Taverns* (New York: Frederick A. Stokes, 1925), p. 238.

trial.⁷³ In *The Night Side of London* (1857), J. Ewing Ritchie recalled the conduct of events:

[h]aving seated himself and bowed to the bar... the Lord Chief Baron called for a cigar and a glass of brandy and water... A jury was selected; the prosecutor opened his case, which, to suit the depraved taste of his patrons, was invariably one of seduction or crim. con. Witnesses were examined and cross-examined, the females being men dressed up in women's clothes, and everything was done that could be to pander to the lowest propensities of depraved humanity... After the defence came the summing up which men about town told you was a model of wit, but in which the wit bore but a small proportion to the obscenity. The jury were complimented on their intelligent and lascivious appearance, all the filthy particulars which had been noted were referred to in Dog Latin, and poetical quotations were plentifully thrown in; and by twelve, amidst the plaudits of the audience, the affair so far as the Judge and Jury Club was concerned, was over.⁷⁴

Sensational adultery cases, as Ritchie observed, provided ready material for the Judge and Jury Society. Such cases were familiarly known as 'crim. con.' (criminal conversation), a form of civil litigation in which a husband sued his wife's lover for property damages.⁷⁵ The reasoning behind the legal action was that a man who slept with another man's wife damaged her body, which was itself regarded as the husband's property. Accordingly, the cuckolded husband could sue his wife's seducer for property damages just as he could sue someone who injured his horse or spoiled a shipment of port. Because of the expense involved in bringing a civil suit, the defendants in crim. con. litigation – that is, the cuckolded husbands – tended to be wealthy gentlemen. The trial proceedings of individual suits were published not only in law reports but also in the popular press and in widely circulated pamphlets. As Lawrence Stone has observed, such transcripts contained the text of love letters read out during the trial in addition to witnesses' accounts of 'looking through keyholes, listening to creaking beds, [and] inspecting bed linen' (*Broken lives*, p. 250). The published court transcripts provided sexual titillation, to be sure, but also the sheer excitement of a legal – and moral – contest.

---

⁷³ S. M. Ellis, ed., *A Mid-Victorian Pepys: The Letters and Memoirs of Sir William Hardman, M.A, F.R.G.S.* (London: Cecil Palmer, 1923), p. 156. Nicholson would periodically interrupt the trial and solemnly instruct the jury to give its 'orders' – that is, to place drink orders with the waiters.

⁷⁴ J. Ewing Ritchie, *The Night Side of London* (London, 1857), qtd in Bradley's introduction to Renton Nicholson, *Rogue's Progress: The Autobiography of 'Lord Chief Baron' Nicholson*, ed. John L. Bradley (1863; Boston: Houghton Mifflin Co., 1965), p. xi.

⁷⁵ Crim. con. was not divorce litigation but only a trial for damages for injury to property. See Lawrence Stone, *Broken Lives: Separation and Divorce in England 1660–1857* (Oxford: Oxford University Press, 1993), pp. 22–5.

By the 1850s, the very predicate for crim. con. litigation – the presumption that a woman's body was her husband's property – was denounced in the middle-class press as 'monstrous', 'abominable', and 'odious'.[76] Until the Divorce Act of 1857 abolished crim. con. litigation, the public's appetite for trial records documenting other people's sexual infidelities was increasingly condemned as being more degraded than infidelity itself. Public morality appeared threatened by the disclosure of isolated incidents of private immorality. For mid-Victorians, as Stone has noted, such legal actions were offensive because they violated the sanctity of the home (*Broken Lives*, pp. 289–90). Crim. con. trials were thus doubly outrageous because they provided blatant sexual titillation and profaned the ideal of domestic life. That crim. con. cases were eventually dramatized – first in song-and-supper rooms and later in actual theatres – need scarcely surprise us. The inherently dramatic nature of legal proceedings made such trials irresistible to performers. From reading lascivious transcripts to acting them out in public was but one short step.[77] 'Baron' Nicholson's antics at the Coal Hole represent not an anomalous, but an exemplary, instance of nineteenth-century scandal culture.[78] And the Olympic's restaging of the 'Judge and Jury Society' demonstrates just how close the affiliations were between burlesque and the 'roystering mob' of London nightlife.[79]

The playbill for *Shylock; or, the Merchant of Venice Preserved* (illustration 21) indicates that the 'Chief Baron lights his Cigar at 9 o'clock precisely' to signal the beginning of the trial scene. That explicit directive was followed in performance, judging from the *Era*'s report that C. Bender, playing the Doge, successfully imitated the 'Lord Chief Baron of a Judge and Jury Society'.[80] In playing Shylock, Robson mimicked 'Herr von Joel', the flunkey from Evans's Supper Rooms, by selling cigars to the assembled patrons (Wagner, *London Inns and Taverns*, p. 228). In September 1853, on one of Robson's benefit nights, the august 'Baron' himself took the part

---

[76] 'The English Law of Divorce', *Westminster Review* 65 (April 1856).
[77] *Othello*, of course, is the Shakespeare play in which topical allusions to 'crim. con.' trials would be entirely appropriate. Indeed, *Othello-Travestie* (1813) features the earliest burlesque reference to an adultery trial, when Othello tells Iago 'first the crim.-con. truth I must discover, / And then, or jealousy or love is over!' ('Ibef', *Othello-Travestie: In Three Acts with Burlesque Notes*, London: J. J. Stockdale, 1813, p. 34).
[78] The London theatrical world was no stranger to crim. con. litigation since in *Cox v. Kean* (1825), one of the century's most notorious trials, Alderman Robert Cox sought damages of £2,000 from Edmund Kean for committing adultery with his wife, Charlotte.
[79] George R. Sims, *My Life: Sixty Years' Recollections of Bohemian London* (London: Eveleigh Nash Co., 1917), p. 2.
[80] *Era* 10 July 1853.

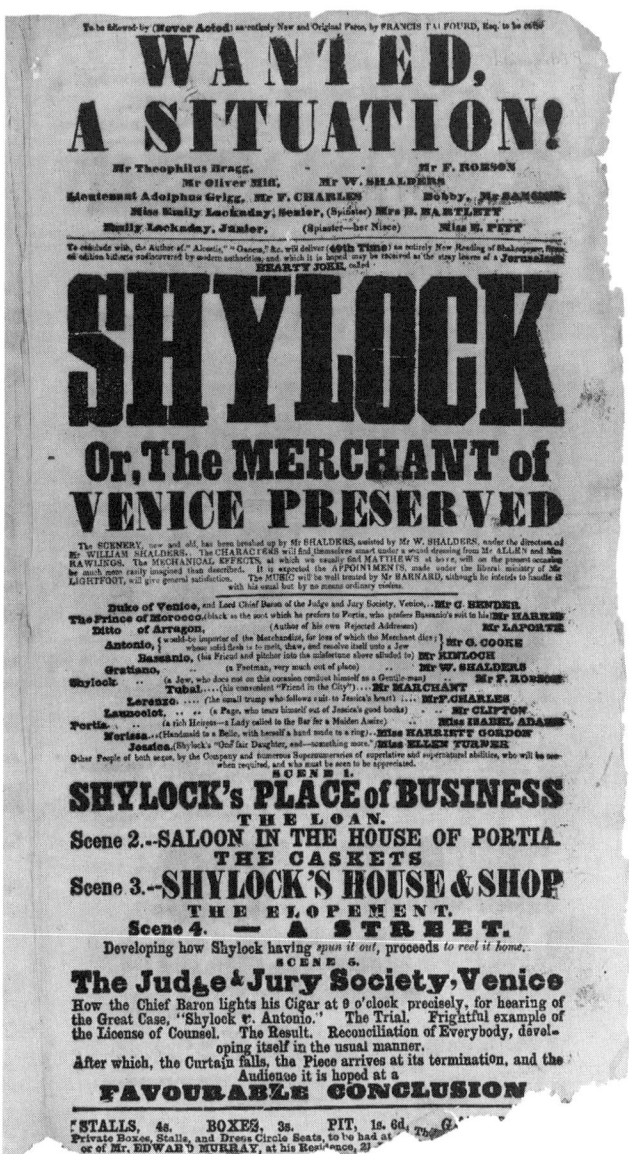

21. Playbill, *Shylock; or, the Merchant of Venice Preserved*, Olympic Theatre, London, 1853. Note the punning misquotation from *Hamlet* in the description of Antonio, 'whose solid flesh is to melt, thaw, and resolve itself unto a Jew'.

of the Doge, thus presiding over what became, for the night, the mock sensational trial '*Shylock* v. *Antonio*' (Cook, 'Frederick Robson', *Gentleman's Magazine* 252, July 1882, p. 722). Admittedly, a crim. con. trial seems out of place in a burlesque of *The Merchant of Venice* since Shylock's suit against Antonio is not about property damages, but breach of contract. By no means, however, was the 'Judge and Jury Society' gratuitously incorporated into the Olympic's production. Bodily damage is of paramount concern in both instances, whether the potential damage to be inflicted upon Antonio or the damaged body of the adulteress. Moreover, both trials featured cross-dressing: Brooks as 'the Protean Witness' and Portia and Nerissa as a lawyer and his clerk. Yet the strongest link between the two performances was forged by the audience itself. Quite simply, the patrons of the 'Judge and Jury Society' were also the principal patrons of the burlesque stage: the 'men about town, revellers, nightbirds, and frolicsome roysterers of the Tom-and-Jerry stamp', as Charles Douglas Stuart and A. J. Park describe the Coal Hole's audience.[81] As described in *Norman Sinclair* (1861), William Edmonstoune Aytoun's autobiographical novel serialized in *Blackwood's Magazine*, a young man with money would find only 'awful temptation' in London's 'theatres, and gardens, and cider-cellars'.[82]

When reviewing *Shylock; or, the Merchant of Venice Preserved*, newspaper and periodical critics alluded to Nicholson's entertainments at the Coal Hole in a largely matter-of-fact manner. The unproblematic assimilation of the 'Judge and Jury Society' into a Shakespeare burlesque tells us not only about the performance's ingenious topicality, but also about its social affiliations. Re-staging the Coal Hole's sensationalized mock trials was precisely what one would expect from the Shakespeare burlesque. Yet the reverse was also true: that Shakespeare just as easily could be exported to the Coal Hole. Compare, for example, 'Baron' Nicholson's lordly presence within a burlesque of *The Merchant of Venice* with 'A Winter's Tale for any Weather' (illustration 22), a contemporary cartoon which depicts Shakespeare's romance set in the Coal Hole. A woman performs on a small stage, illuminated by a row of footlights. She is part classical maiden and part chorus girl. Her white dress and floral wreath clearly invoke the costume which the young Marie Wilton wore when playing the

---

[81] Charles Douglas Stuart and A. J. Park, *The Variety Stage* (London: T. Fisher Unwin, n.d [*c*. 1895]), p. 9.
[82] William Edmonstoune Aytoun, *Norman Sinclair* (Part VIII), *Blackwood's Magazine* 88 (September 1860), p. 379.

22. 'A Winter's Tale for any Weather, In the form of a Pocket Opera', *c*. 1856. Shakespeare's romance relocated from Sicily to the Strand. The sketch seems not to refer to any specific moment in *The Winter's Tale*. The actress dresses like Marie Wilton's Perdita (compare with illustration 23), but the staging of her encounter with a stern Leontes suggests Hermione's trial.

title role in *Perdita* (illustration 23).[83] Yet the details of her costume and appearance – the flowing tresses, the dress which fails to reach her knees, and the dainty leather boots – recall nothing so much as a burlesque

[83] The National Portrait Gallery in London identifies the image (NPG P301 [70]) only as a portrait of Marie Wilton taken by the London photographer Herbert Watkins. There can be no doubt, however, that the portrait depicts Wilton in the role of Perdita, the burlesque 'royal milkmaid'. The actress's own description of her home-made costume, the wooden milkpail which she carries in the photograph, and similarities with the costumes in Kean's production and the 'Winter's Tale' cartoon all provide sufficient evidence to make a correct attribution.

23. Marie Wilton as burlesque Perdita, *Perdita*, Lyceum Theatre, London, 1856. Photograph by Herbert Watkins. As Wilton recalled, she carried a 'wreath of blush roses' and wore a 'charming little dress of white cashmere' adorned with roses made by her mother especially for the production (*Mr. and Mrs. Bancroft On and Off the Stage*, I, p. 45). Note, also, that her legs are modestly encased in thick stockings (compare with illustration 22). Wilton's dress also alludes to the classical costumes used in Kean's revival of *The Winter's Tale*.

coryphée. Whether chaste damsel or voluptuary, the actress performs before an audience consisting of Leontes and his ogling courtiers, one of whom enhances his vision with a pair of binoculars. A mutton-chopped flunkey wearing a Greek tunic over his white-tie uniform stands patiently aside. The various placards posted on the theatre's walls – 'Only One Encore Allowed. By Order.', 'Pose-Plastique Every Evening After The Trial', 'Cyder', 'Cigars', and 'Chops and Steak' – refer unmistakably to Nicholson's 'Judge and Jury' performances, the *poses plastiques* which concluded the evening's entertainment, and the Coal Hole's hearty bill of fare.[84]

As equally confirmed by Leontes' patronage of the Coal Hole and 'Baron' Nicholson's cameo appearance as the Doge, Shakespeare burlesques acknowledged their own entrenched position within cross-referential social practices which, far from promoting rational amusement, fostered alternatives to respectability. That the sexual innuendoes of the burlesque trial scene were omitted when Victoria attended a performance tells us not that royal patronage of the burlesque was the norm but that licentiousness – the element which had to be removed – was the norm. '[T]he burlesque *Shylock* is now an extremely genteel and unexceptional affair', *The Times* dolefully reported on the day of the queen's visit, 'refined, even at the risk of being made too serious, into fitness for the most fastidious occupants of the stalls'.[85] The reviewer's hint of regret suggests that not everybody valued a 'genteel' or 'refined' burlesque. There was indeed something disheartening – even craven – about a burlesque anxious not to offend the 'fastidious occupants of the stalls'. *Shylock; or, the Merchant of Venice Preserved* forswore itself not in replicating the 'Judge and Jury Society', but in eventually renouncing it.

Throughout this chapter we have looked at the different ways in which Shakespeare burlesques repudiated the Victorian middle-class cult of respectability and rational amusement. In doing so, we have seen that those acts of repudiation were undertaken not so much from an oppositional perspective as from a disaffected perspective emanating from within the middle class itself. Burlesque culture arose, then, not as the antithesis of respectability but as its lingering 'shadow'. In the remainder of this chapter I want to offer two examples – T. W. Robertson's comedy *M.P.* (1870) and Marie Wilton's management of the Prince of Wales's Theatre – which demonstrate that burlesques can never be entirely opposed to

---

[84] The satiric rebranding of *The Winter's Tale* as *poses plastiques* recalls the *Era*'s comment that Ellen Kean's 'majestically statuesque' Hermione resembled a '*pose plastique*' (21 September 1856).
[85] *The Times* 3 July 1860.

respectability (just as they can never be entirely opposed to Shakespeare) precisely because they function as the very means by which respectability is problematized.

M.P. opens with a debate on the relative merits of burlesque and Shakespeare, prompted by Chudleigh Dunscombe's decision to inform his father, Dunscombe Dunscombe, MP, that he intends to seek his fortune upon the stage. The news does not go down well.

DUNSCOMBE: ... So you want to strut and bellow as Hamlet or Othello?
CHUDLEIGH: Not at all, my dear sir, that's exploded. Shakespeare is abolished.
DUNS: Shakespeare abolished! Not he! By Jove, sir, even an Act of Parliament couldn't do that; for if it passed the Commons, it would never pass the Lords.
CHUD: I mean that the plays of Shakespeare are not to the taste of the present day.
DUNS: So much the worse for the present day. Who, then, is to the taste of the – evening before next?
CHUD: Burlesque!
DUNS: Who?
CHUD: Burlesque!
DUNS: I never heard of him ... What is a burlesque?
CHUD: It's an entertainment crammed full of fun, and singing, and dancing, and tumbling, and parodies on popular songs, and – it is written in verse.
DUNS: Poetry?
CHUD: Um. Poetry is not exactly the word ...
DUNS: Ah! doggerel.[86]

The cross-generational battle of wits continues, with both father and son making their respective arguments through Shakespearean allusions. Disputing his son's assertion that burlesque remains the sole option for aspiring actors now that 'Shakespeare is abolished', Dunscombe *père* counters that Shakespeare himself exposed the imbecility of amateur actors in *A Midsummer Night's Dream*. Bottom, he pointedly observes, was an 'idiot' (p. 327). No sooner does Chudleigh retort that Bottom was clever enough to win Titania than his father insists that Bottom held no attraction for her until Puck 'raise[d] him in the scale of intellect from an amateur actor to a donkey'.

The timely arrival of Talbot Piers saves the audience from having to endure yet more facile Shakespearean jousting. The unfinished argument, a hallmark of Robertsonian dramaturgy, leaves the spectators

---

[86] T. W. Robertson, *M.P.* (1870), in *The Principal Dramatic Works of Thomas William Robertson* (London: Sampson, Low, 1889), pp. 325–6.

free to contemplate what remains unspoken. And it is precisely the scene's unspoken elements which are its most suggestive. Neither Dunscombe Dunscombe nor Chudleigh Dunscombe acknowledges, or seems about to acknowledge, what must have been obvious to many spectators at the Prince of Wales's Theatre: that Shakespeare's 'Pyramus and Thisbe' was a burlesque. The elder Dunscombe cannot allow that Shakespeare wrote a burlesque since that would compromise his blunt attack on 'confound[ed] burlesque'. Nor can Chudleigh adduce this seemingly advantageous precedent because he has categorically declared that Shakespeare is 'abolished'. If Shakespeare no longer suits the 'taste of the present day', as the would-be actor insists, then neither does Shakespeare's burlesque. And so the scene comes to a standstill: for Chudleigh, Shakespeare was abolished and burlesque 'great fun'; for his father, Shakespeare was immortal and burlesque mere 'doggerel'. But the audience can break the deadlock by remembering that Shakespeare and burlesque, at least in *A Midsummer Night's Dream*, are two sides of the same coin. The distinction between Shakespeare and burlesque is a distinction without a difference.

The audience at the Prince of Wales's Theatre was exceptionally well qualified to take up arguments about the propriety of burlesque since they patronized a theatre whose manageress, a former burlesque star, scrupulously devoted herself to cultivating an audience drawn from the fashionable 'carriage trade'. The theatre itself was only two blocks from Newman Street, where a cluster of Bohemian artists, including George DuMaurier, rented studios and lived in boarding houses. Robertson's *Society*, which premiered at the Prince of Wales's in 1865, depicted a cadre of Bohemian authors with an almost banal sentimentality. Wilton herself, moreover, always gave free passes to the Bohemian members of the Savage Club for the opening nights of Robertson's comedies. Here, then, was an audience well-poised to appreciate the social contradictions of the theatre which they patronized and, moreover, to regard burlesque not as the grotesque antithesis of the legitimate, but as the 'problem' of the legitimate turned back upon itself.

Marie Wilton, however, seems to have perceived none of this. In the decade after she made her London debut, Wilton established herself as the Strand's pre-eminent burlesque 'boy' in works by Byron, Halliday, Talfourd, and Robert Brough. Dickens, after watching her play Pippo in *The Maid and the Magpie*, pronounced her the 'cleverest' and 'most singularly original' actress he had ever seen (qtd in Filon, *The English Stage*, p. 102). In 1865, upon assuming joint-management (along with Byron) of the unfashionable Queen's Theatre in Tottenham Street, Wilton began a successful effort to win over a respectable audience by offering her patrons plays which mirrored their own lives, an acting ensemble increasingly drawn from the middle class, and a comfortable auditorium with carpeted floors, curtains, chintz upholstery, and even lace anti-macassars on the stall seats. As part of her managerial reforms, Wilton (who later shared these responsibilities with her husband, Squire Bancroft) changed the name of the theatre to the Prince of Wales's, started performances at eight o'clock and, eventually, restricted the bill to the performance of a single play, thus ending the longstanding custom of offering half-price admission at nine o'clock (much to the disappointment of 'fast' young men who were fond of turning up at a theatre halfway through the evening). Only too conscious of her status as the head of a theatre which aspired to respectability, Wilton renounced burlesque. After playing the title role in Byron's *Little Don Giovanni* during her first season at the Prince of Wales's, she never accepted another burlesque role.

But the renunciation was never complete, notwithstanding Justin McCarthy's ingratiating assertion that Wilton divested herself of 'all the theatrical peculiarities which naturally belonged to burlesque' once she began to star in Robertson's domestic comedies (*Portraits of the Sixties*, p. 425). Wilton did not forsake such 'theatrical peculiarities' precisely because Robertson wrote scenes of burlesque into his otherwise quaintly realistic 'cup and saucer' domestic comedies. As Filon more accurately remembered, Wilton 'climbed a wall in *School*, used a watering can to baste a mutton chop in *Ours* and imitated a squadron of soldiers in *Caste*' (*The English Stage*, p. 121). She undoubtedly relied on her consummate skills as a burlesque performer to pull off these entertaining star 'turns'. 'If this is not burlesque', Filon quite rightly asks, 'what is it?' At least for her French admirer, Wilton played the burlesque gamine 'all her life' in 'fantastic rôles' written in the 'margin of domestic dramas' (p. 122).

In neither of her memoirs does Wilton skip over the years she spent acting in burlesque; but she regards those years only as useful 'training' for the more legitimate performances she went on to give at the Prince of Wales's and the Haymarket (Bancroft and Bancroft, *Recollections*, p. 18). Of legitimate Shakespeare, the future Lady Bancroft had scant experience.[87] In what was most likely her only performance in a Shakespearean role, the actress appeared in an evening of Shakespeare

[87] Even as a manageress, she produced only one Shakespeare play, *The Merchant of Venice* (Prince of Wales's 1875). Neither Wilton nor her husband acted in the production, which starred Ellen Terry as Portia and Charles Coghlan as Shylock.

scenes jointly produced by West End theatres to commemorate the Tercentenary. Though all the scenes were performed 'straight', the Strand's two offerings – the fifth act of *A Midsummer Night's Dream* and the balcony scene from *Romeo and Juliet* – proudly alluded to its fame as a burlesque house. The comedy featured Shakespeare's own contribution to burlesque while the tragedy recalled the Strand's production five years earlier of *Romeo and Juliet Travestie*. For the Tercentenary celebration, Wilton was Juliet, thus playing a legitimate version of her own burlesque role. In the actress's self-laudatory account, her performance in Shakespeare's balcony scene 'created quite a sensation' and so was reprised for eight additional performances (p. 24). Nowhere, however, does Wilton mention that she had played burlesque Juliet many more times. Attaching a singular importance to her first legitimate Shakespearean venture, Wilton recorded that the 'praise' and 'complimentary letters' she received emboldened her to 'slip out of burlesque as quickly as possible'. The veracity – or falsity – of Wilton's claim we can never establish. But we can nonetheless acknowledge its discursive claim: that through Shakespeare she would escape from the confines of burlesque. And yet the escape into Shakespeare only restored her to burlesque. Wilton never did 'slip out of' burlesque to find herself enfolded in Shakespeare's protective arms. But, then again, how could she? For Shakespeare and the burlesque were inextricably bound together.

CHAPTER 4

Politics 'burlesquified'

At the conclusion of *Romeo and Juliet; or, the Shaming of the True* (1868), Juliet reminds the audience that the performance they have just witnessed cannot be characterized as a vernacular redaction of Shakespeare's original tragedy because 'when Juliet puns and Romeo sings' the burlesque is 'far more like a hundred other things'.[1] As Juliet knows, the burlesque redirects Shakespeare's language toward non-Shakespearean concerns. Some of these 'worldly' concerns we have already encountered. Both the aspirational Apothecary in *Romeo and Juliet Travestie* and Antigonous' dancing bear in *Perdita* mocked the Victorian obsession with respectability. Yet perhaps the most consistent burlesque 'usage' of Shakespeare was political: to invite audiences (or readers) to think through different models of nationhood, national identity, and national origins at a time of gradual democratic reform. The Shakespearean affinities of politically minded burlesques only strengthen their topical force since, in nineteenth-century debates about political reform, Shakespeare provided a consistent frame of reference for thinking about issues of inclusion and exclusion – as the parliamentary transcripts of the 1832 Select Committee on Dramatic Literature and the 1866 Select Committee on Theatrical Licences and Regulations make clear.

In *A Survey of Burlesque and Parody in English* (1931), George Kitchin argued that 'modern' parody – that is, post-Renaissance – 'has tended to become more and more the watchdog of national interests'.[2] Kitchin unequivocally placed burlesque (and other parodic forms) in the service of political conservatism. Yet a careful study of the political topicalities in nineteenth-century Shakespeare burlesques will reveal just how wrongheaded that claim was. As Linda Hutcheon has emphasized, the

[1] Anon., *Romeo and Juliet; or, the Shaming of the True: An Atrocious Outrage* (Oxford: T. and G. Shrimpton, 1868), p. 30.
[2] George Kitchin, *A Survey of Burlesque and Parody in English* (Edinburgh and London: Oliver and Boyd, 1931), p. xiii.

transformational potential of parody can never be 'permanently fixed and defined' (*Theory of Parody*, p. 20). Hutcheon's assessment is particularly relevant to the multiple political perspectives articulated through Shakespeare burlesques. In recognizing that these plays traded on Shakespeare's nationalistic utility, we should not presume that their ideological pronouncements were either uniform or predictable. Less a site of vulgar didacticism than of playful contestation, these comic texts and performances do not so much cite existing political realities in the off-stage world as they use the stage to put alternative political realities into play. In other words, the political operation of Shakespeare burlesques takes place entirely within the symbolic order. And it is only realities which are still potentialities that stand in need of symbolization. What is important in the burlesque, then, is not the release from constructed narratives (that would be impossible anyway) but the recognition that narratives, precisely because they are constructed, situate readers and spectators in the productive gap between representation and the real.

Throughout the nineteenth century, productions of *King John*, whether legitimate or burlesque, bore witness to an enduring obsession with recovering the Middle Ages as a mythologized originary moment for English national character and political identity.[3] The most obvious political relevance *King John* held for a nineteenth-century audience lay in the signing of the Magna Carta. With the characteristic progressivism of Whig historiography, Henry Hallam asserted in his *View of the State of Europe During the Middle Ages* (1818) that the Magna Carta (and, to a lesser extent, the witenagemot established by King Alfred) was the great forerunner of the Glorious Revolution and the first incremental step toward the limitation of English monarchical power. This 'key-stone of English liberty',[4] as memorialized by Hallam, permanently guaranteed that justice may not be 'sold, delayed, or denied'.[5] Such hallowed testimony was not exclusive to constitutional historians. A year after the passage of the Reform Bill of 1832, the *Penny Magazine* informed its mass readership that Britain's 'free constitution' was founded 'upon [the] rock' of Magna Carta which guaranteed that the subject's rights 'were as sacred' as the sovereign's.[6] This

---

[3] Similarly, the legendary status accorded to Alfred the Great in English constitutional history was mocked in Robert Brough's *Alfred the Great; or, the Minstrel King* (Olympic 1859), a parody of Sheridan Knowles' *Alfred the Great; or, the Patriot King* (Drury Lane 1831).
[4] Henry Hallam, *View of the State of Europe During the Middle Ages*, new edn 3 vols. (1818; London: 1872), II, p. 109.
[5] '*Nulli vendemus, nulli negabimus, aut differimus, rectum aut justitiam*' (Article XXX, 'The Great Charter of Liberties', in Richard Thompson, *An Historical Essay on the Magna Charta of King John*, London: John Major, 1829, p. 82).
[6] *Penny Magazine* 15 June 1833.

historical perspective, in which King John stood as a baleful example of unchecked royal authority, was virtually axiomatic for the nineteenth century.

But such a reading of constitutional history was not axiomatic for Shakespeare and his contemporaries. The Magna Carta appears nowhere in *King John* for the very good reason that Shakespeare did not regard the great charter as a cherished document of civil liberty. In fact, the more important event in John's reign was his patriotic defiance of the Roman pontiff. Although less stridently anti-Catholic than Bishop Bale's *Kynge Johan* (*c*. 1539) and *The Troublesome Reign of King John* (1591), Shakespeare's chronicle play nonetheless represents John as a prototype for Henry VIII and the ascendant Tudor monarchy. In the historically conscious nineteenth century, however, the 'John of Shakespeare' and the 'John of history', as the *Theatrical Times* explained, 'could no longer be reconciled'.[7] Audiences expected to see a version of the medieval past which conformed not to Shakespeare's expectations, but to their own. And so the *Critic* praised Kean's revival of *King John* for depicting the triumph of 'right against might' in the victory of the rebellious barons.[8]

The perceived synonymity between Shakespeare's play and the foundation of English civil liberty created a pressure within the theatre to realize onstage the signing of the Magna Carta. The antiquarian revivals staged by Charles Kemble and Planché (Covent Garden 1823) and Macready (Drury Lane 1842) ignored the Magna Carta altogether. Kean, in 1852, acknowledged in his playbill essay that Shakespeare could not have 'allud[ed] to the remarkable political event' which made King John's reign 'all important in the eyes of the constitutional historian'.[9] Shakespeare's silence, Kean asserted, need not prevent contemporary audiences from proudly recalling 'the instrument by which the liberty of England was founded'. Only at the end of the century, however, was the signing of the Magna Carta finally represented onstage – in one of the tableaux from Tree's 1899 revival (Her Majesty's Theatre). In his 1907 edition of the play, Ivor B. John complained that the Magna Carta tableau in Tree's production 'hardly seems justified when we remember that it has nothing to do with the plot or development of the play'.[10] In a sense, he is right; the Magna Carta is irrelevant to the history which Shakespeare tells. Yet it is highly relevant to the history which the

---

[7] *Theatrical Times* 19 August 1848.   [8] *Critic* 15 February 1852.
[9] Playbill, *King John*, Princess's Theatre, London, 9 February 1852 (Princess's Theatre production file, Theatre Museum, London).
[10] Ivor B. John, Introduction, *The Life and Death of King John* (London: Methuen and Co., 1907), p. xxxv.

audience wanted to be told. The tableau found its justification not in the play's 'plot or development', but in the audience's own political development. Tree's interpolation was thus not innovative, but retrospective; it realized onstage what audiences had been thinking about for nearly a century.[11] Even so, it was a late-Victorian burlesque of *King John* which represented the liberties enshrined in the Magna Carta more overtly than any nineteenth-century legitimate revival. On the stage of Her Majesty's Theatre, the Magna Carta remained silent, as if its already clichéd significance could be fully expressed in dumbshow. Only the burlesque *King John* reimagined Shakespeare's English history play so that it spoke in a contemporized, active voice.

The play in question is the anonymous *King John, A Grand, New, Entirely Original, Historical Burlesque in Five Scenes* (c. 1870). Although there is no evidence that the burlesque, which exists only in manuscript, was ever performed – indeed, its aggressive political topicalities would never have been approved by the Lord Chamberlain's office – it was clearly written as a performance text. Like burlesque acting editions, the manuscript includes popular songs (with the customary new lyrics), notations of exits and entrances, indications of end-of-scene dances, detailed stage business (e.g., Prince Arthur riding a bicycle), numerous stage directions, and references to practicable scenery.[12] Of the play's many topical allusions – postal orders, the licensing of pubs, and even Sir Edward Landseer's lions in Trafalgar Square[13] – none refers to the theatre. To be sure, no burlesque script reliably indicates what actually was spoken (or might be spoken) in a performance. Yet it was still unusual for a burlesque written so late in the nineteenth century to be so detached from contemporary theatrical events. But perhaps that was the point. Despite its earlier popularity, *King John* was one of the least frequently performed

---

[11] Perhaps the earliest stage appearance of the Magna Carta was in Henry Milner's *Magna Charta; or, The Eventful Reign of King John* (Coburg 1823). Milner recasts the signing of the Great Charter not as royal acquiescence to aristocratic force but, in a more topically Whiggish spirit, as the reconciliation of the monarch to the people. See Jane Moody's exemplary essay 'Writing for the Metropolis: Illegitimate Performances of Shakespeare in Early Nineteenth-Century London', *Shakespeare Survey* 47 (1994), pp. 61–9.

[12] Anon., *King John, A Grand, New, Entirely Original, Historical Burlesque in Five Scenes* (c. 1870), Fol. Y.d. 303, Folger Shakespeare Library, Washington, DC. Henry Clay Folger purchased the manuscript for £1 10s in 1923 from the London antiquarian booksellers P. J. & A. E. Dobell. The sale catalogue describes the manuscript as 'original' and 'probably unpublished' (P. J. & A. E. Dobell, 'A Catalogue of Autograph Letters, Manuscripts, and Historical Documents' no. 26, London, 1923, p. 15).

[13] As Lady Constance caustically tells Elinor of Acquitaine, '[t]o see you Landseer's Lions would take to flight' (*King John* burlesque, Fol. Y.d. 303, f. 11). The allusion helps to date the manuscript since Landseer's much delayed sculpture did not appear at the base of Nelson's column until 1868.

Shakespearean plays in the late-Victorian era. At the time of Tree's revival, London audiences had not seen the play for twenty-six years. The *King John* burlesque thus appeared at a moment when the legitimate theatre had turned its back on Shakespeare's original play. Unlike *Macbeth Somewhat Removed from the Text of Shakespeare* or *Perdita*, this burlesque is not about the business of theatrical criticism.

But it is about the business of political criticism, as revealed in two key deviations from Shakespeare's original narrative structure. Shakespeare's play opens at court, where John informs the French emissary, Chatillon, that he will not recognize the French king's claim to the English throne and later bestows a knighthood upon the bastard Philip Faulconbridge. Similarly, in the first scene of à Beckett's *King John (with the Benefit of the Act)*, which takes place in 'the Palace', John tells Chatillon that King Philip 'may go, directly to the devil' and then makes the Bastard 'upon the spot a Knight' (BL Add Mss 42,944, fols. 249, 250). The anonymous *King John* burlesque, however, opens not at court but in the 'Fields of Merrie Islington' (Fol. Y.d. 303, f. 2). Peter of Pomfret, standing on a tub, cries out to the assembled Londoners that 'Britons will ne'er be crushed by Tyranny'. Whack'em, the Beadle, cuts short Peter's exhortation to 'shake off a tyrant's shackle' by dispersing the crowd under threat of punishment for 'bellow[ing]' treason (fols. 2, 3). Here is burlesque ingenuity, indeed. Peter of Pomfret does not appear until the fourth act of Shakespeare's play, when the Bastard hauls him before John for preaching in the streets that the king would renounce the throne 'ere the next Ascension-Day at noon' (*King John*, 4.2.151). For that treasonous prophecy, Peter is imprisoned and condemned to die on the very day by which he predicted John would surrender the crown. The prophet utters only one line during his brief scene. The burlesque playwright constructs an astutely contemporized version of the Peter of Pomfret whom Shakespeare describes, but never allows his audience to see: the prophet of political upheaval addressing the 'many hundreds treading on his heels' (*King John*, 4.2.149). To the citizens of London gathered around him in the fields of Islington, burlesque Peter prophesies not that the king will lose his crown but that 'there will come a day / When every Briton shall in full enjoy / The sweets of liberty without alloy' (*King John* burlesque, Fol. Y.d. 303, f. 2).

By expanding the role of a minor character, the burlesque commences not with monarchical politics – 'Now say, Chatillon, what would France with us' (Shakespeare, *King John*, 1.1.1) – but with an oration on electoral reform delivered to a contemporary mass audience. While Shakespeare describes 'the people' as 'strangely fantasied; / Possess'd with rumours, full of idle dreams' (*King John*, 4.2.144–5), the burlesque represents the clarity of their political aspirations as exemplified by the direct call for universal suffrage: 'And more – the day will come – this mark and note, / When every Englishman shall have a vote' (*King John* burlesque, Fol. Y.d. 303, f. 2). Like *Romeo and Juliet Travestie*, this burlesque used the dramaturgical 'emancipation' of a minor character to allegorize the political emancipation of disenfranchised Britons. The *King John* burlesque, however, adopts a more affirmative perspective on electoral reform than did *Romeo and Juliet Travestie*.

The burlesque closes with an event which does not appear in Shakespeare's play. On the plain of Runnymede, John yields to the demands of the rebellious barons and signs 'the nation's charter for Eternity' (*King John* burlesque, Fol. Y.d. 303, f. 43). Before affixing his name, the 'usurping tyrant' (f. 42), as Baron D'eu describes the king, reads aloud the parchment document set before him. Here is a dramatized moment of high political resonance: not just the signing of the Magna Carta, but the public reading – the performance – of that famed historical document. For all its comic contemporization, this moment remains without parallel in the history of nineteenth-century drama. Given the exceptional nature of this burlesque text, we might profitably explore how it rewrites the Magna Carta. As Hallam detailed for his nineteenth-century readers, the original charter secured an 'equal distribution of civil rights to all classes of freemen' largely through the proscriptions of negative law (*View of the State of Europe*, II, pp. 108–9). That is, 'freemen' were protected from arbitrary imprisonment, exile, or seizure of property. Only the verdict of a duly constituted jury could lawfully deprive someone of his liberty. The burlesque Magna Carta invokes this original code of negative freedom through a litany of conditions governed by 'no', 'not', 'unless', and 'except'. Yet as befits a burlesque, the comic interdictions reverse the normal course of events:

> The man that's s'posed to have took what isn't his'n
> Be without ceremony put in prison
> No matter if he's innocent, some one
> Must suffer for the injury that's done.
> No swell may drive, shoot, hunt, fish, dine or walk
> Without its being the daily papers' talk.
> Each country mayor must when a swell comes by
> Treat him to an hour's oratory.
> No Fenian may be captured by the P'lice
> Except on one condition – his Release.

No Policeman may be sent upon a beat
Where are no . . . cooks, beer, or cold meat.
No man may marry if it isn't clear
He's got a hundred and fifty pounds a year.
No man may write upon a subject new
Unless he's bribed the *Saturday Review*.
No man or woman may improve his shape,
As Darwin says he's offspring of an ape.
No girl may claim a pretty foot aright
Unless she's sure her boot is not too tight.
No damsel may for household services tout
Unless she gets her every Sunday out.
No man may take employment anyway
Without he gets half-hol on Saturday.
Lastly let no one our Burlesque revile
Unless he swears he hasn't smiled one smile.
(*King John* burlesque, Fol. Y.d. 303, fols. 43-4)

Some of the clauses are purely nonsensical, some are wry observations on current events, and some a form of class-based social criticism. But all of them are written from the position of subjugation. (Who but a subjugated people would insist upon a charter of rights?) From the burlesque's perspective, the structure and operation of official culture — from the police to the periodical press, from employment conditions to evolutionary theory — is presumed to be inane, inept, or even adversarial. In its inverted critique, the burlesque endorses what it actually opposes. While the original Magna Carta was, for nineteenth-century legal historians, the foundation of the writ of habeas corpus, the burlesque charter opens by contravening that cherished legal principle, allowing the state to imprison (not just to detain) individuals without first securing a conviction. In its reference to Irish republicans, the *faux* Magna Carta alludes to a series of embarrassments for the British government in its attempt to imprison Fenian leaders. James Stephens, leader of the Irish Republican Brotherhood, escaped from a British prison in 1865 with the help of corrupt prison staff. And in 1867, two Fenians arrested in Manchester were rescued in an attack upon a police van.[14] The comic proviso that Irish militants were to be set free as soon as they were arrested speaks to the alarm felt by some Britons at a time when Fenian soldiers attacked police barracks and murdered policemen in the streets. Even so, the burlesque directs its ridicule less at the Fenians than at the law enforcement

---

[14] See E. L. Woodward, *The Age of Reform: 1815–1870* (Oxford: Clarendon Press, 1938), pp. 345–6.

officials unable to capture them – that is, at policemen who are more interested in consuming 'beer' and 'cold meat' than in apprehending criminals.

Similarly, the burlesque only pretends to endorse the 'daily papers'' obsessive interest in tracking the comings and goings of the fashionable set. While the medieval charter arose from the righteous demands of English barons who became mythologized as the guarantors of civil liberties, the burlesque version mocks English swells – the idle, dandified barons of the nineteenth century. The stipulation that newspapers record the gentry's leisure pursuits sardonically comments on the perceived trivialities of higher journalism. At other times, however, the charter addresses the actuality of working-class experiences in its calls for domestic servants (the most common occupational category for Victorian women) to enjoy Sunday as a day of rest and for workingmen, who already had Sundays off, to put in only a half-day on Saturday morning. Partly due to pressure from trade unions, the work week for labourers became increasingly regularized during the 1870s, with the expectation of a half-day on Saturday. The free afternoon – or holiday – was known colloquially as 'half-hol'.[15] With these two references, the play acknowledges that its comic structure does not foreclose the possibility of serious social commentary. Indeed, just the opposite is true: comedy is the means by which the play articulates its political consciousness.

With the exception of working-class employment conditions, the burlesque Magna Carta, far from enshrining rights, seems only to perpetuate frivolity and anarchy. None of the political goals enumerated in the burlesque's opening scene – free trade, free press, and universal suffrage – becomes law in the final scene. We might be tempted, then, to conclude that the comic Magna Carta collapses under the weight of its own nonsense. In the enumeration of legal perversities, we might see only a disheartening retreat from the daring resolve of the opening scene which concludes with a rousing workers' chorus likening the strength of popular opinion to a force of nature:

> But not withstanding we are few, we are resolved to win:
> We'll still hold out, & plot & plan together through thick
>   and thin:
> To the end we're bound to go,
> No wavering to and fro,

---

[15] The guaranteed half-day on Saturday was welcomed by many business owners because it curtailed the traditional high rates of absenteeism on Monday and Tuesday. These de facto holidays became known as St Monday and Holy Tuesday.

> Straight on to the goal of our fondest ambition
> Like cataracts we will flow.
>
> (*King John* burlesque, Fol. Y.d. 303, fols. 8–9)

We might further confirm the burlesque's self-effacement by pointing to the numerous instances when the play distances itself from direct political action. 'No Guy Fawkeses we', the barons who plot to capture King John disarmingly sing:

> We don't mean to blow
> M.P.s down below, on their building. No, no
> ... No selfish desire assembles us here,
> You need have no fear, the very idea!
>
> (fols. 22–3)

And while the tyrannical monarch capitulates to calls for the end of 'hard taxation', 'undue restraints', and abuse of the 'people's rights' (f. 42), the play enacts the ultimate reconciliation of the crown to the people. 'I was a Brute, once eager you to sit on', John confesses; but '[n]ow you'll find me to the core a Briton: / Though John of hist'ry never thus changed side. / Quite different in King John burlesquified' (f. 44). Far from demanding that tyranny be held accountable, the citizens of London end the play by professing in song their enduring loyalty to the crown:

> Hip Hip Hurrah
> Rule Bri-tann-i-a
> You'll see that though we spoil a crown
> We loyal are, O,
> God Save the Queen,
> May nothing come between,
> Her happiness and ours e're next we are seen!
>
> (f. 49)

To read these passages as signs of political fecklessness is, I argue, to misread them. Once we understand the traditionally nationalistic rhetoric of Victorian working-class radicalism we can see quite readily that the burlesque alliance with the crown does not dilute, but actually intensifies, the play's political consciousness. As Margot Finn has revealed in *After Chartism*, working-class radicals in nineteenth-century Britain placed patriotism above internationalism.[16] Marxist theories of labour notwithstanding, being British always mattered more than being part of an international proletariat. Gareth Stedman Jones has similarly

---

[16] Margot Finn, *After Chartism* (Cambridge: Cambridge University Press, 1993), p. 80.

maintained that while the Victorian working class remained sceptical of intrusive middle-class reformers, its response was not 'political combativity' but 'enclosed and defensive conservatism'.[17] The late-Victorian burlesque of *King John* paints just this picture of radical working-class politics. The aggrieved residents of 'Merrie Islington' seek redressment not in violence and revolution, but in peaceful protest and patriotic assembly. 'No Guy Fawkeses we', the conspirators reassuringly trolled. Political emancipation, the burlesque advises, would entail no cataclysmic, continental-style revolution but rather the renewal of ancient English liberty – the very liberty first guaranteed more than 600 years earlier in the Magna Carta.

The renewed bond between the monarch and his subjects emerges not as the inevitable next step in a progressive historical narrative of political emancipation but as the consummation of a burlesque narrative. Through its comic irrationality, the burlesque does not rewrite English constitutional history so much as it constructs a more appealing theatricalized alternative. At first glance, the chorus's concluding refrain ('Hip Hip Hurrah' . . .) seems an entirely conventional ending to a burlesque or extravaganza: patriotism affirmed, the monarch saluted, and the audience bid farewell until the next performance. But let us look again. Through this song the burlesque fast forwards, as it were, from the thirteenth to the nineteenth century, replacing John Plantagenet with Victoria of Saxe-Coburg and Gotha. The burlesque does not merely wish Victoria happiness but invokes a state of mutual, undisturbed happiness between her and her people: 'May nothing come between, / Her happiness and ours'. The burlesque's view of a monarch united with her subjects is precisely what the original Magna Carta itself envisioned – a 'just solicitude for the people', as Hallam recorded, 'which infringed upon no essential prerogative of the monarchy' (*View of the State of Europe*, II, p. 108).[18] There is no denying that the play parodically rewrites the founding document of English liberty. But the nonsense of *King John*

---

[17] Gareth Stedman Jones, *Languages of Class: Studies in English Working Class History 1832–1982* (Cambridge: Cambridge University Press, 1983) p. 183.

[18] Such an affirmative depiction of monarchy looks back to *Perdita; or the Royal Milkmaid*, whose very title suggests a controlling theme of monarchical restoration. In *Perdita*, Polixenes approvingly alludes to Victoria reviewing troops upon their return from the Crimea when he tells Leontes that the highlight of his visit was witnessing 'the return of your brave troops victorious / From well-fought battle fields. When, thro' their ranks, / Their sov'reign passed, bestowing well won thanks' (W. Brough, *Perdita*, p. 7). The allusion was hardly an instance of gratuitous patriotism since the Crimean War was notoriously unpopular. In an otherwise informative essay, Wells wrongly maintains that this speech alludes to the queen's presentation of the first sixty-two Victoria Crosses at a ceremony in Hyde Park ('Shakespearian Burlesques', p. 57). That ceremony did not occur until 26 June 1857, nine months after *Perdita* had opened.

'burlesquified' acts as the very enabling mechanism for a contemporized reaffirmation of the great charter's original precepts. Such a parody was far more resolute than the humbug of the periodical press which, as one reader of the *Theatrical Times* charged, only 'babble[d]' of 'liberty' (2 December 1848).

Why, in the years around 1870, would a Shakespeare burlesque enact scenes of accommodation between crown and country? Although the 1850s was a decade marked by comparatively few calls for political reform, the 1860s witnessed a renewed interest in political emancipation, with explicit calls for direct parliamentary representation of the urban working class. The Reform League was founded in 1865 to campaign for universal male suffrage. In defiance of the Parks Regulation Meeting Act, the League held a mass meeting in London's Hyde Park on 23 July 1866. It quickly turned riotous. The police, under orders from Lord Derby's conservative government, locked the park's gates in an attempt to prevent the meeting from taking place. The government was legally permitted to close Hyde Park whenever it wished since the public enjoyed access to it only by royal favour. Presuming its right to peaceful assembly – a right which did not exist – a crowd of more than 20,000 broke through the park's railings. Police already stationed within the park chased out most of the protesters. A determined few remained throughout the night, and within twenty-four hours nearly all the protesters had gone home.[19]

Yet as political historians such as T. A. Jenkins have observed, while the Hyde Park Riots were not 'decisive' in the campaign for political reform – they were principally about the right to assembly – they certainly accelerated its pace.[20] The riots did put a human face on the seemingly abstract question of electoral reform, convincing conservative ministers of the urgent need to face the issue head on.[21] The importance of the riots in Victorian political culture, as James Vernon argues, lies in the radical use of public space to 'challenge official definitions of the constitution'.[22] Nineteenth-century 'reformers sought to create new political arenas',

---

[19] See F. B. Smith, *The Making of the Second Reform Bill* (London: Cambridge University Press, 1966), pp. 121–33.

[20] T. A. Jenkins, *Parliament, Party and Politics in Victorian Britain* (Manchester: Manchester University Press, 1996), p. 97. Such an assessment roughly accords with Arnold's conservative view in *Culture and Anarchy* (1869) that the 'Hyde Park rioter' has 'no visionary schemes of revolution and transformation' (Matthew Arnold, *Culture and Anarchy*, 1869, ed. Samuel Lipman, New Haven: Yale University Press, 1994, p. 50).

[21] The Royal Parks and Gardens Regulation Act (1872) allowed a space in the north-east corner of Hyde Park – the famed 'Speaker's Corner' – to be reserved for public speaking. This was not, however, the space which the Reform League had intended to use.

[22] James Vernon, *Politics and the People: A Study of English Political Culture, c. 1815–1867* (Cambridge: Cambridge University Press, 1993), p. 214.

Vernon contends, 'by reclaiming old constitutional rights with which to contest restrictive and exclusive definitions of the public political sphere' (*Politics and the People*, p. 184). The burlesque uses its re-imagined Hyde Park Riots – conveniently re-located to suburban Islington – to advocate broad electoral reform. Through Peter of Pomfret's call that 'every Englishman shall have a vote' (*King John* burlesque, Fol. Y.d. 303, f. 2), the burlesque surpasses the level of emancipation achieved with the passage of the Reform Bill of 1867.[23]

A further, perhaps less obvious, political topicality at work in the burlesque was its generalized allusion to the Magna Charta Association, one of the largest grass-roots organizations in nineteenth-century radical politics. As Richard Price relates, the Association's 'eclectic appeal to tradition' encompassed supporting the power of the House of Lords, advocating a stronger monarchy, and invoking the ancient rights of 'freeborn Englishmen'.[24] Similarly, as Vernon demonstrates in his study of nineteenth-century 'popular constitutionalism', radical politics invoked a rhetoric of ancient liberty – for which the Magna Carta was a founding document – to decry the erosion of self-government, peaceful assembly, and freedom of expression by centralized state corruption (*Politics and the People*, p. 321). Such corruption lay not in the upper echelons of power but in the intricate, daily workings of state bureaucracy. The burlesque shares just such a view of national politics. King John ends the play not as a villain but as the defender of individual freedom. Nor does the nobility appear guilty, for the conspirators whose tricks bring about John's change of heart are themselves barons. Consistent with the rhetoric of political radicalism, the play's corrupt characters are not the ruling elites, but their flunkies: Whack'em and his fellow Beadles, who 'hector beggars, cripples and / Silence an angry crowd by wave of hand' (*King John* burlesque, Fol. Y.d. 303, f. 20).

While the exact date for the composition of the *King John* burlesque remains a mystery (although 1870 seems about right), the circumstances which informed its composition are clear enough. At a time when political debate, as Richard Price explains, sought to determine precisely where 'the line could be drawn between the respectable and the residual

---

[23] The bill enfranchised roughly two-thirds of the male working-class population and made the working class the majority of the national electorate. Derby, the Prime Minister, called the bill a 'leap in the dark' since it was more radical than even its proponents had anticipated. The burlesque also functions as a proto-suffrage play. In response to the lone female voice which asks, 'And women?', Peter of Pomfret replies 'Yes, God bless'm, that [i.e., the right to vote] they shall [have]. / From Mrs Prodgers down to our Sal' (*King John* burlesque, Fol. Y.d. 303, f. 2).

[24] Richard Price, *British Society, 1680–1880: Dynamism, Containment and Change* (Cambridge: Cambridge University Press, 1999), p. 287.

classes' (*British Society*, p. 282), the burlesque stands for the politics of inclusion. In this play there exist no 'residual' classes. But there does exist a class whose historic rights have been abused, whose devotion to the crown cannot be doubted, and who deserve 'the sweets of Liberty without alloy'. And yet the appeal of 'burlesquified' *King John* lay not in the seeming actuality of its dramatized events, but in their artificiality. The burlesque's virtue was to offer neither the 'John of Shakespeare' nor the 'John of history' – they could never be reconciled – but the John of fantasy. The play offers a super-factual narrative – history as it ought to have occurred – in which John does not accede to the barons' demands under compulsion but rather blithely 'change[s] side[s]' and so recasts himself as the guardian of individual liberty. The burlesque stages not a false history but a true myth of origins for a political reality which had yet to be realized.

James Morgan's *Coriolanus; a Burlesque* (1846), also unlikely ever to have been performed, offers a strikingly different outlook on political reform.[25] Since *Coriolanus* was one of the least popular Shakespearean plays on the nineteenth-century stage, it is remarkable that a burlesque version exists at all. Indeed, *Coriolanus; a Burlesque* appears to be the only parody of Shakespeare's Roman play written in the entire century. Morgan, in his preface, acknowledges that he did not write the burlesque 'with a view to Stage Representation' (p. 5). Had the play ever been submitted to the Lord Chamberlain's Office it would certainly have been heavily censored given its explosive topical references to the Anti-Corn Law League.[26] Yet like the anonymous *King John* burlesque, Morgan's play reads as a theatrical script. The text includes descriptions of costumes, properties, and scenery, numerous stage directions in precise theatrical jargon (e.g., 'R.U.E.' for stage right upstage entrance), interpolated songs and dances, spectacle (a triumphal entry with five divisions of Roman soldiers), and metatheatrical commentary. The publisher, S. A. Hurton, also treated *Coriolanus; a Burlesque* as a script since the title page calls attention to the 'entrances / and exits, – relative positions of the / performers on the stage, – and the / whole of the stage business'. The burlesque's readiness for performance, as it were, invites us to examine it in light of contemporary productions of *Coriolanus*.

[25] James Morgan, *Coriolanus; a Burlesque* (Liverpool: S. A. Hurton, 1846).
[26] As George Colman testified before Bulwer-Lytton's Select Committee in 1832, the Examiner of Plays would remove any political reference 'applied to the existing moment, and which is likely to be inflammatory' (*Report from the Select Committee on Dramatic Literature*, London: House of Commons, 1832, p. 66).

Between 1789 and 1901, John Philip Kemble, Macready, Edmund Kean, Phelps, and Irving all played Coriolanus on the London stage. Of this distinguished company, only Kemble met with any lasting success – attributable, no doubt, to the tragedian's own patrician *hauteur*. From 1860 to 1901 there was not a single London production. Outside the metropolis, however, productions of *Coriolanus* were more common.[27] In the second half of the century, the play survived *only* in the provinces, principally as a star vehicle for Charles Dillon, G. V. Brooke, and William Creswick. John Vandenhoff, to whom Morgan dedicated the burlesque, was perhaps the most successful provincial Coriolanus between 1820 and 1850. In Liverpool, where *Coriolanus; a Burlesque* was published, Vandenhoff amassed an especially loyal following of theatregoers who held him in 'affectionate regard' and honoured him on his retirement in 1848.[28] Given the declining theatrical fortunes of *Coriolanus*, we ought not to be surprised that *Coriolanus; a Burlesque* evinces little interest in satirizing the conventions of legitimate Shakespeare. Indeed, the dedication to Vandenhoff indicates a more respectful attitude toward the legitimate stage than was usually found in nineteenth-century burlesques.

Coriolanus; a Burlesque professed great interest in the contemporary politics of food. It was published in the same year – 1846 – that Parliament finally repealed the protectionist Corn Laws, a potent symbol of 'Old Corruption' instituted more than thirty years earlier to protect the interests of aristocratic landowners. That a *Coriolanus* burlesque traded on political topicality was only to be expected since Shakespeare's original play has been read as an extended topical allusion to the Enclosure Act, the Midlands insurrection of 1607, and James I's battle with Parliament over royal prerogative.[29] Poor harvests and exorbitant food prices marked the early years of James' reign, with riots breaking out in the Midlands in 1607. Instigated by peasants, the riots were quashed by the local gentry who quickly recognized that the rioters' goal was to overturn the Enclosure Act which enabled the gentry to amass large estates by terminating the common ownership of land by subsistence farmers. The politics of food was no less explosive in the mid nineteenth century than it was in the early seventeenth century. As Jonathan Bate has astutely observed, the conflict over the supply of food in *Coriolanus* became a mirror image

---

[27] See John Ripley's 'Chronological Handlist of Performances', in his *'Coriolanus' on Stage in England and America, 1609–1994* (Madison, NJ: Fairleigh Dickinson University Press, 1998), pp. 343–66.

[28] George Vandenhoff, *Leaves from an Actor's Notebook* (New York and London: D. Appleton and Co., 1860), p. 33.

[29] See, for example, Shannon Miller, 'Topicality and Subversion in William Shakespeare's *Coriolanus*', *Studies in English Literature 1500–1900* 32 (1992), pp. 286–310.

of 'popular discontent' in Britain during the years (1815–46) when the Corn Laws were in force (*Shakespearean Constitutions*, p. 166). The citizens' complaint that the Roman patricians '[s]uffer [the people] to famish' by hoarding grain (*Coriolanus*, 1.1.79) was certainly echoed generations later by Britons who suffered under the effects of the Corn Laws.

Through its topical allusions to the Anti-Corn Law League, the pressure group which campaigned to repeal protectionist legislation, *Coriolanus; a Burlesque* transforms the politics of republican Rome into the politics of early-Victorian Britain. To that extent, the burlesque fully accords with Shakespeare's own dramaturgy. Morgan rewrites Shakespeare's *Coriolanus* just as Shakespeare rewrites (Sir Thomas North's translation of Jacques Amyot's translation of) Plutarch's *Lives*. It bears recalling that in Plutarch's account the Roman plebeians revolt mainly over usury; only after Coriolanus had been rejected for a consulship does the shortage of food become an issue. Shakespeare, however, conflates the two insurrections and places them in the first scene. The audience thus learns within the first few minutes of the performance that food is scarce, the Senate refuses to intervene, and Coriolanus opposes distributing the corn reserves. The parallels with the 1607 Midlands food riots could hardly have been more evident. Morgan, as a burlesque author, uses topical allusion rather than historical parallel to craft a story of Coriolanus which documents the nineteenth century's own crisis over the supply and cost of food. While Shakespeare's play uncannily anticipated nineteenth-century debates on rural poverty, Morgan's burlesque exploited the historical links for direct political purposes.

In 1815, after the conclusion of the Napoleonic Wars, the British government instituted the Corn Laws to protect the nation's agricultural interests against foreign competition in the production and sale of grain products. The strongly protectionist statutes, whose principal beneficiaries were land-owning aristocrats, remained in force for more than thirty years and became the foundation of Tory economic policy. Through a combination of economic depressions and poor harvests in the 1830s, the price of bread steadily rose as wages steadily fell. The result was starvation and misery on a massive scale. With no mechanism in place for market forces to lower the price of bread by increasing supply, the Corn Laws became a potent symbol for aristocratic stewardship gone wrong. These misfortunes and economic hardships set the stage for the 'Hungry Forties', a decade in which the nation finally faced the 'Condition-of-England' question which Carlyle had first posed in his essay 'Chartism' (1839).

One answer came from the Anti-Corn Law League. Founded in 1838 by a group of Manchester industrialists, Richard Cobden and John Bright chief among them, the League was one of the great political pressure groups of the nineteenth century. Though in part inspired by the theories of Adam Smith and other political economists, the League operated more as a 'popular radical campaign', Alastair Reid has observed, attempting to persuade various sectors of British commercial life – manufacturers and workers no less than politicians – that the only solution to the nation's economic hardship lay in repealing the outdated Corn Laws and introducing free trade.[30] Apart from direct pressure on Parliament, the League embraced a range of public activities from publications and lectures to tea parties. For manufacturers, who provided most of the League's financial backing, the appeal of overturning protectionist legislation was obvious: when food prices declined, so, too, would the pressure placed on them to increase wages. For workers themselves, a decrease in the cost of food would instantly escalate their standard of living. Aristocrats and other landowners, the bedrock of Tory government, were fervently committed to preserving the Corn Laws for the equally obvious reason that artificially inflated prices kept their profits at the highest possible level.

By the 1840s, the Anti-Corn Law League – never an exponent of class warfare – managed to bring together a number of different interests in opposing agricultural protection: industrialists, nonconformists, radicals, and even some landowners converted by the gospel of free trade. The devastation of the Irish potato famine made the repeal of the Corn Laws desirable even to the Tory Prime Minister, Robert Peel, since the country would soon need to import as much food as possible at the best prices. By perpetuating the Corn Laws, Peel's government would be seen to enforce the scarcity of food and thus to condemn its own populace to starvation. The 1846 repeal of the Corn Laws represented the triumph not of trade unions, but of what Cobden called the 'intelligent middle and industrious classes' over the 'landed oligarchy'.[31] Indeed, Cobden never denied that the League consisted of 'a middle-class set of agitators' who relied on 'those means by which the middle-class usually carries on its movements'.[32] As the historian Charles Whibley observed early in

---

[30] Alastair J. Reid, *Social Classes and Social Relations in Britain 1850–1914* (Cambridge: Cambridge University Press, 1995), p. 11.

[31] Richard Cobden, speech of 15 January 1845, in *Speeches on the Questions of Public Policy by Richard Cobden, M.P.*, ed. John Bright and J. E. Thorold Rogers 2 vols. (London: T. Fisher Unwin, 1908), I, p. 256.

[32] Qtd in Charles Whibley, *Political Portraits* (London: Macmillan and Co., Ltd, 1917), p. 262.

the twentieth century, Cobden 'cared as little for the people as he cared for the landed gentry' and he 'strain[ed] every nerve to transfer the power to the middle class' (*Political Portraits*, pp. 306–7). John Bright addressed the matter more directly, affirming that members of the League 'wished for no violence . . . [and] would not have the Corn Laws or any other law removed by the shedding of one drop of blood'.[33] Although the League's goals had been articulated by political radicals, those goals were realized not through a grassroots workers' revolt, as Dror Wahrman explains, but through a gradual political alignment of middle-class and manufacturing interests which centred on the fundamental rightness and benefits of free trade (*Imagining the Middle Class*, p. 410).

Coriolanus had always proven irresistible to anyone interested in politics, and no more so than when the scent of revolution was in the air. As Hazlitt shrewdly observed in 1816, anyone reading *Coriolanus* 'may save himself the trouble of reading Burke's *Reflections*, or Paine's *Rights of Man*, or the Debates in both Houses of Parliament since the French Revolution or our own'.[34] When A. C. Swinburne argued in 1880 that *Coriolanus* was 'rather a private and domestic than a public or historical tragedy' he was flatly contradicting over a hundred years of theatrical practice.[35] To appreciate, then, the full political resonance of *Coriolanus; a Burlesque* we must understand the politics of Shakespeare's original play, in its stage history as well as its subject matter. The contrasting images of the solitary patrician and the plebeian mob were the political flashpoints of seemingly every production. Kemble's 1789 Drury Lane revival premiered five months before the fall of the Bastille and was quickly withdrawn, not to be staged again until 1792. While theatre historians generally agree that after 1789 stage crowds were always seen as potentially revolutionary, they cannot agree whether the tone of Kemble's production was revolutionary or reactionary. David Rostron has argued that the crowd scenes fuelled domestic fears that a continental-style revolution would take place in England.[36] By contrast, Bate maintains that Kemble's 'firm handling' of mutinous plebeians 'served as an image of control, a proclamation that London would not go the way of Paris' (*Shakespearean*

---

[33] Qtd in C. R. Fay, *The Corn Laws and Social England* (London: Cambridge University Press, 1932), pp. 94–5.
[34] *Examiner* 15 December 1816.
[35] A. C. Swinburne, *A Study of Shakespeare* (London: Chatto and Windus, 1880), p. 187. 'I cannot but think that enough at least of time has been spent if not wasted by able and even eminent men on examination of *Coriolanus* with regard to its political aspect or bearing upon social questions.'
[36] David Rostron, 'Contemporary Political Comment in Four of J. P. Kemble's Shakespearean Productions', *Theatre Research* 12.2 (1972), p. 114.

Constitutions, p. 64). Three years after Kemble's 1817 retirement, Edmund Kean offered a new interpretation. Forsaking the memory of Kemble's aristocratic demeanour, Kean gave his Drury Lane audience a plebeian Coriolanus. Hazlitt, with the memory of the Peterloo Massacre still fresh in his mind, affirmed that Kean's acting 'is not of the patrician order; he is one of the people, and what might be termed a *radical* performer' (*Works*, XVIII, p. 290).

Kean's embodiment of a plebeian Coriolanus marks a significant change in the play's reception history for it allows audiences to view the stage crowd as the play's central, galvanizing force. Whether that force was democratic or anarchistic was still a matter of contention. Macready's 1838 Covent Garden revival is a case in point. As Martin Meisel has incisively observed, the stage crowd for this production was 'a French Revolutionary crowd' adapted to English concerns about 'popular democracy' and the extension of the franchise.[37] The Covent Garden audience, *John Bull* commented, was only too willing to recognize the contemporary 'struggle for power' behind the splendour of Roman history.[38] The crowd represented no mere 'mob of barbarians', the journal elaborated, but rather 'the onward and increasing wave ... of men who have spied their way to equal franchises, and are determined to fight their way to the goal'. For the *Morning Chronicle*, however, the stage crowd did indeed represent a mob motivated only by 'wild impulses', 'fickle waywardness', and 'baseness'.[39] In John Forster's conservative appraisal, the stage crowd appeared not as disenfranchised Britons on the verge of gaining their freedom, but rather as 'agents of catastrophe' and a rabble 'truly fearful to think of encountering'.[40] He insisted that *Coriolanus* could not be read as a cautionary tale on the abuses of patrician government. Not because there were no such abuses; but because Coriolanus was no patrician. This was a nice distinction indeed. By insisting that Coriolanus was not an enemy of the people, Forster depoliticized the play at a time when its political resonance was becoming ever more acute. Fearing the barely contained violent impulses of the 'starving, discontented, savage, cowardly, fickle, tumultuous Roman people', Forster quickly detached *Coriolanus* from any enactment of civil unrest.

However much Forster, in the year of the People's Charter, resisted transforming a potentially revolutionary stage mob into the image of a

---

[37] Martin Meisel, *Realizations: Narrative, Pictorial, and Theatrical Arts in Nineteenth-Century England* (Princeton: Princeton University Press, 1983), p. 227.
[38] *John Bull* 19 March 1838.   [39] *Morning Chronicle* 22 March 1838.
[40] *Examiner* 18 March 1838.

free citizenry, that inarguably democratic transformation reached something of an unanticipated climax in Phelps' 1848 revival of *Coriolanus* at Sadler's Wells. The 'mob' supernumeraries, as the actor Edward Righton recalled, performed with an unusual 'intensity' in the scene when they banished Coriolanus (qtd in Scott, *Drama of Yesterday and Today*, I, p. 287). After Phelps took his customary bow during the end-of-act curtain call, an unprecedented cry for the 'Supers' arose from the spectators. The astonished actor–manager quickly realized that his audience was clamouring for the stage 'mob' to take its own bow. Phelps, admitting that he 'never saw better acting in [his] life', immediately acquiesced (p. 288). And so the curtain fell and rose again to reveal the 'supers' alone on stage, taking the call demanded by the spontaneous acclamation of an enthusiastic audience. The elevation of supernumeraries to the rank of theatrical stars, at least for the nonce, was no doubt richly satisfying for a local audience which included their friends, neighbours, and associates.[41] From a metatheatrical perspective, the curtain call testifies not only that the Sadler's Wells' audience identified with the stage crowd but, more significantly, that the audience projected its own perception of the drama's political narrative onto the actuality of the performance itself.[42] The *Theatrical Times*, in its review, offered the historicist insight that Shakespeare's seeming endorsement of the 'Roman aristocracy' accorded more with the opinions of his own day, than with 'the public spirit of the present age'.[43] An actor like Phelps, the journal declared, could not persuade an audience that Coriolanus was a man of 'high principle and upright intention'. In the 'unusual spectacle', as Righton characterized the event, of the audience demanding recognition for much-maligned stage extras, we can see an affirmative convergence of onstage and offstage worlds.

Published in the months leading up to the repeal of the Corn Laws, Morgan's *Coriolanus; a Burlesque* directly intervenes in the exceptionally charged political discourse in which legitimate productions of *Coriolanus* had long played a part. Roman citizens are recast as League members

---

[41] In a contrasting view, George Cooke, who played a knight in Charles Kean's *Richard II*, complained to the actor–manager that his efforts to 'elevate' his non-speaking role 'to the dignity of *a part*' were derided by the 'herd of wretches who go on the stage as supernumeraries' (George Cooke, a letter to Kean, 21 December 1857, Fol. Y.c. 602 (1), Folger Shakespeare Library, Washington, DC).

[42] As Gilbert Abbott à Beckett observed, the 'career' of the supernumerary was marked by 'abject subservience' to more powerful theatrical constituencies (Gilbert Abbott à Beckett, *The Quizziology of the British Drama* (London: Punch Office, 1846), p. 16).

[43] *Theatrical Times* 7 October 1848.

whom Coriolanus disparages as '"corn-law" rogues' (Morgan, *Coriolanus; a Burlesque*, p. 24). Predictably, the burlesque patrician opposes free trade in grain, rejects the reforms which the Anti-Corn Law League advocates, and supports the protectionist statutes which make him rich but condemn the less fortunate to starve. As Coriolanus informs the citizens in one of the play's few puns, '[t]o praise you goes against the grain' (p. 6). Morgan also turns references to the price of grain in Shakespeare's text into topical allusions. 'Let us kill' Coriolanus, urges one rebellious Roman in the original play, 'and we'll have corn at our own price' (*Coriolanus*, 1.1.10–11). In the corresponding burlesque scene, the mutinous citizens are encouraged to '[s]trike Marcius down, and then reduce his power, / Should he resist, let's grind him into flour' (*Coriolanus; a Burlesque*, p. 5). The violent image of the patrician ground into flour is the ironic, brutal punishment for an aristocrat content to let the people go hungry. Through such unmistakably topical dialogue, the burlesque clearly presents itself as a sustained commentary on the contemporary politics of food.

But what was the purpose of this commentary? What could *Coriolanus; a Burlesque* accomplish that a contemporary legitimate production of *Coriolanus* could not? The burlesque's comparative advantage, I propose, lies in its highly coloured depiction of the Anti-Corn Law League. In the anachronistic burlesque, the League's members consist largely of ordinary Roman workers, the common rabble whom Coriolanus dismisses as 'plebeian scum' (p. 24). This much at least is faithful to the narrative as Morgan found it, for Shakespeare himself depicts only two social orders: the patrician and the plebeian. What is pointedly missing from the burlesque is any representation of the industrialists who founded the League and ensured its survival.[44] Nor does the play acknowledge, let alone dramatize, the middle-class commitment to economic reform and free trade which was chief among the forces leading to Peel's revocation of the protectionist statutes. Morgan uses the Roman orders of patrician and plebeian not to deny the topicality of his political references but to direct those references toward a particular set of prejudiced interests. More specifically, the burlesque uses anachronistic Roman social orders to transform the Anti-Corn Law League from a middle-class pressure group into a grassroots workers' movement. The burlesque blatantly distorts political realities since workers comprised the League's

[44] In 1843 the newspaper editor and political activist Feargus O'Connor told his fellow Chartists that the League was 'composed of the owners of machinery' (Feargus O'Connor, ed., *The Trial of Feargus O'Connor* (1843), qtd in Paul A. Pickering and Alex Tyrrell, *The People's Bread: A History of the Anti-Corn Law League* (London and New York: Leicester University Press, 2000), p. 141).

least sympathetic constituency. Indeed, resolutely working-class groups generally favoured protectionist laws because they feared that an increase in food imports would push domestic agricultural workers into the already saturated urban labour markets. The Chartists, in particular, remained sceptical of the League's middle-class political activities, regarding them, as E. L. Woodward has explained, as 'an attempt to divert the working class from the struggle to obtain political rights' (*Age of Reform*, p. 114). It bears remembering that the Anti-Corn Law League was a single-issue organization with one clear goal. By contrast, the six points of the People's Charter centred on parliamentary and electoral reform. The League never committed itself to the broad-based political reform which Chartists advocated. Indeed, Chartists routinely disrupted League meetings.[45]

Morgan's play thus re-stages the conflict over the repeal of the Corn Laws as something it never was: a struggle between citizen-workers and the aristocracy. In another of the play's rare puns, Menenius instructs Coriolanus that he must be guided by the people's 'voice', prompting the proud warrior to retort that the people's 'vice' should be taken from them (Morgan, *Coriolanus; a Burlesque*, p. 21). Since the stage pronunciations of 'voice' and 'vice' were identical, we must read this exchange not merely as yet another instance of elitist scorn, but as the play's aggressive characterization of all populist discourse as fundamentally vicious. By emphasizing the working class, the burlesque does not so much empower a disaffected segment of the population as it trades on stereotypical fears of working-class violence and anarchistic intrigue – the same fears evoked by Macready's 1838 production – to discredit the Anti-Corn Law Leaguers. The burlesque, in short, makes the 'mutinous' Leaguers behave as if they were Chartists (p. 6). For free-traders who sought to repeal the Corn Laws it would have been disastrously counter-intuitive to connect the League with working-class dissent. The fears of violence and revolution aroused by such movements as Chartism were precisely what the League needed to renounce. For conservative proponents of the landed gentry, however, it made eminent sense to associate the League with the Chartists. Through a classic strategy of guilt by association, the League would be equally vulnerable to charges, however false, of covert revolutionary activity. To find ample precedent for his dramaturgical connivance, Morgan had only to glance at the conservative periodical press.

---

[45] Donald Grove Barnes, *A History of the English Corn Laws from 1660–1846* (London: George Routledge & Sons, Ltd, 1930), pp. 247–8.

An 1842 essay from the *Quarterly Review* on 'Anti-Corn Law Agitation' is instructive.[46]

In a rambling, seventy-page diatribe, the Tory journal attempts to uncover the Anti-Corn Law League's 'real objectives' (p. 245). However much the League 'affected to belong to the middle class', the *Quarterly Review* insisted, it was still a covert 'revolutionary' movement which, like Chartism, incited workers 'to pull down the aristocracy' (pp. 259, 251). Because the League had 'fraternised with the old Jacobin spirit of enmity to our existing institutions', it would 'join the new revolutionary banner, that substitutes for the vague motto of "The Rights of Man" the more intelligible but equally deceptive war-cry of "Cheap Bread"' (pp. 244–5). Exploiting the fears provoked by Chartist rallies, the *Quarterly Review* repeatedly warns that the 'conjunct agitation' of the Chartists and the Leaguers can result only in 'violence and sedition' (p. 272). *Coriolanus; a Burlesque*, though far less stridently, argues the same case. By trading on stereotypical fears of mob rule the burlesque calumniates opponents of the Corn Laws by rebranding them as labourers who 'plot and intrigue' to overthrow the government (Morgan, *Coriolanus; a Burlesque*, p. 6). The play's innovation lies not in imputing revolutionary aims to the Anti-Corn Law League – the conservative press was already doing just that – but in manipulating Shakespeare's text to make the imputation seem historically inevitable. Of course the manipulation went both ways. As Jeremy Crump has revealed, workingmen's political movements in the mid nineteenth century – such as the Shakespeare Chartist Association – frequently invoked Shakespeare as, in the words of one labourer, 'the people's bard'.[47] The counter-strategy of *Coriolanus; a Burlesque* was to divorce Shakespeare from any populist alliance by discrediting working-class political movements as revolutionary intrigue and, moreover, by reaffirming the patrician elements within Shakespeare's original play. *Coriolanus; a Burlesque* represents the conservative extreme of nineteenth-century Shakespearean parody.[48]

Despite being the only recorded nineteenth-century burlesque of *Coriolanus*, Morgan's parody occupies not an anomalous, but a central,

---

[46] 'Anti-Corn Law Agitation', *Quarterly Review* 71 (December 1842), pp. 244–314.

[47] Jeremy Crump, 'The Popular Audience for Shakespeare in Nineteenth-Century Leicester', in *Shakespeare and the Victorian Stage*, ed. Richard Foulkes (Cambridge: Cambridge University Press, 1986), p. 276.

[48] *Coriolanus; a Burlesque* does not feature the wide-ranging topical allusions (with the exception of the Anti-Corn Law League) and intricate wordplay prominent in other Shakespeare burlesques. Social improprieties are equally absent. We might reasonably expect, for example, that the fight between Coriolanus and Aufidius would be staged as a boxing match. Yet in a play full of detailed stage directions there is no indication that the fight was meant to be either comic or contemporized.

position in the contested political reception of Shakespeare's Roman play. Its rhetorical disabling of the middle-class Anti-Corn Law League and its apprehensions of working-class political movements stand in unexpected counterpoint to an increasingly populist perspective on Shakespeare's play, from *John Bull*'s glimpse of an extended franchise in Macready's 1838 revival to the unprecedented recognition of the 'supers' at Sadler's Wells a decade later. Given that burlesques were the most vulgar form of nineteenth-century popular performance, we might find it remarkable that a burlesque should be the preferred vehicle for affirming – and contemporizing – the most reactionary impulses of Shakespeare's tragedy. We might be tempted to disregard *Coriolanus; a Burlesque* as inauthentic – as a burlesque that gets it wrong – because of its conservatism. Yet such an over-determined reading only denies this comic theatrical form its constitutive openness, its distinctive strategies of nonconformity and dissent. Morgan's play provides us with a further reminder that the burlesque's topical idiom guarantees its social immediacy, but does not pre-ordain its politics.

To get a fuller sense of the ideological singularity of *Coriolanus; a Burlesque*, let us examine some of Robert Brough's related satiric verse. Sala, his fellow journalist, described Brough as an 'irreconcilably democratic Republican',[49] while Yates recalled that the playwright and poet harboured a 'deep vindictive hatred of wealth and rank and respectability'.[50] Nine years after the publication of Morgan's burlesque, Brough completed his *Songs of the 'Governing Classes'* (1855), a series of lyrics written in a 'spirit of vulgar declamation' to advance the cause of radical and revolutionary politics.[51] His verse includes satiric portraits of imaginary aristocratic politicians who 'vote / Your rights and mine away' and 'have us shot like vicious dogs, / Should we in murm'ring rise!' ('The Marquis of Carabas', *Songs of the 'Governing Classes'*, p. 23). The collection, which Filon predicted would be found in 'anarchist anthologies of the future' (*The English Stage*, p. 111), singles out the 'absolute existence' of the aristocracy as the principal cause of 'political injustice' and the 'grovelling moral debasement' of the people (R. Brough, Preface, *Songs of the 'Governing Classes'*, p. xi). It can hardly surprise us that when

---

[49] G. A. Sala, *The Life and Adventures of George Augustus Sala* 2 vols. (London: n.p., 1895), I, p. 329.
[50] Yates, *Recollections and Experiences*, II, p. 314.
[51] Robert Brough, *Songs of the 'Governing Classes', and other Lyrics. Written in a Seasonable Spirit of 'Vulgar Declamation'* new edn (London: Vizetelly & Co., 1890). The title alludes to *The Governing Classes of Great Britain* written by his friend and fellow Bohemian Edward M. Whitty, to whom Brough dedicated his collection of poems. Brough knew just how incendiary these verses were for he omitted them from his list of publications when applying for a grant from the Royal Literary Fund (Nigel Cross, *The Common Writer: Life in Nineteenth-Century Grub Street*, Cambridge: Cambridge University Press, 1985, p. 97).

Brough turned his hand to radical political ballads he drew inspiration from *Coriolanus*, a play which gave equal scope for anti-aristocratic sentiment.

Brough prefaces his poem 'Sir Menenius Agrippa, the Friend of the People' with an excerpt from the opening scene of Shakespeare's play in which Menenius attempts to reassure citizens armed with 'bats and clubs' that the patricians have 'most charitable care' of them (*Coriolanus*, 1.1.55, 64). Like his Shakespearean counterpart who was popularly believed to have 'always loved the people' (*Coriolanus*, 1.1.51), Brough's Sir Menenius takes pride in being called a 'Leveller' and a 'stark staring Democrat' ('Sir Menenius Agrippa', lines 5, 6). Yet as Brough gradually discloses, the politics which the pseudo-radical baronet advocates are the politics of hypocrisy. Sir Menenius' public endorsement of several Chartist reforms – extension of the franchise, secret ballots, and annual parliaments – only disguises his true patrician bearing. He represents a constituency 'remote from his home', earns a yearly rental income of £65,000, and wears 'very old coats' when on the hustings only to don a clean suit 'at the club' (lines 13, 36). He sympathetically confides to his constituents that peers form an 'exclusive and arrogant class' who are 'not a throb with the mass' (line 30), yet is himself about to be elevated to the peerage. The savvy politician may indeed be 'a popular man' (line 8), but his popularity rests on no firmer foundation than a calculated charade: the studied inattention to his own rumpled clothes, unkempt hair, and 'begrime[d]' fingernails (line 17).

Brough's invocation of *Coriolanus* in his *Songs of the 'Governing Classes'* was hardly the writer's first overtly radical use of Shakespearean allusion. Seven years earlier, two unknown Liverpudlian youths – Robert and William Brough – wrote a burlesque of *The Tempest* sympathetic to republican and revolutionary interests. Its reading of Shakespeare's play, though timely, was not entirely innovative. For in spite of a seeming emphasis on sensual pleasures and exotic imaginings, *The Tempest* has always been staged as a political play. By writing a burlesque crammed with allusions to Chartism, anti-slavery campaigns, and continental revolutions, the Broughs strove to turn that original politicization to more immediate advantage. To appreciate fully the theatrical climate in which the Broughs' *The Enchanted Isle* was performed, let us briefly review the salient facts of *The Tempest*'s stage history from the Restoration to the Victorian era.

Apart from the nineteen years (1757–76) when Garrick staged a heavily cut version of *The Tempest* as it appeared in the First Folio, the

Dryden–Davenant–Shadwell musical version remained the basis for stage performance until Macready's 1838 Covent Garden revival finally restored to the theatre something approximating Shakespeare's original text. The theatre's enduring fascination with *The Tempest* as a vehicle for spectacle, scenery, and song did not, however, occlude an appreciation for the play's political content. From 1670 to 1700, when it was the most frequently performed Shakespearean play, the Dryden–Davenant–Shadwell adaptation offered theatregoers sensitive to the evolving nature of monarchical rule a model not of absolutism but of 'limited' kingly rule which, as Katharine Eisaman Maus argues, secured justice and civil order without coercive force.[52] In the Restoration, Prospero figured as a surrogate Stuart in an allegory about political exile and return. As Michael Dobson has noted, Prospero entered on the eighteenth-century stage as an emblem of 'paternal jurisdiction' sanctioned by nature and left it as an emblem of counter-revolution.[53] By the second half of the nineteenth century, *The Tempest* had become the logical play through which to stage the cluster of social concerns engendered by Britain's burgeoning empire, particularly race, slavery, and the 'white man's burden'.[54]

Within this long history of ideologically aware performances are two undeservedly neglected moments of burlesque: Duffet's *The Mock-Tempest* and the Broughs' *The Enchanted Isle*. As Dobson astutely observes, the one thing Duffet's burlesque does not deform is Prospero's commanding position as a Foucauldian agent of surveillance, discipline, and punishment ('Remember / First to Possess his Books', p. 101). The mock-Prospero is not a metaphorical, but a literal, jailer – the warden of London's Bridewell Prison. Duffet's play thus remains complicit with the model of state power enacted in *The Enchanted Island*. Nearly 200 years would pass before a British audience watched a version of *The Tempest* which radically challenged prevailing notions of executive authority.

To understand how a republicanized burlesque of *The Tempest* came to be performed in 1848 we need to recall that critical interpretations of Shakespeare's play in the preceding fifty years had not been entirely in thrall to Romantic stereotypes of poetic drama unfettered by social reality. Coleridge, confining the play to the recesses of private imagination,

---

[52] Katharine Eisaman Maus, 'Arcadia Lost: Politics and Revision in the Restoration *Tempest*', *Renaissance Drama* n.s. 13 (1982), p. 204.

[53] Michael Dobson, ' "Remember / First to Possess his Books": The Appropriation of *The Tempest* 1700–1800', *Shakespeare Survey* 43 (1991), p. 107.

[54] See, for example, Alden T. Vaughan and Virginia Mason Vaughan, *Shakespeare's Caliban: A Cultural History* (New York: Cambridge University Press, 1991), pp. 102–14, 183–90; and Trevor R. Griffiths, ' "This Island's Mine": Caliban and Colonialism', in *Critical Essays on Shakespeare's 'The Tempest'*, ed. Alden T. Vaughan and Virginia Mason Vaughan (New York: G. K. Hall, 1998), pp. 130–51.

asserted in an 1818 lecture that *The Tempest* was 'independent of all historical facts and associations'.⁵⁵ Yet he also regarded Caliban as a fearful image of Jacobinism. By contrast, Hazlitt proposed that Caliban was no French-style revolutionary but rather the island's legitimate monarch whom Prospero had wrongfully deposed. In Hazlitt's ultra-royalist analogy – itself a parody of claims for the legitimacy of the Bourbon restoration – Caliban becomes the 'Louis XVIII. of the enchanted island in *The Tempest*'.⁵⁶ By shifting the play's focus from the exemplary model of royal power embodied by Prospero to the conflict between usurper and usurped enacted by Prospero and Caliban, Hazlitt's topical reading created a critical space in which the Broughs' even more aggressively topical reading could emerge through the deformations of burlesque.

The date of the production is telling. The revolutions of 1848, a series of uprisings in France, Germany, the Austrian Empire, and parts of Italy, sought either to establish constitutional governments or to secure independence for particular nationalities. 'Tranquility has been shaken in the two kingdoms' (i.e., the Bourbon Kingdom of the two Sicilies) by 'factious movements', the *Theatrical Times* warned a month after the Liverpool premiere of the Broughs' burlesque; '[t]he spirit of faction is detrimental to society; it is a link disjoining itself from the great chain'.⁵⁷ As a paralysing fear of continental-style revolution gripped the British Isles, the nationalistic, indeed counter-revolutionary, face of the theatre grew strikingly visible. In that single year, an irate and xenophobic audience, in the greatest theatrical riot since 1809, hissed a visiting French troupe off the Drury Lane stage during a performance of Dumas' *The Count of Monte Cristo*; Benjamin Webster, manager of the Haymarket, petitioned Parliament to limit the number of foreign companies appearing on London stages; on the eve of a Chartist rally, the *Sunday Times* sharply criticized the royal family for bestowing its patronage on French and Italian opera; the radical publisher Effingham Wilson composed the first serious manifesto for a British national theatre, *A House for Shakespeare: A Proposition for the Nation*; and Queen Victoria made a series of high-profile state visits to West End theatres to establish herself as the nation's leading patron of the drama. It would be impossible to imagine a conjuncture of events more auspicious for political theatre than this.

Set against all these conservative measures is a seditious burlesque of *The Tempest* which echoes John Bright's cry, from a week after a failed

---

⁵⁵ *Coleridge's Shakespearean Criticism*, ed. Thomas Middleton Rayner 2 vols. (London: Constable & Co., Ltd, 1930), I, p. 131.
⁵⁶ *Yellow Dwarf* 15 February 1818; rpt in Hazlitt, *Works*, XIX, p. 207.
⁵⁷ *Theatrical Times* 21 September 1848.

Chartist rally, that the working class 'must oust the dominant class' or else be destroyed.[58] As the *Illustrated London News* recognized, the burlesque invoked the 'late Continental disturbances, together with our own semi-serious riots and rebellions'.[59] The play's radicality can hardly surprise us. For who, after all, would write a burlesque of *The Tempest* to advance the cause of counter-revolution given that legitimate productions of Shakespeare's play had been doing just that since the Restoration? Foremost among the allusions to contemporary European politics which ran throughout performances of *The Enchanted Isle* was Paul Bedford's 'skit upon Louis-Phillip [*sic*]' in his impersonation of Alonzo.[60] The comparison between the deposed French monarch and Alonzo was only too apt. After the downfall of the bourgeois July Monarchy in February 1848, the 'citizen-king' and his wife escaped to England, travelling aboard a British steamer under the names of Mr and Mrs Smith.[61] Never coy about its political timeliness, the Adelphi production described Alonzo as 'one of the numerous instances now-a-days of a Monarch all abroad and quite at sea'.[62] As shown in illustration 24, Alonzo, the centre figure, appears as a dancing fat man wearing over-sized blue pantaloons, a pink kerchief tied tightly around his thick neck, and a tin crown teetering upon his head. He is a *buffo* monarch, a trait certainly enhanced by Bedford's corpulence. Yet the island harbours another deposed king. Prospero, too, appears as an 'exiled monarch'; not the deposed Duke of Milan, but the dethroned King of Naples.[63] As his *cartes de visite* confirm, Prospero accepts his diminished status as an 'F.M.' (p. 26) or Former Majesty. His situation within the play does not, however, entirely correlate with contemporary events since the Bourbon king of Naples and the Two Sicilies, the autocratic Ferdinand II, remained on his throne throughout the period of civil unrest in 1848.[64] And yet it is only by understanding Prospero as a surrogate for Ferdinand II – 'King

[58] John Bright, 18 April 1848, qtd in Michael Bentley, *Politics without Democracy: Great Britain 1815–1914* (Totowa, NJ: Barnes & Noble Books, 1984), p. 134.
[59] *Illustrated London News* 25 November 1848.
[60] *Theatrical Times* 25 November 1848.
[61] In the week of *The Enchanted Isle*'s London premiere, *Punch* used a Shakespearean parody to comment on the downfall of Louis-Philippe: 'France is a stage, / And all her heroes little more than players, / Her Kings their exits have, and entrances; / And the Republic runs its round of parts' (25 November 1848). The exiled king died in England two years later.
[62] Playbill, *The Enchanted Isle*, Adelphi Theatre, London, 20 November 1848 (Adelphi Theatre production file, Theatre Museum, London).
[63] Robert Brough and William Brough, *The Enchanted Isle; or, Raising the Wind Upon the Most Approved Principles*... (London: National Acting Drama Office, n.d.), p. 2. The original manuscript is unaccountably absent from the Lord Chamberlain's Collection in the British Library.
[64] Revolutionary themes also appear in Robert Brough's non-Shakespearean burlesques. In *Masaniello* (1857), the eponymous fisherman revolutionary exclaims to his comrades 'Liberty!

24. Finale, Robert and William Brough's *The Enchanted Isle*, Adelphi Theatre, London, 1848. Ariel, Alonzo, and Prospero dance in the foreground while Ferdinand and Miranda embrace behind them, surrounded by a fairy chorus. Prospero wears a magician's cloak adorned with stars and crescent moons over his professorial attire. The backdrop depicts the magically restored Naples Direct Steamer immediately prior to its return voyage.

Bomba' – that the political immediacy of Caliban's revolutionary uprising becomes apparent.⁶⁵ *The Enchanted Isle* thus operates out of the rift between its dramatic narrative and the contemporary political narrative which it can only imperfectly allegorize. Prospero is, variously, a deposed king, an ersatz king, and no king at all.

As performed by Richard John Smith, Prospero occasionally alludes to his former state, singing that he was '[t]he rightful monarch of Naples' until his brother 'got up a popular manifestation / and forced me to sign my abdication' (p. 11). More frequently, however, Prospero performs magic acts in the 'style of street conjurors' to prophesy his own restoration. 'All the dread agents of my mystic power', he divines, '[f]oretell the approach of an auspicious hour. / The stars, my cups and balls, the learned pig, / My hocus-pocus, card tricks, thimble-rig' (p. 11). And yet the antics of a boulevard sorcerer provide no basis for *realpolitik*. Whatever political aura surrounds the Former Majesty quickly fades as his 'impotent art' compels us to see him not as an exiled monarch but as 'Signor Prosperino' – a fashionable stage conjuror, an international theatrical star. Indeed, throughout most of the burlesque, Prospero appears in a black academic gown, mortarboard, judicial wig, and spectacles, recalling the *faux* respectability which Victorian magicians accorded to themselves by appearing onstage as learned 'professionals' in formal attire. Prospero's actions within the play itself are performed as an ongoing theatrical magic act. In front of his cell hangs a sign announcing the forthcoming departure of 'Signor' Prospero: 'Blaze of Triumph!! Positively the last week of Sig. Prospero, the celebrated Wizard of the Isle!! who is about to Break his Staff and Drown his Book!!' (p. 4). This is no mere placard, but a theatrical handbill announcing the impending completion of a successful 'run' by a theatrical star (ironically, much like *The Tempest* has been read as Shakespeare's own valediction to the theatre). In a satiric reference to John Henry Anderson, the 'Great Wizard of the North', Prospero styles himself the impressively global 'Wizard of the North, South, East, and West Winds' (p. 2). His commanding title also alludes to the comedian Charles Mathews, who adopted the epithet 'Wizard of the South-South-West-by-East' in his burlesque of Anderson's celebrated Gun Trick. As one reviewer noted, Smith's 'general conjuror-like

---

freedom! tyranny is floor'd! / Run hence, proclaim it! have it shouted-roar'd!' (*Masaniello; or the Fish'oman of Naples*, London: Thomas Hailes Lacy, n.d., p. 28).

⁶⁵ The play is unable to sustain its own allusions since Prospero also declares that he 'escaped to this isle *in the name of Smith*' (R. Brough and W. Brough, *The Enchanted Isle*, p. 11), a clear reference to the false name under which Louis-Philippe had travelled to England.

appearance' and similarity to the 'Wizard of the North' induced 'roars of laughter' from the Adelphi's appreciative spectators.[66]

Whether in dialogue, costume, or stage business, the allusions which surround Prospero have less to do with continental monarchs and more to do with continental conjurors. Monarchical restoration matters so little in *The Enchanted Isle* that Prospero punningly informs Alonzo, as the reconciled brothers prepare to board the magically repaired Naples Direct Steamer on their homeward voyage, that he 'would not rob [Alonzo] of half a crown, / Much less a whole one' (p. 32). The aggrieved ex-sovereign blithely renounces any claim to his throne, leaving it safely occupied by his usurping brother. This is the Broughs' ending – not Shakespeare's – and it categorically prevents us from reading *The Enchanted Isle* as a legitimating allegory of monarchical restoration and patriarchal rule. Such a reading would have been anathema to Robert Brough, who instead ends the burlesque emphasizing that the King of Naples is an illegitimate ruler and Prospero an ineffectual rival who has ceded all his power. The magically repaired steamer about to embark cannot symbolize political repatriation because Prospero has renounced his claim to sovereignty.[67] As for the future of the proverbial enchanted isle, Prospero leaves unanswered the abandoned Caliban's anxious question '[i]f you're all leaving thus, / "What's to be done for the people" – meaning us?' (p. 31). The only possible 'us' at that moment in the performance is the audience since Caliban is the one person on stage not about to board the steamer. To that searching question Prospero makes no reply because he holds no authority over either Caliban or the audience. He holds our attention, yes; not through brute coercion, but through the magician's amusing diversions.

Ariel, for his part, emerges not as the island's chief sprite, but as its chief law-enforcement officer who swears in a deputation of fairies as 'Special Constables' to keep the peace in the 'disturbed state of the times' (p. 3). Seven months before *The Enchanted Isle* opened at the Adelphi, the Chartists held a mass rally on Kennington Common in south London. Emboldened by the socialist rhetoric of the revolution which led to Louis-Philippe's exile two months earlier, the Chartists assembled to escort their petition across the Thames to the House of Commons. They never got

---

[66] Unidentified newspaper review (Adelphi Theatre production file, Theatre Museum, London).

[67] The *Theatrical Times* did read this image from a conservative perspective, explaining that the wreck of the Naples Direct Steamer on which Alonzo had been a passenger alludes 'to the wreck of the kingdom of France' (25 November 1848). Only a royalist would liken a revolution to a shipwreck.

there. The government, determined to prevent the spectacle of workers marching into central London, blocked their movements. At the age of seventy-nine, the Duke of Wellington deployed troops throughout the city to maintain order. Special constables (William Gladstone among them) were appointed for the day. These pre-emptive tactics were successful, for the protesters amassed in smaller than anticipated numbers and did not attempt to cross the river. The workers' petition to end political servitude eventually found its way to Parliament, delivered by a mere handful of Chartists arriving by carriage. The failure of the rally does not mean that no one took it seriously. Palmerston's request that ammunition be sent to Osborne House to protect Victoria indicates, as Michael Bentley observes, just how threatening Chartist rallies could be (*Politics without Democracy*, p. 134).

As recent critics of *The Tempest*'s stage history have noted, Caliban first becomes a significant character in the play's political reception in the nineteenth century, when debates on colonialism, the dissemination of Western 'civilization', and evolution highlight the importance of this hitherto secondary character. Well before the legitimate stage offered ideologically informed characterizations of Caliban, the Broughs' burlesque depicts him as a figure of developing political consciousness – from oppressed slave to disaffected worker to militant revolutionary. No sooner is Caliban imprisoned for his treasonous plots than he is left to his own devices in a recreated state of nature. Caliban's explicitly revolutionary goals are achieved in spite of his efforts, and at the end of the play he faces a lifetime of liberty with a decided lack of confidence in his own capacity for self-governance. But until this point in the play he has engaged in active resistance to Prospero's autocratic rule. At least from Caliban's perspective, the magician really is a tyrant. In a review from the *Theatrical Times*, 'fraternity' and 'fraternise' appear with specific and exclusive reference to Caliban.[68] Since 'fraternity' was a recognizable codeword for French-style revolution, this review confirms a perception of Caliban as an active revolutionary. Yet Caliban begins the play less a revolutionary than a disgruntled slave. He first enters polishing Miranda's Wellington boots, imploring her to stop calling him a 'slave' (R. Brough and W. Brough, *The Enchanted Isle*, p. 14). Caliban then invokes the successful slogan of the Anti-Slavery Society by asking his master's daughter 'Ain't I a man and a brother?' The scene

---

[68] *Theatrical Times* 19 August 1848 and 25 November 1848. The *Dramatic and Musical Review* recorded its impressions of a 'democratic Caliban' (December 1848).

is purposefully anachronistic since slavery had been abolished throughout the British Empire in 1838. When alone on stage, Caliban sings to the audience, whom he regards as 'Sons of freedom', of having been 'kicked and cuffed about' by his cruel master. He soon confronts Prospero, declaring that '[t]he love of liberty upon me seizes; / My bosom's filled with freedom's pure emotions, / And on the "Rights of Labour" I've strong notions' (p. 16). The anachronistic slave now becomes a contemporary Chartist. Prospero, unmoved by his servant's 'democratic' pronouncements, quickly calls in Ariel's 'Fairy Specials' to beat Caliban back into submission. 'Thus disaffection should be timely checked', Prospero smugly advises the audience, much as the Special Constables checked the disaffection of Chartists during their rally on Kennington Common in April 1848.

At length, the play's political allusions turn from the rights of English workers to the revolution of European peasants. Caliban, having escaped from Ariel's violent constables, wears a Cap of Liberty, brandishes a red flag, and spiritedly sings *La Marseillaise*. 'I'll have a revolution', he flatly announces to the audience, '[p]roclaim my rights – demand a constitution' (p. 19). He soon enlists two of the shipwrecked Italians – Easa di Baccastoppa and Smuttifaccio – in a plot to 'take the island' (p. 20). Historical references to the French Revolution notwithstanding, Caliban's plot to overthrow Prospero and gain control of the island alludes directly to the Sicilian revolutionaries who, in the early months of 1848, unsuccessfully sought to expel the Neapolitans from their island and restore self-governance by re-establishing their 1812 constitution. Ariel thus sings of calming the 'dreadful hurricane' which 'in its fury swallows up the king and all his ministers ... all Naples would regret it' (p. 12). Prospero becomes, then, a stand-in for the despotic Ferdinand II who, with the support of the British government, ruled the island of Sicily from Naples. As the news of Caliban's revolutionary plot spreads across the island, Ariel warns his deputies that '[t]reason's afloat' and, perhaps obliquely referring to Palmerston's call to guard the queen at the time of the Chartist rally, commands them to '[p]rotect the crown' (p. 20). The detachment of fairies quickly apprehends the conspirators, binds them in chains, and delivers them to Prospero. The 'stoker' Smuttifaccio, despite his appearance as a Sicilian rebel, also draws the play's focus back to England since his coal-besmirched countenance (his 'smutty face') invites comparisons with England's 'great unwashed'. To the strains of *La Marseillaise*, now played *legato*, Caliban reluctantly admits that his cap of liberty 'won't fit' and that the three prisoners should 'surrender', 'quietly submit', and 'to [Prospero's] government send in adhesion' (p. 29). But no sooner does Prospero compel the revolutionaries to capitulate than he leaves the island, granting liberty to Caliban – not Ariel – as casually as he renounces all claim to his former throne.

Here the intertwined allegories of French and Italian revolutions cease, and the Broughs dramatize an imaginary turn of events. Not only does Ferdinand II – in the theatrical guise of Prospero – relinquish control of Sicily and leave the indigenous islanders to govern themselves, but he also abdicates his Neapolitan throne. It bears remembering that the burlesque was written no later than the summer of 1848, when the outcome of uprisings in Sicily and Naples was far from clear. *The Enchanted Isle* certainly envisions its preferred outcome: a complete victory for the Italian revolutionaries. Yet can we really speak of the play's preferences? After all, the logic of the burlesque narrative ends in equivocation. Naples remains an absolute monarchy, ruled by Prospero's brother Alonzo. Caliban's freedom is neither a constitutional right nor a spoil of victory but the mere bequest of his departing sovereign. Gratuitous in the strictest sense, his freedom only confirms the power of autocrats to dictate who shall be free.

The few critics who have studied *The Enchanted Isle* typically argue that the play's anti-climactic resolution effectively suppresses any revolutionary impulses which may be shared by – or instilled in – the audience. Such accounts rightly focus on the defeated Caliban's final address to the audience:

> Excuse me, pray; my lawless acts completing,
> With stirring language I'll inflame this meeting.
> (*to audience*) Be noisy – and excuse the observation –
> Get up a *devil* of a *demon*stration;
> But not with *arms* – no, only with the *hand*.
> (*Indicating clapping.*)
> That's all we want. And, please to understand,
> Tho' noise 'mongst you we're wishing to increase –
> Here on the stage we wish to *keep the piece!*
> (R. Brough and W. Brough, *The Enchanted Isle*, pp. 31–2)

Trevor Griffiths, for example, maintains that the speech warns the audience not to confuse Caliban's 'plea for applause' with 'an incitement to riot' ('"This Island's Mine"', p. 133). Rather, the audience must sublimate its own political 'enthusiasm' within a 'purely aesthetic dimension'. In other words, the forcibly disarmed Caliban ends the play by disarming his audience, ensuring that it substitutes clapping hands for gun shots and preserves the stage as a depoliticized zone of comic delectation. To '*keep the piece*' onstage requires that the audience 'keep the peace' offstage.

Such a reading is untenable, I believe, not the least because it remains insensitive to the structural ambiguities of the burlesque genre.[69] No burlesque ever possesses complete freedom to determine the course of its own narrative because it always depends upon a previously traced original narrative. Moreover, Griffiths' reading ignores the overt radicalism of Robert Brough's other writings. No one as feral as Brough, a man who came of political age in the 'Hungry Forties', would countenance a play which promotes subjugation. A year before *The Enchanted Isle*, Brough translated Jean de Béranger's *Songs of the Empire, the Peace, and the Restoration*, written after the 1830 return of the Bourbon monarchy. In the poem 'The Deluge', Béranger predicts that the surging waves of the 'People' will eventually submerge royal dynasties: 'Unhappy monarchs! they must all be drown'd' (*Béranger's Songs*, p. 161). Such a violent image provides us with a model for a republican reading of *The Tempest* – or, indeed, *The Enchanted Isle* – in which the storm at sea is not the first step in Prospero's cabalistic strategy to restore himself to the Duchy of Milan but the death knell for monarchy itself. The driving force behind the storm is not the calculating tyrant–magician, but the irrepressible sentiments of a people struggling to be free. Certainly, I am not proposing a causal link between *The Enchanted Isle* and Brough's translation of Béranger. But I am proposing that by studying these texts in conjunction we can avoid reductive interpretations of the burlesque which render it uncharacteristically passive. Let us remember that Brough was desperate to be taken '*au sérieux*' (Preface, *Songs of the 'Governing Classes'*, p. x). Fearful that readers would dismiss his political verse as harmless satire, Brough was anxious that his 'earnest convictions' not be 'passed by as a collection of ephemeral squibs written in the spirit of the merest tomfoolery' (p. ix). 'I have certainly made jokes for a livelihood', he admitted, 'but I do not see that I am thereby disqualified from giving serious utterance to my feelings on vital questions'.

The satirist's affirmation of the underlying sobriety of his writings becomes even more relevant when we assess the political acuity of his

---

[69] Brough's *Alfred the Great; or, the Minstrel King* advances a similarly ambiguous outlook on revolution. Oswith, Alfred's aide-de-camp, punningly discloses when taken prisoner by the Danes that '[t]he air of Continental revolution / I fear won't suit my British Constitution'. The playful assertion means both that the unwritten British constitution can withstand the threat of anarchy and that Britons do not have the individual resolve – are not constitutionally suited – to bring about their own emancipation (Robert Brough, *Alfred the Great; or, the Minstrel King. An Historical Extravaganza*, London: Thomas Hailes Lacy, n.d., p. 12).

theatrical burlesques. In the peaceful conclusion to *The Enchanted Isle* we see not, as Griffiths would have it, the defeat of burlesque – its capitulation to harmless buffoonery – but rather the laying bare of its very dynamic in which symbolic reality and empirical reality are carefully distinguished. The Broughs' revolution unfolds within an 'aesthetic dimension', as Griffiths rightly states; but the revolution is not unavailing for that. The aesthetic has ideologies of its own. Through Caliban's punning injunction to '*keep the piece*', the burlesque discloses that its radical politics operate entirely within the symbolic order, that the performance will never be released from the confines of representation. Although the burlesque unabashedly trades in political topicalities, it does not serve a chiefly propagandistic function for any specific revolutionary agenda. Actual riots and rebellions throughout Europe were effecting far more change than could be brought about by a riot in the Adelphi Theatre. Like the anonymous burlesque of *King John*, the Broughs' burlesque of *The Tempest* re-imagines political possibilities which have standing only within the world constituted by the play itself. Because these imagined realities have no empirical standing they cannot – by definition – be transferred from the stage to the stalls, where they might be 'taken up' by the audience and carried outside the theatre. To explain that theatrical symbols and political actualities are distinct is not, however, to presume the worthlessness of symbols. Rather, it is to explain that the distinctive value of performative imaginings lies in their ability to bring into a virtual existence a reality which has yet to find an immediate, codifiable existence. To fault *The Enchanted Isle* for not inciting an actual revolution is to misperceive how burlesques operate. Burlesque laughter occurs in the space between the audience's empirically ordained reality and the performance's rhetorically imagined reality.

The uncompromised ideological vigour of *The Enchanted Isle* becomes more pronounced still when we set the burlesque alongside contemporary stage adaptations of *The Tempest*. The Halévy–Scribe opera invites direct comparison. In his prolix apology for *La Tempesta*, Morris Barnett argued that a lavish and spectacular opera was the most appropriate theatrical form for Shakespeare's play because his 'scene is laid in regions of pure fancy, peopled by personages derived not from observation and the worldly wisdom of the comic dramatist, but from the pure inspiration and unshackled genius of the poet'.[70] It would be difficult to imagine a more Romantic account of *The Tempest* than this, in which the play's lush

---

[70] Morris Barnett, *'The Tempest' as a Lyrical Drama* (London: J. Mitchell, 1850), p. 16.

idealism sprang directly from Shakespeare's private inspiration. When juxtaposed with this account of disinterested aestheticism, the hard-hitting political punch of the Broughs' *The Enchanted Isle* must strike us – even in the face of Caliban's failed *coup d'état* – all the more forcefully. That the Broughs' play, under the new title *La! Tempest! Ah!*, was performed as a spoof of the opera *La Tempesta* reminds us just how antagonistic the burlesque remained toward socially irresolute treatments of Shakespeare's play.

But irresolution may still have won the day. Burnand's *Ariel*, produced nearly forty years after the Broughs' burlesque, was derided by *Dramatic Notes* for being as 'tasteless as a mild cigarette' and as 'insipid as a lemon squash' (October 1883, p. 48). A politically conscious burlesque might have been entitled *Prospero* or, more daringly, *Caliban*. By contrast, the title *Ariel* confirms that the performance had been successfully absorbed within the late-Victorian cult of spectacular fairy extravaganzas. Of course the 'mashers' in the Gaiety audience could not have cared less. No longer the 'Sons of freedom', as Caliban addressed the Adelphi audience in 1848, the docile young men of the Gaiety in 1883 only too gladly succumbed to the charms of Nellie Farren's Ariel, allowing themselves to be lulled into submission by female sensuality. A burlesque composed 'for the special patrons of the Gaiety', *Dramatic Notes* declared, was no better than 'pap food for overgrown infants'.

Yet the infantilized audience took its cue from the infantilized world depicted on the stage. Ariel was not the only inane character in the play since Caliban himself appeared less a freedom-fighter than a whining schoolboy. Not entirely mindless, this puerile characterization satirizes the emerging view of Caliban as the evolutionary link between *Homo sapiens* and the lower primates.[71] As Sir Daniel Wilson argued in the first Darwinian reading of *The Tempest*, Caliban represents the 'half-human link between the brute and man'. Mindful, perhaps, of Wilson's 1873 treatise, Burnand depicts Caliban not as the primitive progenitor of mankind but as an immature schoolboy.[72] As the playwright himself remarked, his burlesque Caliban was a 'backward boy' (Fol. Y.c. 327 1a–d).

[71] In Matthew Monck's *Prospero; or, the King of the Caliban Islands* (Imperial Theatre, 1883) the revolutionary conspiracy is reversed as Prospero, Ferdinand, Miranda, Gonzalo, and Alonzo plot to 'revel in a revolution' to overthrow Caliban (British Library Add Mss 53,308 T, f. 30). Their song – 'Caliban, Caliban, we will kill Caliban / That foolish, mis-shapen, baboonish young man / That monkey, that ape, that Catamaran / We'll kill Caliban' – provides further evidence that theatrical realizations of the so-called 'missing link' Caliban appeared first on the burlesque stage.

[72] Daniel Wilson, *Caliban: The Missing Link* (London: Macmillan and Co., 1873), p. 14.

In the performance, Caliban bemoans his failed attempt to master geography, Latin, and Greek in 'Dr. Prospero's School' and describes himself in a song as a mere 'blunderhead, woodeny, / Dunderhead, puddeny, / Terrible backward boy!' (Burnand, *Ariel*, BL Add Mss 53,301 J, fols. 10, 24). By the end of the play, however, Caliban learns to read. He also learns to wash his face and comb his hair. There is a transformational narrative here, but it is more about etiquette than evolution. The comic potential of depicting Caliban as a 'blunderhead' is, at best, feeble; it is little more than the ritualized ranting of an overgrown English public schoolboy. Of greater significance, however, is that Burnand forecloses the play's potential for political satire by failing to rise above the tedium of adolescent pranks. So harmless is this burlesque Caliban that, far from plotting to overthrow Prospero, he actually assists his teacher in preparing the apparitional banquet to trick Alonzo, Sebastian, and Antonio.

Here, then, is a burlesque of *The Tempest* which amounts to little more than an insipid fairy extravaganza performed before an infantilized audience. Burnand's play has much more in common with the lush exoticism of the Halévy–Scribe opera than with the pointed political topicality of the Broughs' burlesque. *Ariel* substituted the pleasures of an inward-looking aesthetic for political activity directed at the external world. No longer tempest-tossed, but tempest-tamed.

Bibliography

I. NINETEENTH-CENTURY SHAKESPEARE BURLESQUES

A'Beckett, Gilbert Abbott. *King John (with the Benefit of the Act)*. London: W. Strange, 1837. British Library Add Mss 42,944, fols. 249–61b.

Anon. *Hamlet; or, Not Such a Fool as He Looks*. Cambridge: W. Metcalfe and Son, 1882.

Julius Caesar Travestie . . . By an Amateur. Brighton: Curtis and Sons, n.d.

King John. A Grand, New, Entirely Original, Historical Burlesque in Five Scenes. Fol. Y.d. 303. Folger Shakespeare Library, Washington, DC.

King Richard III According to an Act of Parliament. 1854. British Library Add Mss 52,947 B.

Kynge Lear and Hys Faythfulle Foole. Burlesque in One Act. 1860. British Library Add Mss 52,994 C.

Macbeth. A Burlesque. Nottingham: J. N. Dunn, 1866.

Macbeth Bottled into a Burletta. 1842. British Library Add Mss 42,962, fols. 427–49b.

Macbeth Modernised. London: n.p., 1838.

Richard the Third Travesty. London: E. Duncombe, 1823.

Romeo and Juliet; or, the Shaming of the True: An Atrocious Outrage. Oxford: T. and G. Shrimpton, 1868.

Romeo and Juliet Travesty. London: T. Hookham, Jun., 1812.

A Thin Slice of Ham let! Cut for Fancy Fare. London: Jason Wade, n.d.

Barton, [—]. *Hamlet According to an Act of Parliament*. 1853. British Library Add Mss 52,943 M.

Beckington, Charles. *Hamlet the Dane; A Burlesque Burletta*. Newcastle-upon-Tyne: M. Moss, 1847.

Blanchard, E. L. *The Merchant of Venice (very far indeed) from the Text of Shakespeare. A Burlesque Operatic Extravaganza in One Act*. 1843. British Library Add Mss 42,968, fols. 688–700.

Brough, Robert, and William Brough. *The Enchanted Isle; or, Raising the Wind Upon the Most Approved Principles*. London: National Acting Drama Office, n.d. British Library Add Mss 43,028, fols. 515–58b (prologue only).

Brough, William. *Perdita; or, the Royal Milkmaid*. London: Thomas Hailes Lacy, n.d. British Library Add Mss 52,961 K.

Brougham, John. *Much Ado about a Merchant of Venice*. New York: Samuel French, n.d.
A Recollection of O'Flannigan and the Fairies. New York: Samuel French, n.d. [*c*. 1856].
Burnand, F. C. *Antony and Cleopatra; or, His-tory and Her-story in a Modern Nilo-metre*. London: Strand, 1866.
Ariel, a Burlesque Fairy Drama in Three Acts and Four Tableaux. 1883. British Library Add Mss 53,301 J.
Our Own Antony and Cleopatra. London: E. Rimmel, 1873.
The Rise and Fall of Richard III; or, a New Front to an Old Dickey. London: Phillips, n.d.
'By, William'. *Richard III. Travestie; in Three Acts with Annotations*. London: Sherwood, Neely & Jones, 1816.
Byron, H. J. *The Rival Othellos*. 1861. British Library Add Mss 54,163 I.
Chalmers, John E. *King Leer and His Darters*. 1848. British Library Add Mss 43,001, fols. 393–409.
Coyne, J. Stirling. *New Grand, Historical, Bombastical, Musical and Completely Illegitimate Tragedy to be Called 'Richard III'*. 1844. British Library Add Mss 42,973, fols. 2–19.
This House to be Sold: (The Property of the late William Shakspeare) Inquire Within. London: National Acting Drama Office, 1847. British Library Add Mss 43,005, fols. 890–916.
Craig, Robert. *Hamlet; or, Wearing of the Black*. Fol. D.a. 68. Folger Shakespeare Library, Washington, DC.
Dowling, Maurice G. *Othello Travestie: an Operatic Burlesque Burletta in Two Acts*. London: J. Duncombe & Co., n.d.
Romeo and Juliet, as the Law Directs. An Operatic Burlesque Burletta. London: J. Duncombe and Co., n.d. British Library Add Mss 42,941, fols. 761–78.
Gilbert, W. S. *Rosencrantz and Guildenstern*. *Fun* 12–26 December 1874. Reprinted in *Original Plays by W. S. Gilbert*. 3rd ser. London: Chatto and Windus, 1903.
Gordon, George L., and G. W. Anson. *Hamlet à la Mode*. 1876. British Library Add Mss 53,173 D.
Griffin, G. W. H. *Shylock, a Burlesque, as Performed by the Griffin & Christy's Minstrels*. New York: Happy Hours Co., n.d.
Gurney, Richard. *Romeo and Juliet Travesty*. London: T. Hookham, Jr, *et al.*, 1812.
Halliday, Andrew. *Romeo and Juliet Travestie; or, the Cup of Cold Poison*. London: Thomas Hailes Lacy, n.d. British Library Add Mss 52,986 G.
Hazelwood, Colin. *New King Richard the Third; a Burlesque Extravaganza*. 1873. British Library Add Mss 53,200 B.
'Ibef'. *Othello Travestie*. London: J. J. Stockdale, 1813.
'Lloyd, Horace Amelius' [pseud. William Hughes Logan]. *Rummio and Judy*. Edinburgh: John Menzies, 1841.

Malone, [—]. *Macbeth According to an Act of Parliament.* 1853. British Library Add Mss 52,939 I.
Richard the Third. A Burlesque Operatic Edition of Master Shakespeare's Celebrated Tragedy with Additional Notes. 1854. British Library Add Mss 52,947 B.
Mathews, Charles. *Othello, the Moor of Fleet Street.* 1833. British Library Add Mss 42,920, fols. 77–95. Ed. Manfred Draudt. Tübingen: Francke, 1993.
Monck, Matthew. *Prospero; or, the King of the Caliban Islands.* 1883. British Library Add Mss 53,308 T.
Moore, Rush. *Macbeth Travestie in Three Acts.* Calcutta: S. Greenway, 1820.
Morgan, James. *Coriolanus; a Burlesque.* Liverpool: S. A. Hurton, 1846.
Northall, W. K. *Macbeth Travestie. In Two Acts.* New York: William Taylor & Co., 1847.
Plowman, Thomas Forder. *Romeo Redivivus.* Oxford: Slatter and Rose, 1881.
Poole, John. *Hamlet Travestie: In Three Acts, with Burlesque Annotations.* London: J. M. Richardson, 1811.
Poole, John F. *Richard III, The Crookedest Man in New York.* Tony Pastor Collection, Harry Ransom Humanities Research Center, The University of Texas at Austin, Austin, TX.
Romeo and Juliet; or, the Beautiful Blonde who Dyed for Love. New York: n.p., 1869.
Rice, George Edward. *Hamlet Prince of Denmark; an Old Play in a New Garb.* Boston: Ticknor, Reed, and Fields, 1852.
Selby, Charles. *Kynge Richard ye Third; or, Ye Battel of Bosworth Field.* London: Thomas Hailes Lacy, n.d. British Library Add Mss 42,973, fols. 391–413.
Spry, R. *Macbeth, a Burlesque.* 1857. British Library Add Mss 52,967 N.
Talfourd, Francis. *Hamlet Travestie.* Oxford: J. Vincent, 1849.
Macbeth Somewhat Removed from the Text of Shakespeare. London: Thomas Hailes Lacy, n.d.
The Merchant of Venice Travestie. A Burlesque in One Act. Oxford: E. T. Spiers, 1849.
Shylock; or, The Merchant of Venice Preserved. London: Thomas Hailes Lacy, n.d. British Library Add Mss 52,941 I.
Wells, Stanley (ed.). *Nineteenth-Century Shakespeare Burlesques.* 5 vols. London: Diploma Press, 1977.

II. MANUSCRIPT SOURCES

Birmingham Shakespeare Library

Promptbooks
Macbeth Travestie (Francis Talfourd), *Shylock; or, the Merchant of Venice Preserved* (Francis Talfourd), *Othello Travestie* (Maurice Dowling), *Kynge Richard ye Third* (Charles Selby), *The Rise and Fall of Richard III* (F. C. Burnand), *Romeo and Juliet Travestie* (Andrew Halliday).

British Library

Additional Manuscripts
  Lord Chamberlain's Plays (see titles listed above)

Folger Shakespeare Library

F. C. Burnand Letters
Charles Kean Letters
Tom Taylor Letters
Dramatic Records Scrapbooks
Theatrical Miscellany Scrapbooks
Promptbooks
  Hamlet Prince of Denmark; an Old Play in a New Garb (George Edward Rice), *Hamlet; or, Wearing of the Black* (Robert Craig), *Hamlet Travestie* (John Poole), *Kynge Richard ye Third* (Charles Selby), *Macbeth Somewhat Removed from the Text of Shakespeare* (Francis Talfourd), *Macbeth Travestie* (W. K. Northall), *Much Ado about a Merchant of Venice* (John Brougham)

Harry Ransom Humanities Research Center, The University of Texas at Austin

Robert Brough Letters
Tony Pastor Collection
Promptbooks
  Burlesque Macbeth (anon.), *Romeo and Juliet; or, the Beautiful Blonde who Dyed for Love* (John F. Poole), *Richard III, The Crookedest Man in New York* (John F. Poole)

Harvard Theatre Collection

'Hugo Vamp's Comic Dramatic Shakespearean Scenas'
  Hamlet, the Black Prince of Denmark, Kynge Rycharde Ye Thyrde, The Merchant of Venice, Ye Song of Macbeth
Promptbooks
  Hamlet Travestie (John Poole), *King John (with the Benefit of the Act)* (Gilbert Abbott à Beckett), *Kynge Richard ye Third* (Charles Selby), *Macbeth Travestie* (Francis Talfourd), *Othello Travestie* (Maurice Dowling), *Perdita; or, the Royal Milkmaid* (William Brough), *Richard III. Travestie* ('William By'), *Romeo and Juliet Travestie* (Andrew Halliday), *Shylock; or, the Merchant of Venice Preserved* (Francis Talfourd), *This House to be Sold* (J. Stirling Coyne)

Theatre Museum, London

Production and Building Files
  Adelphi, Covent Garden, Drury Lane, Gaiety, Haymarket, Her Majesty's, Lyceum, Olympic, Princess's, Strand

III. NEWSPAPERS AND PERIODICALS

The Academy
All the Year Round
Athenaeum
Belgravia
Bell's Life in London
Bell's Weekly Messenger
Bentley's Miscellany
Blackwood's Magazine
Contemporary Review
Cornhill Magazine
Court Journal
Critic
Daily News
Dramatic Mirror
Dramatic Notes
Dublin University Magazine
Era
Examiner
Fraser's Magazine
Gentleman's Magazine
Household Words
Illustrated London News
Illustrated Times
John Bull
Leader
Literary Gazette
Lloyd's Weekly
Morning Advertiser
Morning Chronicle
Morning Post
New Monthly Magazine
The New York Times
Observer
Penny Magazine
People's Journal
Players
Punch
Quarterly Review
Saint Paul's
Saturday Review
The Spectator
Standard
Tallis's Dramatic Magazine
The Theatre
Theatrical Journal
Theatrical Observer
Theatrical Times
The Times
Under the Clock
Universal Review
Welcome Guest
Westminster Review

IV. PRE-TWENTIETH-CENTURY BOOKS, ESSAYS, AND PLAYSCRIPTS

A'Beckett, Arthur William. *Green-Room Recollections*. London: Simpkin, Marshall, Ltd, 1896.

A'Beckett, Gilbert Abbott. *The Quizziology of the British Drama*. London: Punch Office, 1846.

Adams, W. Davenport. *A Book of Burlesque: Sketches of English Stage Travestie and Parody*. London: Henry & Co., 1891.

Anon. *Hamlet, A Comic Song*. London, c. 1853.

Archer, William. *About the Theatre*. London: T. Fisher Unwin, 1886.

    English Dramatists of To-Day. London: Sampson Low, 1882.

Arnold, Matthew. *Culture and Anarchy*. 1869. Ed. Samuel Lipman. New Haven: Yale University Press, 1994.

    The Poetical Works of Matthew Arnold. Ed. C. B. Tinker and H. F. Lowry. London: Oxford University Press, 1963.

Barnett, Morris. '*The Tempest' as a Lyrical Drama*. London: J. Mitchell, 1850.

Bedford, Paul. *Recollections and Wanderings of Paul Bedford*. London: Strand, 1867.
Bertram, J. G. *Glimpses of Real Life as Seen in the Theatrical World and in Bohemia*. Edinburgh: William P. Nimmo, 1864.
Blanchard, E. L. *Life and Reminiscences of E. L. Blanchard*. 2 vols. London: n.p., n.d.
Brough, Robert. *Alfred the Great; or, the Minstrel King. An Historical Extravaganza*. London. Thomas Hailes Lacy, n.d.
   Masaniello; or the Fish'oman of Naples. London: Thomas Hailes Lacy, n.d.
   Songs of the 'Governing Classes', and other Lyrics. Written in a Seasonable Spirit of 'Vulgar Declamation'. 1856. London: Vizetelly & Co., 1890.
Brough, Robert (ed. and trans.). *Béranger's Songs of the Empire, the Peace, and the Restoration*. London: Addey and Co., 1856.
Burnand, F. C. *The 'A.D.C.' Being the Personal Reminiscences of the University Amateur Dramatic Club Cambridge*. 2nd edn. London: Chapman and Hall, 1880.
   Patient Penelope; or, the Return of Ulysses. London: Thomas Hailes Lacy, n.d.
Carlyle, Thomas. *On Heroes, Hero-Worship, and the Heroic in History*. London: James Fraser, 1841.
Cole, John. *Life and Theatrical Times of Charles Kean, F. S. A*. 2 vols. London: Richard Bentley, 1859.
Coleman, John. *Memoirs of Samuel Phelps*. London: Remington & Co. Publishers, 1886.
   Players and Playwrights I Have Known. London: Chatto and Windus, 1888.
A Collection of Poems Written upon several Occasions By several Persons. London, 1673.
Cook, Dutton. *Nights at the Play*. 2 vols. London: Chatto and Windus, 1883.
   On the Stage: Studies of Theatrical History and the Actor's Art. London: Sampson Low, 1883.
Donne, William Bodham. *Essays on the Drama*. London: John W. Parker and Son, 1858.
Downes, John. *Roscius Anglicanus, or an Historical Review of the Stage*. London, 1708.
Dryden, John, and William Davenant. *The Tempest, or the Enchanted Island. A Comedy*. London, 1674.
Duffet, Thomas. *Epilogue. Being a new Fancy after the old, and most surprising way of 'Macbeth'* ... London, 1674.
   The Mock-Tempest: or The Enchanted Castle. Acted at the Theatre Royal. London, 1675.
Eliot, George. *Impressions of Theophrastus Such*. 1879. Edinburgh and London: William Blackwood and Sons, 1901.
Erle, T. W. *Letters from a Theatrical Scene-Painter*. London: Marcus Ward & Co., 1880.
Fairholt, F. W. *The Grimaldi Shakspere*. London: J. Russell Smith, 1853.
Filon, Augustin. *The English Stage*. London: John Milne, 1897.
Foot, Jesse. *The Life of Arthur Murphy*. London: J. Faulder, 1811.
'Full Report of the Trial "*Cox* v. *Kean*"'. London: J. Duncombe, n.d.

Hallam, Henry. *View of the State of Europe During the Middle Ages*. 1818. New edn 3 vols. London: John Murray, 1872.
Halliday, Andrew (ed.). *The Savage-Club Papers*. London: Tinsley Bros, 1867.
Hamilton, Walter (ed.). *Parodies of the Works of English and American Authors*. 6 vols. London: Reeves and Turner, 1885.
Hazlitt, William. *Characters of Shakespear's Plays*. London: C. H. Reynell, 1817.
  The Complete Works of William Hazlitt. Vol. VI. Ed. P. P. Howe. 21 vols. London: J. M. Dent and Sons Ltd, 1931.
  A View of the English Stage. London: Robert Stodart, 1818.
Hollingshead, John. *Gaiety Chronicles*. London: Archibald Constable & Co., 1891.
  My Lifetime. 2 vols. London: Sampson Low, Marston & Co., 1895.
Hotten, J. C. *The Slang Dictionary*. 1859. London: Chatto and Windus, 1891.
Hutton, Laurence. *Curiosities of the American Stage*. New York: Harper and Bros., 1891.
Johnson, Samuel. 'Preface to Shakespeare'. 1765. London, 1778.
Knight, Charles. *Studies of Shakspere*. London: Charles Knight, 1849.
Knowles, Sheridan. *The Dramatic Works of James Sheridan Knowles*. Vol. I. London: Edward Moxon, 1841.
Langbaine, Gerald. *An Account of the English Dramatick Poets*. Oxford, 1691.
Macdonnell, Patrick. *An Essay on the Play of 'The Tempest'*. London: John Fellowes, 1840.
Marston, Westland. *Our Recent Actors*. London: Sampson Low, 1888.
Mathews, Brander, and Laurence Hutton (eds.). *Actors and Actresses of Great Britain and the United States*. New York: Cassell & Co., 1886.
Mathews, Charles James. *Letter from Mr. Charles Mathews to the Dramatic Authors of France*. London: J. Mitchell, 1852.
Mayhew, Henry. *London Labour and the London Poor*. 3 vols. London: C. Griffin and Co., 1861.
  The Wandering Minstrel. London: John Dicks, n.d.
Merivale, Charles. *Autobiography*. London: Edward Arnold, 1899.
Morley, Henry. *Journal of a London Playgoer from 1851 to 1866*. London: George Routledge & Sons, 1866.
Nicholson, Renton. *Rogue's Progress: The Autobiography of 'Lord Chief Baron' Nicholson*. 1863. Ed. John L. Bradley. Boston: Houghton Mifflin Co., 1965.
Pemberton, T. Edgar. *The Life and Writings of T. W. Robertson*. London: Richard Bentley, 1893.
Pepys, Samuel. *The Diary of Samuel Pepys*. Ed. Robert Latham and William Matthew. 11 vols. Berkeley and Los Angeles: University of California Press, 1970–8.
Phelps, Henry P. *Hamlet from the Actors' Standpoint*. New York: Edgar S. Werner, 1890.
Phelps, W. May. *The Life and Life-Work of Samuel Phelps*. London: Sampson Low, 1886.
Planché, James Robinson. *The Camp at the Olympic*. 1853. British Library Add Mss 52,942 M.

Costumes of Shakespeare's Tragedy of 'Hamlet' Selected and Arranged from the Best Authorities... London: John Miller, 1825.
The Discreet Princess; or, the Three Glass Distaffs. London: Thomas Hailes Lacy, n.d.
The Drama at Home; or, An Evening with Puff. London: S. G. Fairbrother, 1844.
The Extravaganzas of J. R. Planché, 1825–1871. 5 vols. London: Samuel French, 1879.
The Golden Fleece. London: S. G. Fairbrother, n.d.
Plays by James Robinson Planché. Ed. Donald Roy. Cambridge: Cambridge University Press, 1986.
Recollections and Reflections. 2 vols. London: Sampson Low, Marston & Co., Ltd, 1872.
Pollock, Frederick (ed.). *Macready's Reminiscences.* New York: Harper & Brothers, 1875.
Report from the Select Committee on Dramatic Literature. London: House of Commons, 1832.
Report from the Select Committee on Theatrical Licences and Regulations. London: House of Commons, 1866.
Robertson, T. W. *The Principal Dramatic Works of Thomas William Robertson.* London: Sampson Low, 1889.
Robinson, Henry Crabb. *The London Theatre 1811–1866: Selections from the Diary of Henry Crabb Robinson.* Ed. Eluned Brown. London: The Society for Theatre Research, 1966.
Russell, William Clark (ed.). *Representative Actors.* London: Frederick Warne, n.d.
Sala, G. A. *The Life and Adventures of George Augustus Sala.* London: n.p., 1895.
Robson: A Sketch. London: John Camden Hotten, 1864.
Scott, Clement. *The Drama of Yesterday and Today* 2 vols. London: Macmillan, 1899.
Scribe, Eugène, and Fromental Halévy. *La Tempesta. An Entirely New Grand Opera in Three Acts.* London: J. Mitchell, 1850.
Smith, Albert. *Why Our Theatres Are Not Supported*... London: n.p., 1848.
Smith, Albert (ed.). *Sketches of London Life and Character.* London: Dean & Son, n.d.
Stuart, Charles Douglas, and A. J. Park. *The Variety Stage.* London: T. Fisher Unwin, n.d. [c. 1895].
Swinburne, A. C. *A Study of Shakespeare.* London: Chatto and Windus, 1880.
Thackeray, W. M., et al. *The Comick Almanack 1844–1853.* 2nd ser. London: Chatto and Windus, n.d.
Thompson, Richard. *An Historical Essay on the Magna Charta of King John.* London: John Major, 1829.
Ulrici, Hermann. *Shakspeare's Dramatic Art.* Trans. A. J. W. Morrison. London: Chapman Brothers, 1846.
Vamp, Hugo [pseud. John Robert O'Neill]. 'Kynge Rycharde Ye Thyrde – Hys Historie, as Literally Per-verted from the Text of Shakespeare'. London: Davidson's Musical Treasury, n.d.

Vandenhoff, George. *Leaves from an Actor's Notebook*. New York and London: D. Appleton and Co., 1860.
Watson, Aaron. *The Savage Club*. London: T. Fisher Unwin, 1907.
Wenckstern, Otto. *Saunterings in and about London*. London: Nathaniel Cooke, 1853.
Wheler, R. B. *Historical and Descriptive Account of the Birth-place of Shakespeare*. Stratford-upon-Avon: James Ward, 1824.
History and Antiquities of Stratford-upon-Avon ... Stratford-upon-Avon: J. Ward, 1806.
Whyte, Frederic. *Actors of the Century*. London: George Bell and Sons, 1898.
Wilson, Daniel. *Caliban: The Missing Link*. London: Macmillan and Co., 1873.
Yates, Edmund. *Edmund Yates: His Recollections and Experiences*. 3rd edn 2 vols. London: Richard Bentley and Son, 1884.

V. BOOKS AND ARTICLES

A'Beckett, Arthur William. *The à Becketts of 'Punch'; Memories of Father and Sons*. New York: E. P. Dutton and Co., 1903.
Allen, Robert C. *Horrible Prettiness: Burlesque and American Culture*. Chapel Hill: The University of North Carolina Press, 1991.
Altick, Richard D. *Punch: The Lively Youth of a British Institution, 1841–1851*. Columbus: Ohio State University Press, 1997.
The Shows of London. Cambridge, MA: Belknap Press, 1978.
Bailey, Peter. *Leisure and Class in Victorian England*. 2nd edn. London: Methuen, 1978.
Popular Culture and Performance in the Victorian City. Cambridge: Cambridge University Press, 1998.
Bakhtin, Mikhail. *The Dialogic Imagination*. Ed. Michael Holquist. Trans. Caryl Emerson and Michael Holquist. Austin: The University of Texas Press, 1981.
Bancroft, Marie, and Squire Bancroft. *The Bancrofts: Recollections of Sixty Years*. London: J. Murray, 1909.
Mr. and Mrs. Bancroft On and Off the Stage. London: Richard Bentley and Son, 1904.
Barnes, Donald Grove. *A History of the English Corn Laws from 1660–1846*. London: George Routledge & Sons, Ltd, 1930.
Barton Baker, H. *History of the London Stage*. 2nd edn. London: G. Routledge & Sons, Ltd, 1904.
Bate, Jonathan. 'Parodies of Shakespeare'. *Journal of Popular Culture*. 19.1 (Summer 1985), pp. 75–89.
Shakespearean Constitutions: Politics, Theatre, Criticism 1730–1830. Oxford: Clarendon Press, 1989.
Bate, Jonathan (ed.). *The Romantics on Shakespeare*. London: Penguin Books, 1992.
Bentley, Michael. *Politics without Democracy: Great Britain 1815–1914*. Totowa, NJ: Barnes & Noble Books, 1984.
Besant, Walter. *London in the Nineteenth Century*. London: A&C Black, 1909.

Best, G. F. A. *Mid-Victorian Britain, 1851–75*. London: Weidenfeld and Nicholson, 1979.
Bond, Donald F. *The Spectator*. 5 vols. Oxford: Clarendon Press, 1965.
Bond, Richmond P. *English Burlesque Poetry, 1700–1750*. Cambridge, MA: Harvard University Press, 1932.
Booth, Michael. *Prefaces to English Nineteenth-Century Theatre*. Manchester: Manchester University Press, 1980.
  Theatre in the Victorian Age. Cambridge: Cambridge University Press, 1991.
Booth, Michael (ed.). *English Plays of the Nineteenth Century*. 5 vols. Oxford: Clarendon Press, 1976.
Borgeson, Jess, Adam Long, and Daniel Singer. *The Compleat Works of Wllm Shkspr (abridged)*. New York: Applause Books, 1994.
Bouton, Archibald L. (ed.). *Matthew Arnold: Prose and Poetry*. New York: Charles Scribner's Sons, 1927.
Brailsford, Dennis. *Sport, Time and Society: The British at Play*. London: Routledge, 1991.
Braunmuller, A. R., and Michael Hattaway (eds.). *The Cambridge Companion to English Renaissance Drama*. Cambridge: Cambridge University Press, 1990.
Bristol, Michael D. *Big-Time Shakespeare*. London and New York: Routledge, 1996.
  Carnival and Theater. New York and London: Methuen, 1985.
Burnand, F. C. *Records and Reminiscences*. 2 vols. London: Methuen & Co., 1904.
Caesar, Terry. '"I Quite Forgot What – Say a Daffodilly": Victorian Parody'. *ELH* 51 (1984), pp. 795–818.
Cherry Red Productions, www.cherryredproductions.com .
Child, Harold. 'Stage History', in *King John*. The New Cambridge Shakespeare. London: Cambridge University Press, 1936.
Clinton-Baddeley, V. C. *The Burlesque Tradition in the English Theatre after 1660*. London: Methuen & Co., Ltd, 1952.
Cohn, Ruby. *Modern Shakespeare Offshoots*. Princeton: Princeton University Press, 1976.
Coleridge, Samuel Taylor. *Coleridge's Shakespearean Criticism*. Ed. Thomas Middleton Rayner. 2 vols. London: Constable & Co., Ltd, 1930.
Cross, Nigel. *The Common Writer: Life in Nineteenth-Century Grub Street*. Cambridge: Cambridge University Press, 1985.
Culler, Jonathan (ed.). *On Puns: The Foundation of Letters*. Oxford: Basil Blackwell, 1988.
Davis, Jim, and Victor Emeljanow. 'New Views of a Cheap Theatre: Reconstructing the Nineteenth-Century Theatre Audience'. *Theatre Survey* 39.2 (1998), pp. 53–72.
Davis, Tracy C. *Actresses as Working Women*. London: Routledge, 1991.
  The Economics of the British Stage 1800–1914. Cambridge: Cambridge University Press, 2000.
Davison, Peter. *Popular Appeal in English Drama to 1850*. London and Basingstoke: The Macmillan Press Ltd, 1982.
Dentith, Simon. *Parody*. London and New York: Routledge, 2000.

Diamond, Elin. 'Stoppard's *Dogg's Hamlet, Cahoot's Macbeth*: The Uses of Shakespeare'. *Modern Drama* 29 (1986), pp. 593–600.
DiLorenzo, Ronald Eugene (ed.). *Three Burlesque Plays of Thomas Duffet*. Iowa City: University of Iowa Press, 1972.
Dobell, A. E., and P. J. Dobell. 'A Catalogue of Autograph Letters, Manuscripts, and Historical Documents'. No. 26 London, 1923.
Dobson, Michael. '"Remember / First to Possess his Books": The Appropriation of *The Tempest* 1700–1800'. *Shakespeare Survey* 43 (1991), pp. 99–107.
Doyle, Anne T. *Elkanah Settle's 'The Empress of Morocco' and the Controversy Surrounding It, A Critical Edition*. New York and London: Garland Publishing, Inc., 1987.
Draudt, Manfred. '"Committing Outrage Against the Bard": Nineteenth-Century Travesties of Shakespeare in England and Austria'. *Modern Language Review* 88 (1993), pp. 102–9.
Dryden, John. *The Works of John Dryden*. Ed. Edward Niles Hooker and H. T. Swedenberg, Jr, *et al*. Berkeley and Los Angeles: University of California Press, 1956.
Ellis, James. 'The Counterfeit Presentment: Nineteenth-Century Burlesques of *Hamlet*'. *Nineteenth Century Theatre Research* 11.1 (Summer 1983), pp. 29–50.
Ellis, S. M. (ed.). *A Mid-Victorian Pepys. The Letters and Memoirs of Sir William Hardman, M.A, F.R.G.S.* London: Cecil Palmer, 1923.
Elson, John James (ed.). *The Wits; or, Sport upon Sport*. 1663, 1672. Ithaca: Cornell University Press, 1932.
Fay, C. R. *The Corn Laws and Social England*. London: Cambridge University Press, 1932.
Finn, Margot. *After Chartism*. Cambridge: Cambridge University Press, 1993.
Fischlin, Daniel, and Mark Fortier (eds.). *Adaptations of Shakespeare*. London: Routledge, 2000.
Fitzgerald, Percy. *Shakespearean Representation; its Laws and Limits*. London: Elliot Stock, 1908.
Foulkes, Richard. *The Shakespeare Tercentenary of 1864*. London: The Society for Theatre Research, 1984.
Foulkes, Richard (ed.). *Shakespeare and the Victorian Stage*. Cambridge: Cambridge University Press, 1986.
Granville-Barker, Harley. 'Exit Planché – Enter Gilbert'. *London Mercury* 25.149/150 (March and April 1932), pp. 457–66, 558–73.
Griffiths, Trevor R. '"This Island's Mine": Caliban and Colonialism', in *Critical Essays on Shakespeare's 'The Tempest'*. Ed. Alden T. Vaughan and Virginia Mason Vaughan. New York: G. K. Hall, 1998, pp. 130–51.
Guffey, George Robert (ed.). *After 'The Tempest'*. Los Angeles: William Andrew Clark Memorial Library, 1969.
Hannoosh, Michele. 'The Reflexive Function of Parody'. *Comparative Literature* 41.2 (Spring 1989), pp. 113–27.
Hewitt, Barnard. 'Mrs. John Wood and the Lost Art of Burlesque Acting'. *Theatre Journal* 13.2 (May 1961), pp. 82–5.

Holland, Peter (ed.). *A Midsummer Night's Dream*. Oxford: Clarendon Press, 1994.
Hunting, Penelope. *A History of the Society of Apothecaries*. London: The Society of Apothecaries, 1998.
Hutcheon, Linda. *A Theory of Parody: The Teachings of Twentieth-Century Art Forms*. New York and London: Methuen, 1985.
Jacobs, Henry E., and Claudia D. Johnson. *An Annotated Bibliography of Shakespearean Burlesques, Parodies, and Travesties*. New York: Garland Publishing, Inc., 1976.
Jaggard, William. *Shakespeare Bibliography*. Stratford-upon-Avon: The Shakespeare Press, 1911.
Jenkins, Anthony. *The Making of Victorian Drama*. Cambridge: Cambridge University Press, 1991.
Jenkins, T. A. *Parliament, Party and Politics in Victorian Britain*. Manchester: Manchester University Press, 1996.
John, Ivor B. (ed.). *The Life and Death of King John*. London: Methuen and Co., 1907.
Joyce, Patrick. *Democratic Subjects*. Cambridge: Cambridge University Press, 1994.
Jump, John. *Burlesque*. London: Methuen, 1972.
Kattwinkel, Susan (ed.). *Tony Pastor Presents: Afterpieces from the Vaudeville Stage*. Westport, CT: Greenwood Press, 1998.
Kitchin, George. *A Survey of Burlesque and Parody in English*. Edinburgh and London: Oliver and Boyd, 1931.
Lehnert, Martin. 'Arthur Murphy's *"Hamlet"'* Parodie (1772) auf David Garrick'. *Shakespeare Jahrbuch* 102 (1966), pp. 97–167.
Levine, Lawrence. *Highbrow/Lowbrow: The Emergence of Cultural Hierarchy in America*. Cambridge, MA: Harvard University Press, 1988.
MacDonald, Joyce Green. 'Acting Black: *Othello*, *Othello* Burlesques, and the Performance of Blackness'. *Theatre Journal* 46 (1994), pp. 133–46.
Mackinnon, Alan. *The Oxford Amateurs*. London: Chapman and Hall, Ltd, 1910.
Mahood, M. M. *Bit Parts in Shakespeare's Plays*. Cambridge: Cambridge University Press, 1992
  Shakespeare's Wordplay. London: Methuen and Co. Ltd, 1957.
Marcus, Leah. *Puzzling Shakespeare: Local Reading and its Discontents*. Berkeley: University of California Press, 1988.
Maus, Katharine Eisaman. 'Arcadia Lost: Politics and Revision in the Restoration *Tempest*'. *Renaissance Drama* n.s. 13 (1982), pp. 189–209.
Mazer, Cary. *Shakespeare Refashioned*. Ann Arbor: UMI Research Press, 1981.
McCarthy, Justin. *Portraits of the Sixties*. London: T. Fisher Unwin, 1903.
McCord, Norman. *English History 1815–1906*. Oxford: Oxford University Press, 1991.
Meisel, Martin. *Realizations: Narrative, Pictorial, and Theatrical Arts in Nineteenth-Century England*. Princeton: Princeton University Press, 1983.
Merchant, W. Moelwyn. *Shakespeare in Art*. Nottingham: Nottingham Art Gallery, 1961.
Merivale, Herman C. *Bar, Stage, and Platform*. London: Chatto & Windus, 1902.

Moody, Jane. 'Writing for the Metropolis: Illegitimate Performances of Shakespeare in Early Nineteenth-Century London'. *Shakespeare Survey* 47 (1994), pp. 61–9.
Mugglestone, Lynda. *'Talking Proper': The Rise of Accent as Social Symbol*. Oxford: Clarendon Press, 1995.
Müller-Schwefe, Gerhard. *Corpus Hamleticum*. Tübingen: Francke, 1987.
Müller-Schwefe, Gerhard (ed.). *Shakespeare im Narrenhaus*. Tübingen: Francke, 1990.
Nicoll, Allardyce. *A History of Early Nineteenth-Century Drama 1800–1850*. 2 vols. Cambridge: Cambridge University Press, 1930.
  A History of Late Nineteenth-Century Drama 1850–1900. 2 vols. Cambridge: Cambridge University Press, 1946.
Odell, G. C. D. *Shakespeare from Betterton to Irving*. 2 vols. New York: Charles Scribner's Sons, 1920.
'One of the Old Brigade'. *London of the Sixties*. London: Everett & Co., 1909.
Orgel, Stephen. 'The Authentic Shakespeare'. *Representations* 21 (Winter 1988), pp. 1–25.
  '"Counterfeit Presentments": Shakespeare's Ekphrasis', in *England and the Continental Renaissance*. Ed. Edward Chaney and Peter Mack. Woodbridge: The Boydell Press, 1990.
Parker, Patricia. *Shakespeare from the Margins: Language, Culture, Context*. Chicago: University of Chicago Press, 1996.
Parker, R. B. (ed.). *Coriolanus*. Oxford: Clarendon Press, 1994.
Pickering, Paul A., and Alex Tyrrell. *The People's Bread: A History of the Anti-Corn Law League*. London and New York: Leicester University Press, 2000.
Powell, Jocelyn. *Restoration Theatre Production*. London: Routledge & Kegan Paul, 1984.
Price, Richard. *British Society, 1680–1880: Dynamism, Containment and Change*. Cambridge: Cambridge University Press, 1999.
Reid, Alastair. *Social Classes and Social Relations in Britain 1850–1914*. Cambridge: Cambridge University Press, 1995.
Rinear, David L. *The Temple of Momus: Mitchell's Olympic Theatre*. Metuchen, NJ: The Scarecrow Press, Inc., 1987.
Ripley, John. *'Coriolanus' on Stage in England and America, 1609–1994*. Madison, NJ: Fairleigh Dickinson University Press, 1998.
Robinson, J. W. (ed.). *Theatrical Street Ballads*. London: The Society for Theatre Research, 1971.
Roche, Senga Wallace. 'Travesties and Burlesques of Shakespeare's Plays on the British Stage during the Nineteenth Century'. Unpublished Ph.D. dissertation. University of London, 1987.
Rose, Margaret. *Parody: Ancient, Modern, and Post-modern*. Cambridge: Cambridge University Press, 1993.
  Parody/Meta-Fiction. London: Croom Helm, 1979.
Rostron, David. 'Contemporary Political Comment in Four of J. P. Kemble's Shakespearean Productions'. *Theatre Research* 12.2 (1972), pp. 113–19.

Rowell, George. *The Victorian Theatre 1792–1914: A Survey.* 2nd edn. Cambridge: Cambridge University Press, 1978.
Rowell, George (ed.). *Victorian Dramatic Criticism.* London: Methuen, 1971.
Salomon, Jacob Bonnist. 'Dramatic Burlesques of Shakespeare in Great Britain Before 1900: A Stage History and Analysis'. Unpublished Ph.D. dissertation. University of Pennsylvania, 1975.
Saltz, David Z. 'When is the Play the Thing? – Analytic Aesthetics and Dramatic Theory'. *Theatre Research International* 20.3 (Autumn 1995), pp. 266–76.
Sands, Mollie. *Robson of the Olympic.* London: The Society for Theatre Research, 1979.
Schoch, Richard W. '"Chopkins, Late Shakespeare": The Bard and his Burlesques, 1810–1866'. *ELH* 67 (2000), pp. 973–91.
  Shakespeare's Victorian Stage: Performing History in the Theatre of Charles Kean. Cambridge: Cambridge University Press, 1998.
Scott, Harold. *The Early Doors: Origins of the Music Hall.* London: Nicholson & Watson, 1946.
Senelick, Laurence. *The Age and Stage of George L. Fox: 1825–1877.* Hanover, NH: University Press of New England, 1988.
Shafer, Yvonne. 'George L. Fox and the *Hamlet* Travesty'. *Theatre Studies* 24/25 (1977–9), pp. 79–93.
Sharp, R. Farquaharson. 'Travesties of Shakespeare's Plays'. *Library* 1 (June 1920), pp. 1–20.
Shattock, Joanne, and Michael Wolff (eds.). *The Victorian Press: Samplings and Soundings.* Leicester: Leicester University Press, 1982.
Shattuck, Charles H. *The Shakespeare Promptbooks.* Urbana: University of Illinois Press, 1964.
  William Charles Macready's 'King John'. Urbana: University of Illinois Press, 1962.
Sims, George R. *My Life: Sixty Years' Recollections of Bohemian London.* London: Eveleigh Nash Co., 1917.
Smith, F. B. *The Making of the Second Reform Bill.* London: Cambridge University Press, 1966.
Spence, Christopher (ed.). *Five Restoration Adaptations of Shakespeare.* Urbana: University of Illinois Press, 1965.
Stedman Jones, Gareth. *Languages of Class: Studies in English Working Class History 1832–1982.* Cambridge: Cambridge University Press, 1983.
Stephens, John Russell. *The Censorship of English Drama 1824–1901.* Cambridge: Cambridge University Press, 1980.
Stern, Tiffany. *Rehearsal from Shakespeare to Sheridan.* Oxford: Clarendon Press, 2000.
Stone, Lawrence. *Broken Lives: Separation and Divorce in England 1660–1857.* Oxford: Oxford University Press, 1993.
Summers, Montague. *Shakespeare Adaptations.* London: Jonathan Cape, 1922.
Summers, Montague (ed.). *The Rehearsal.* Stratford-upon-Avon: The Shakespeare Head Press, 1914.

Thomas, James Michael. *The Art of the Actor–Manager: Wilson Barrett and the Victorian Theatre*. Ann Arbor: UMI Research Press, 1984.
Thompson, F. M. L. *The Rise of Respectable Society*. Cambridge, MA: Harvard University Press, 1988.
Trussler, Simon (ed.). *Burlesque Plays of the Eighteenth Century*. Oxford: Oxford University Press, 1969.
Vaughan, Alden T., and Virginia Mason Vaughan. *Shakespeare's Caliban: A Cultural History*. New York: Cambridge University Press, 1991.
  The Tempest. The Arden Shakespeare. Walton-upon-Thames: Thomas Nelson and Sons Ltd, 1999.
Vernon, James. *Politics and the People: A Study of English Political Culture, c. 1815–1867*. Cambridge: Cambridge University Press, 1993.
Wagner, Leopold. *London Inns and Taverns*. New York: Frederick A. Stokes, 1925.
Wahrman, Dror. *Imagining the Middle Class*. Cambridge: Cambridge University Press, 1995.
Watson, E. B. *From Sheridan to Robertson*. Cambridge, MA: Harvard University Press, 1926.
Wearing, J. P. *American and British Theatrical Biography*. Metuchen, NJ: Scarecrow Press, 1979.
Wells, Stanley. 'Burlesques of Charles Kean's *The Winter's Tale*'. *Theatre Notebook* 16 (1962), pp. 78–83.
  'Shakespeare in Planché's Extravaganzas'. *Shakespeare Survey* 16 (1963), pp. 103–17.
  'Shakespearian Burlesques'. *Shakespeare Quarterly* 16 (1965), pp. 49–61.
Wheeler, David (ed.). *'Coriolanus': Critical Essays*. New York and London: Garland Publishing, Inc., 1995.
Whibley, Charles. *Political Portraits*. London: Macmillan and Co., Ltd, 1917.
Williams, Raymond. *Keywords: A Vocabulary of Culture and Society*. New York: Oxford University Press, 1985.
Willson, Robert F., Jr. *'Their Form Confounded': Studies in the Burlesque Play from Udall to Sheridan*. The Hague: Mouton, 1975.
Wilson, J. Dover (ed.). *King John*. The New Cambridge Shakespeare. London: Cambridge University Press, 1936.
Woodward, E. L. *The Age of Reform: 1815–1870*. Oxford: Clarendon Press, 1938.
Worthen, W. B. *Shakespeare and the Authority of Performance*. Cambridge: Cambridge University Press, 1997.
Young, Arlene. *Culture, Class and Gender in the Victorian Novel*. Basingstoke: Macmillan Press Ltd, 1999.

Index

Page numbers in italics denote references to illustrations.

Shakespeare burlesques are listed by author and by source text (e.g., *Rosencrantz and Guildenstern* is listed under 'Gilbert, W. S.' and 'Shakespeare, burlesques of *Hamlet*')

A'Beckett, Arthur William, 114
A'Beckett, Gilbert Abbott:
   King John (with the Benefit of the Act) (1837), 31–3, *32*, 38, 155
acting styles, 52, 53–4, 59–63, 85–6, 90, 100–1, 105, 167–8
Adams, W. Davenport, 37, 57
Addison, Joseph, 17
Adelphi Theatre, 14, 131, 179–80
alcohol, 126–9
Allcroft, F. W., 89
Allen, Robert C., 33
allusions *see* burlesque, language of
Anderson, John Henry, 179–80
Anti-Corn Law League, 165, 166–7, 169–73
antiquarianism, 31, 65, 87–9, 153–4
apothecaries, 119–24, 119 n. 35, 123 n. 41
Archer, William, 13, 38
aristocracy 171, 173–4
Arnold, Matthew, 74, 161 n. 20
Athenaeum, 76
audience:
   at burlesque theatres, 12–13, 13 n. 28, 29, 38–9, 45, 47, 48, 55, 100, 103, 107–15, 125–6, 129, 143, 180, 185, 186
   at legitimate theatres, 111, 169, 176
   at minor theatres, 107–8

Bailey, Peter, 80
Baker, H. Barton, 14, 14 n. 30, 100
Bakhtin, Mikhail, 19
Bancroft, Marie *see* Wilton, Marie
Bancroft, Squire, 149
Bardolatry:
   burlesque critique of, 3–4, 6–7, 27, 28, 52, 55, 67, 73, 85–6, 92
   hypocrisy of, 74–7, 83–5

Barnett, Morris, 185
Barrett, Wilson, 10–11, 14 n. 29, 86–7
Barton:
   Hamlet According to an Act of Parliament (1853), 12, 34, 91, 124, 125, 126
Bate, Jonathan, 20, 164–5, 167–8
Beaumont, Francis, 22–3
Bedford, Paul, 76–7, 177
beer *see* alcohol
Bell, Robert:
   Macbeth Modernised (1838), 11, 60, 124, 127
Bell's Life in London, 125
Bentley, Michael, 181
de Béranger, Pierre Jean, 184
Besant, Walter, 134
Blanchard, E. L.:
   The Merchant of Venice (very far indeed) from the Text of Shakespeare (1843), 11, 34, 127–8, 129
Blanchard, Thomas, 1, 2
Bliss, Lee, 23
Bohemianism, 135–8, 148
Booth, Michael, 14 n. 30, 16 n. 34, 107
boxing, 34, 124–6
Branagh, Kenneth, 21 n. 48
breakdown dance, 14 n. 30
Bright, John, 166–7, 176
Britannia Theatre, 14
Brooke, G. V., 85
Brough, Robert, 118, 136, 138
   Béranger's poems, translation of, 184
   burlesque plays:
      Alfred the Great (1859), 152 n. 3, 184 n. 69
      The Enchanted Isle (with W. Brough) (1848), 13, 91–2, 91 n. 65, 174, 177–86, *178*, 183
      Masaniello (1857), 177 n. 64

203

Brough, Robert (*Cont.*)
  La! Tempest! Ah! (with W. Brough) (1850), 91–2, 186
  political views of, 173–4, 180, 184
  Songs of the 'Governing Classes', 173–4, 173 n. 51, 184
Brough, William:
  Perdita (1856), 43–4, 63 n. 10, 92–5, 105, 110–11, *112*, 115–17, 117, 123 n. 41, 124 n. 42, 143–4, 144 n. 83, *145*, 160 n. 18
  see also Brough, Robert: *The Enchanted Isle* and *La! Tempest! Ah!*
burlesque:
  acting styles in, 14–15, 59–63, 103, 104
  ambivalence toward original text, 21, 55–6, 59, 63, 66–9, 70–3, 94–5
  in America, 3 n. 2, 3 n. 3
  audiences for, 12–13, 13 n. 28, 29, 38–9, 45, 47, 48, 55, 100, 103, 107–15, 125–6, 129, 143, 180, 185, 186
  Bardolatry, critique of, 3–4, 6–7, 27, 28, 52, 55, 67, 73, 85–6, 92
  bibliographies of, 10 n. 18
  and Bohemianism, 29
  and class, 80–1, 107–15, 118–19, 162–3, 170–1
  conventions of, 12, 14–15, 14 n. 30
  costumes for, 31, *32*, 60–1, *62*, 69, 144–5, 114 n. 83, *145*, 179
  criticism of, 19–21, 26–7, 70, 102
  defence of, 4, 57–8, 65–6
  definitions of, 17–19, 17 n. 37, 21 n. 47
  documentary evidence for, 17
  in Elizabethan and Jacobean drama, 22–3
  and ethnicity, 29 n. 65, 89 n. 57
  and historiography, 92–3
  iconography of, 8, *9*, *35*, 75, *76*, *79*, *133*, *144*
  intelligibility of, 28, 31–3, 37–8, 39–41, 42, 45–7
  irony of, 59–63
  language of:
    dialect, 38, 43–4, 45–6, 98, 99 n. 80
    puns, 42–8, 42 n. 21, 43 n. 23, 44 n. 26
    quotations, 66–9
    revisions, 48–56
    slang, 37, 44, 44 n. 25, 124, 129, 129–31
    topicality, 28, 33–41, 44, 50–1, 54, 154, 154 n. 13, 164, 172 n. 48, 177, 180 n. 67
  metatheatricality of, 27, 31–3, 34–7, 52–6, 69, 71, 105, 111, 154–5, 179–80
  and the middle class, 80, 107–15, 170–1
  and modernism, 19
  and the monarchy, 159–61, 160 n. 18
  non-English language, 11 n. 22
  origins of, 23–4
  performers of, 15
  politics, perspective on, 29, 151–2, 186–7
  popularity of, 4–6, 13
  populist rhetoric of, 119–24, 159–61, 171
  as private theatricals, 110
  promptbooks of, 16, 16 n. 34, 48–9, 49–50, 49 n. 34, *50*
  and racial stereotypes, 29 n. 65
  and respectability, 80–1, 113–18, 119–24, 128, 130–5, 143, 146–50
  and revolution, 177, 177 n. 64, 179, 180, 181–4, 184 n. 69, 186 n. 71
  scripts of, 15, 43 n. 23, 48–56, 52 n. 39, 110
  self-ridicule of, 103–6
  and Shakespeare:
    critique of, 92–3
    defence of, 4, 57–8, 65–6, 91–5
  and song, 15, 36, 99–100
  theatres, 14
  theories of, 18–19, 20–1
  types of, 4
Burnand, F. C., 134 n. 57, 136
  burlesque plays:
    Antony and Cleopatra; or, His-tory and Her-story in a Modern Nilo-metre (1866), 11
    Ariel (1883), 70–3, 71 nn. 17, 18, *72*, 72 n. 22, 186–7
    Our Own Antony and Cleopatra (1873), 70 n. 18
    The Rise and Fall of Richard III; or, a New Front to an Old Dickey (1868), 44
  as Cambridge undergraduate, 109
  defence of burlesque, 4
Byron, H. J.:
  and the Prince of Wales's Theatre, 148–9
  The Rival Othellos (1861), 85, 85 n. 51

Cambridge University, 109
Carlyle, Thomas, 74, 95, 165
Carr, J. Comyns:
  A Fireside Hamlet (1884), 11, 14, 14 n. 29
censorship, 36–7, 163
Chartism, 170 n. 44, 171–2, 174, 176, 177, 180–1, 182
Cibber, Colley, 58 n. 4
Cider Cellars, The, 34, 128, 138, 139, 139 n. 69
Clarke, John ('Little'), 109, 125
Clinton-Baddeley, V. C., 60
Coal Hole, The, 128, 130, 131, 134, 134 n. 60, 139, 139 nn. 69, 71, 143, 146
Cobden, Richard, 166–7
Cockney, 38, 44, 45–6
  see also burlesque, language of

Index

Coleridge, Samuel Taylor, 101, 175–6
Collier, J. P., 8
Colman (the Younger), George, 163 n. 26
Comic Almanack, 7, 135
Conway, Mrs F. B., 49, 51, 52, 54
Cook, Dutton, 98, 102
Corn Laws, 164–7, 169–73
Covent Garden Theatre, 14, 114
Cowden-Clarke, Charles, 18, 20 n. 43
Cowell, Sam, 7, 132, 132 n. 55
Coyne, J. Stirling:
  New Grand, Historical, Bombastical, Musical and Completely Illegitimate Tragedy to be called Richard III (1844), 10, 12, 13, 34, 127
  This House to be Sold (1847), 78–84, 78 n. 38, 81 n. 44, *82*, 83 n. 45, 85 n. 48
Craig, Robert:
  Hamlet; or, Wearing of the Black (c. 1866), 60, 126–7
crim. con., 140–3, 140 n. 75, 141 nn. 77, 78
Crimean War, 160 n. 18
crowd scenes, 168–9
Cruikshank, George, 7
Crump, Jeremy, 172
Culler, Jonathan, 42

Dallas, E. S., 45, 47, 87, 89, 98, 102, 130
Davenant, Sir William, 24
  The Enchanted Isle (1667), 26, 26 n. 59, 175
  Macbeth (1674), 24, 25
Dekker, Thomas, 22
DeLeon, T. C., 16, 60, 63 n. 11, 69
Dentith, Simon, 18
dialect *see* burlesque, language of
dialogism, 19
Diamond, Elin, 6
Dillon, Charles, 105
Dillon-Croker, T. F., 37–8
divorce law, 140–1
Dixon, W. Hepworth, 76, 79–80, 79 n. 41
Dobson, Michael, 175
Donne, W. B., 20, 20 n. 44, 74, 114–15
Doran, John, 101
Dorset Garden Theatre, 24, 25
Dowling, Maurice:
  Othello Travestie (1834), 11
  Romeo and Juliet as the Law Directs (1837), 36, 124
Downes, John, 24, 24 n. 54
Draudt, Manfred, 16 n. 34
drolls, 23
Drury Lane Theatre, 14, 114, 167, 176
Dryden, John, 25, 25 n. 56, 26–7
  The Enchanted Island (1667), 26, 26 n. 59

Duffet, Thomas:
  The Empress of Morocco (1673), 24–5, 24 n. 55, 95
  The Mock-Tempest (1675), 25–6, 27, 73, 73 n. 24, 175
Duke's Men, The, 24–6

East End *see* London
electoral reform, 120, 120 n. 37, 155–6, 162, 162 n. 23, 168, 173, 174
Eliot, George, 20
Ellis, James, 37
The Empress of Morocco (Duffet, 1673), 24–5, 24 n. 55, 95
The Empress of Morocco (Settle, 1671), 24
Erle, T. W., 108
Evans's Supper Rooms, 132, 134, 134 n. 57, 141

Fairholt, F. W., 8–9
Farren, Ellen ('Nellie'), 71, 86, 186
Farren, William, 98 n. 73
'fast', 117–18, 128, 131–5
  see also burlesque, and respectability
Fechter, Charles, 52, 85, 90, 105
Fenians, 157
Ferdinand II, king of Naples and the Two Sicilies, 177, 182, 183
Filon, Augustin, 16, 38, 149, 173
Finn, Margot, 159
Fletcher, John, 22–3
Folger Shakespeare Library, 154 n. 12
Forrest, Edwin, 52
Forster, John, 168
Fox, George L., 16, 60–2, *62*, 69
France:
  revolution of 1789, 167, 182
  revolution of 1830, 184
  revolution of 1848, 176, 177 n. 61, 180 n. 67, 182–3
Furnivall, F. J., 73

Gaiety Theatre, 13 n. 28, 14, 70, 71, 86, 186
Garrick, David, 27 n. 63, 53–4, 74
'gent', 80–1
  see also burlesque, and respectability
Gilbert, W. S.:
  Rosencrantz and Guildenstern, 10, 59–60, 68–9, 105
Gordon, Harriet, 117–18
Granville-Barker, Harley, 94
Grecian Saloon, 14
Griffiths, Trevor, 183–4, 185
Grimaldi Shakespeare, The, 8
Gurney, Richard:
  Romeo and Juliet Travesty, 124

Halévy, Fromental, 91–2, 185
Hallam, Henry, 152, 156, 160
Halliday, Andrew:
  Romeo and Juliet Travestie; or the Cup of Cold Poison (1856), 8 n. 15, 15, 36, 58–9, 66, 119–24, 119 n. 35, 124, 125, 126
  Savage Club, 138
Hamilton, Walter, 31, 38
Hannoosh, Michele, 103
Haymarket Theatre, 92
Hazlitt, William, 57, 100, 168, 176
Hewitt, Barnard, 16
historicism, 92–3, 153–4
Holland, Peter, 22
Hollingshead, John, 13 n. 28, 70–1, 73, 136
Hotten, J. C., 130
'Hugo Vamp's Comic Dramatic Shakesperean Scenas' *see* Vamp, Hugo
Hutcheon, Linda, 17, 151–2
Hyde Park Riots, 161, 161 n. 20

'Ibef':
  Othello Travestie (1813), 141 n. 77
Imperial Theatre, 186 n. 71
Ingoldsby, Thomas, 7–8
Irving, Henry, 10, 40, 85 n. 51, 114
Italy, revolution of 1848, 176, 177–9

Jenkins, T. A., 161
Jerrold, Douglas, 108
John, king of England, 153, 159, 163
  as a burlesque character, 31–3, *32*, 155, 156, 159, 160, 162, 163
Johnson, Samuel, 42, 42 n. 18
Jonson, Ben, 22
Joyce, Patrick, 113
'Judge and Jury Society', 139–40, 140 n. 73, 141–3, 146
Jump, John, 18

Kean, Charles, 36
  burlesques of his productions:
    Macbeth, 6, 6 n. 9, 87–9, *88*
    Richard III, 10
    The Winter's Tale, 92–4, 93 n. 69, 105, 109, 111
  Princess's Theatre, manager of, 5, 13, 65, 85, 87–9, 90, 114, 153, 169 n. 41
  roles:
    Hamlet, 86
    Macbeth, 6
Kean, Edmund, 89 n. 58, 100–1, 141 n. 78, 168
Kean, Ellen, 146 n. 84
Kemble, John Philip, 167–8
King's Men, The, 24–6
Kitchin, George, 151

Knight of the Burning Pestle, The (c. 1607), 22–3, 119 n. 35

Langbaine, Gerald, 25–6, 26 n. 57
Lewes, G. H., 90
localizations *see* burlesque, language of; London, burlesque references to
London:
  burlesque references to, 26, 34, 118–19, 127–8, 155
  East End, 14, 98, 98 n. 79, 107, 118, 126
  West End, 127–8, 132–5, 136, 148
  see also Bohemianism
Lord Chamberlain's Office *see* censorship
Louis-Philippe, king of France, 177, 177 n. 61, 179 n. 65
Lyceum Theatre, 92, 105

M.P. (Robertson, 1870), 146–8
MacDonald, Joyce Green, 29 n. 65
Macready, W. C., 114, 168, 175
Magna Carta, 152–4, 152 n. 5, 154 n. 11, 156–7, 158, 159, 162
  burlesques of, 154–63
Magna Charta Association, 162
Mahood, M. M., 119
Malone:
  Macbeth According to an Act of Parliament (1853), 6 n. 9, 87–9, *88*, 89 n. 57, 117
Man in the Moon, 78
Marcus, Leah, 40
Martineau, Harriet, 79 n. 41
Mathews, Charles, 179
  Othello, the Moor of Fleet Street (1833), 12, 16 n. 34
Maus, Katharine Eisaman, 175
Mayhew, Henry, 127–8
McCarthy, Justin, 98, 138, 149
Meisel, Martin, 168
middle class, 107–15, 134, 166–7, 170–1
Milner, Henry, 154 n. 11
Monck, Matthew:
  Prospero; or, the King of the Caliban Islands (1883), 186 n. 71
Moody, Jane, 154 n. 11
Morgan, James:
  Coriolanus; a Burlesque (1846), 11, 163–5, 169–73, 172 n. 48
Morley, Henry, 101
Mugglestone, Linda, 130
Müller-Schwefe, Gerhard, 5 n. 6
Murphy, Arthur, 27 n. 63

National Shakspeare Committee, 76
Nicholson, 'Baron' Renton, 139–40, 140 n. 73, 141–3, 146

Olympic Theatre, 14, 59, 63, 109–10, 115, 141
O'Neill, J. R. *see* Vamp, Hugo
Oxford University, 108, 108 n. 6

Park Theater (Brooklyn), 49–56
Parker, Patricia, 43, 48
parody:
    definitions of, 17–18, 17 n. 37
    theories of, 17, 19
Pastor, Tony, 51 n. 38, 105
Peel, Robert, 166
Pepper's Ghost, 34–6, 34 n. 9, *35*
Phelps, Samuel, 5, 75 n. 34, 114
    productions at Sadler's Wells:
    Coriolanus, 169
pictorialism, 87–90, 154
Planché, J. R.:
    Camp at the Olympic, The (1853), 114
    Golden Fleece, The (1845), 93 n. 68
    Love and Fortune (1859), 58
Poole, John:
    Hamlet Travestie (1810), 10, 12, 49 nn. 33, 34, 51 n. 37, 52 n. 39, 57–8, 59, 124
    revival at the Park Theater (1870), 49–56, 49 n. 35
Poole, John F.
    Romeo and Juliet; or, the Beautiful Blende Who Dyed for Love (1869), 42, 51 n. 38
postmodernism, 19
pre-Raphaelites, 109
Price, Richard, 162, 162–3
Prince of Wales's Theatre, 148–9, 149 n. 87
Princess's Theatre, 86–7
promptbooks, 16, 16 n. 34, 48–9, 49–50, 49 n. 34, *50*
Punch, 75–6, *77*, 177 n. 61
puns *see* burlesque, language of

Reduced Shakespeare Company, 21 n. 48, 37, 39 n. 15
Reform League, 161
Reid, Alastair, 166
Rejected Addresses, 7
revolutions of 1848, 176, 177, 177 n. 61, 182–3
Righton, Edward, 169
Ripley, John, 164 n. 27
Ritchie, J. Ewing, 134, 140
Robertson, T. W., 14–15
    M.P. (1870), 146–8
Robinson, Henry Crabb, 108 n. 6
Robson, Frederick, 4–5, 17, 95, 95 n. 72, *96*, 109, 109–10, 110 n. 15, 114
    acting style, 98, 100–3
    compared to Edmund Kean, 100–1
    critical opinions of, 98, 100, 101–3

    roles:
        burlesque Macbeth, 95, 98
        burlesque Shylock, *97*, 98–101, 102–3, 141
Rose, Margaret, 17, 66
Rostron, David, 167
Russian Formalists, 19
Ryman, Addison, 105

Sadler's Wells Theatre, 13, 16 n. 34, 114, 115
Sala, G. A., 109, 115, 135, 173
Saltz, David Z., 21
Salvini, Tommaso, 6, 10, 85 n. 51
Savage Club, 136, 148
Scarron, Paul, 23
Scott, Clement, 132
Scribe, Eugène, 91–2, 185
Selby, Charles:
    Kynge Richard ye Third; or, Ye Battel of Bosworth Field (1844), 10, 31 n. 1, 38, 58 n. 4, 124, 139 n. 69
Select Committee on Dramatic Literature (1832), 151, 163 n. 26
Shadwell, Thomas, 91 n. 66
Shafer, Yvonne, 63 n. 11
Shakespeare, William:
    adaptations of, 21, 92
    and authenticity, 57–9, 63–5, 66, 87, 93–4
    burlesques of:
        Antony and Cleopatra: *Antony and Cleopatra; or, His-tory and Her-story in a Modern Nilo-metre* (Burnand, 1866), 11 *Our Own Antony and Cleopatra* (Burnand, 1873), 70 n. 18
        Coriolanus: *Coriolanus; a Burlesque* (Morgan, 1846), 11, 163–5, 169–73, 172 n. 48
        Hamlet: *A Fireside Hamlet* (Carr, 1884), 11, 14, 14 n. 29; *Hamlet According to an Act of Parliament* (Barton, 1853), 12, 34, 91, 124, 125, 126; *Hamlet the Hysterical* (Snow, 1874), 10, 40; *Hamlet! The Ravin' Prince of Denmark!!* (Anon., 1866), 36, 39, 67, 110, 124; *Hamlet Travestie* (John Poole, 1810), 10, 12, 49–56, 49 nn. 33, 34, 35, 51 n. 37, 52 n. 39, 57–8, 59, 124; *Hamlet; or, Wearing of the Black* (Craig, *c*. 1866), 60, 126–7; *Rosencrantz and Guildenstern* (Gilbert, 1891), 10, 59–60, 68–9, 105; *A Thin Slice of Ham let!* (Anon., *c*. 1850), 34; *Very Little Hamlet* (Yardley, 1884), 11, 11 n. 20, 86–7
    King John: *King John (with the Benefit of the Act)* (G. A. A'Beckett, 1837), 31–3, *32*, 38, 155; *King John Burlesque* (Anon., *c*. 1870), 154–63, 154 n. 13, 162 n. 23
    King Lear: *Kynge Lear and Hys Faythfulle Foole* (Anon., 1860), 11

Shakespeare, William (*Cont.*)
  Macbeth: Epilogue, *The Empress of Morocco* (Duffet, 1673), 95; *Macbeth According to an Act of Parliament* (Malone, 1853), 6 n. 9, 87–9, *88*, 89 n. 57, 117; *Macbeth Bottled into a Burletta* (Anon., 1842), 127; *Macbeth Modernised* (Bell, 1838), 11, 60, 124, 127; *Macbeth Somewhat Removed from the Text of Shakespeare* (Talfourd, 1847), 43, 44 n. 26, 59, 63–5, *64*, 108, 108 n. 6, 111
  The Merchant of Venice: *The Merchant of Venice (very far indeed) From the Text of Shakespeare* (Blanchard, 1843), 11, 34, 127–8, 129; *Shylock; or, the Merchant of Venice Preserved* (Talfourd, 1853), 11, 43, 45, 89–90, 89 n. 58, *97*, 98–100, 98 n. 73, 110, 117, 131, 139, 139 n. 70, 141–3, *142*
  Othello: *Othello, the Moor of Fleet Street* (Mathews, 1833), 12, 16 n. 34; *Othello Travestie* (Dowling, 1834), 11; *Othello Travestie* ('Ibef', 1813), 141 n. 77; *The Rival Othellos* (Byron, 1861), 85, 85 n. 51; *Salthello Ovini* (Anon., 1875), 10
  Richard III: *Kynge Richard ye Third; or, Ye Battel of Bosworth Field* (Selby, 1844), 10, 31 n. 1, 38, 124, 139 n. 69; *New Grand, Historical, Bombastical, Musical and Completely Illegitimate Tragedy to be called Richard III* (Coyne, 1844), 10, 12, 13, 34, 127; *The Rise and Fall of Richard III; or, a New Front to an Old Dickey* (Burnand, 1868), 44
  Romeo and Juliet: *Romeo and Juliet as the Law Directs* (Dowling, 1837), 36, 124; *Romeo and Juliet; or, the Shaming of the True* (Anon., 1868), 151; *Romeo and Juliet; or, the Beautiful Blende Who Dyed for Love* (John F. Poole, 1869), 42, 51 n. 38; *Romeo and Juliet Travestie* (Halliday, 1859), 8 n. 15, 15, 36, 58–9, 66, 119–24, 119 n. 35, 124, 125, 126; *Romeo and Juliet Travesty* (Gurney, 1812), 124
  The Tempest: *Ariel* (Burnand, 1883), 70–3, 71 nn. 17, 18, *72*, 72 n. 22, 186–7; *The Enchanted Isle* (R. and W. Brough, 1848), 13, 91–2, 91 n.65, 174, 177–86, 178; *La! Tempest! Ah!* (R. and W. Brough, 1850), 91–2, 186; *The Mock-Tempest* (Duffet, 1674), 25–6, 27, 73, 73 n. 24, 175; *Prospero; or, the King of the Caliban Islands* (Monck, 1883), 186 n. 71
  The Winter's Tale: *Perdita* (W. Brough, 1856), 43–4, 63 n. 10, 92–5, 105, *112*, 115–17, 117, 123 n. 41, 124 n. 42, 143–4, 144 n. 83, *145*, 160 n. 18

parodies, non-theatrical, 7–9, 35–6, 110–11, 132 n. 55, 143–6
iconography of, 8, *9*, *35*, 75, *76*, 79, *133*, *144*
plays:
  Coriolanus, 164–5, 164 n. 27, 167–9, 167 n. 35, 174
  Hamlet, 1–2, *2*, 14 n. 29, 40, 53, 54–6, 60–2, *61*, 86–7, 105
  King John, 31, 152–6
  Love's Labour's Lost, 22
  The Merchant of Venice, 99, 143, 149 n. 87
  A Midsummer Night's Dream, 12, 22, 58, 90, 147, 148, 150
  Romeo and Juliet, 22, 95 n. 72, 119–21, 150
  The Tempest, 70, 91–2, 174–6, 177, 181, 184, 185–6, 186
  The Winter's Tale, 111, 135, 143–6, 146 n. 84
Stratford birthplace, 78–80, 79 n. 41, *79*, 81–3, 81 n. 44, *82*, 83 n. 45
see also Coyne, *This House to be Sold*
Tercentenary (1864), 76, 78, 78 n. 38, 150
topicality, uses of, 40–1
wordplay in, 43, 48
Sharp, R. Farquaharson, 10 n. 18
slang *see* burlesque, language of
slavery, 175, 181–2
Smith, Albert, 107, 119 n. 35
Smith, Richard John, 179
Snow, W. R.:
  Hamlet the Hysterical (1874), 10, 40
Stedman Jones, Gareth, 159–60
Stoppard, Tom, 6
Strand Theatre, 14, 36, 89, 122, 148, 150
Summers, Montague, 27
supernumeraries, 169, 169 nn. 41, 42
Surrey Theatre, 107, 108
'swells', 128, 158
see also burlesque, and respectability
Swinburne, A. C., 167, 167 n. 35

Talfourd, Francis, 136, *137*
  Macbeth Somewhat Removed from the Text of Shakespeare, 43, 44 n. 26, 59, 63–5, *64*, 108, 108 n. 6, 111
  Shylock; or, the Merchant of Venice Preserved, 11, 12, 43, 45, 89–90, 89 n. 58, *97*, 98–100, 98 n. 73, 110, 117, 131, 139, 139 n. 70, 141–3, *142*
Tempesta, La (1850), 185–6
Tercentenary (1864) *see* Shakespeare, William
Thackeray, W. M., 110
Theatre Comique (New York), 105
Thomas, Moy, 70

Thompson, F. M. L., 113
Thumb, Tom, 75, *76*
Toole, J. L., 78, 78 n. 38
topicality *see* burlesque, language of
travesty, 17 n. 37, 18, 55
Tree, Herbert Beerbohm, 14, 14 n. 29, 153
Trussler, Simon, 18
Tupper, Martin, 15

Ulrici, Hermann, 42 n. 21

Vamp, Hugo, 132
Vandenhoff, John, 164
Vernon, James, 161
Victoria, queen of England, 110, 110 n. 15, 111, 146, 159, 160, 160 n. 18, 176, 181
'Villikins and his Dinah', 95 n. 72

Wahrman, Dror, 113, 167
Webster, Benjamin, 176
Wells, Stanley, 14, 21 n. 50, 160 n. 18
West End *see* London
Wheler, R. B., 78 n. 39, 81 n. 44
Williams, Raymond, 130
Wilson, Daniel, 186
Wilson, Effingham, 176
Wilton, Marie, 5, 15, 48, 143–4, 144 n. 83, *145*, 148–50, 149 n. 87
Woodward, E. L., 171
wordplay *see* burlesque, language of
working class, 107–8, 118–19, 124, 124 n. 42, 126, 127–8, 158, 158 n. 15, 159–60, 166–7, 171
Worthen, W. B., 28 n. 64
Wright, Edward, 131
Wright, Mrs Edward, 69

Yardley, William:
  Very Little Hamlet, 11, 11 n. 20, 86–7
Yates, Edmund, 109, 136, 173